The Orphans' Nine Commandments

A MEMOIR

William Roger Holman

With a Foreword by Ted Blevins

TCU PRESS   Fort Worth

Library of Congress Cataloging-in-Publication Data
Holman, William Roger, 1925-
The Orphans' Nine Commandments: A Memoir.
ISBN 978-0-87565-355-6
1. Holman, William Roger, 1925- 2. Orphans—Biography.
3. Orphans—Oklahoma—Biography.
4. Bechan, Roger, 1925- I. Title.
HV 990.052 046 2500
362.79 H

Printed in the United States of America on acid-free paper.

TCU Press
P.O. Box 298300
Fort Worth, TX 76129
817.257.7822
http://www.prs.tcu.edu
To order books: 1.800.826.8911

TO BARBARA SWITZER HOLMAN

Foreword

The Orphans' Nine Commandments, A Memoir is set in the Great
Depression in Oklahoma—one of the most depressed states of the
era. It is a story of resilience and of the right people, at just the right
time, in the life of William Roger Holman.

On a bright summer afternoon in May 1932, Anna Bechan, a single mother, takes her six-year-old son, Roger, on a trolley ride to the
city. They visit her friend, Uncle Paul, and have a check-up by their
family physician. The following day Mother Bechan abandons Roger
at the Oklahoma Society for the Friendless, a bleak orphanage.
Reverend Wheeler, the court-appointed guardian, earns fees by brokering the boy through six foster homes and three orphanages. Each
home struggles to survive the '30s and '40s, creating a tumultuous
family of the marvelous, the loving, the eccentric, the ill-tempered,
and the cruel.

William Roger Holman navigates each placement just as he did
when he took a sailing adventure on Belle Isle Lake and befriended a
former slave, fisherman, and frog doctor, who sang folk songs as he
served a meal of possum-and-sweet potato stew. This is just one of

the unforgettable characters who helped him build a bridge from the darkness to the resilient. A child abandoned, William Roger Holman quickly honed the skills to pick out the unforgettable characters who shaped his life almost like the buoys that later helped guide his sailboat in international water adventures, a lifelong avocation spearheaded by the first sailing adventure on Belle Isle Lake. Characters like Katy Schickram, the president of the board at the Drumright City Library, who quickly sized up a boy full of adventure. Week after week she placed in his hands books of adventure that fueled his natural curiosity and welded an attachment to books that soon became the vision and hope of his remarkable life. He devised a scheme to meet Kansas City Babe, the town madam, because he wanted to quench his curiosity: what would she look like; how would she smell; what would he do? Finally, this young man of resilience, curiosity, and emerging vision found his small place in a large world.

Holman, shadowed by an Indentured Contract, takes the reader into his complicated world. He makes us wonder along with him, which of the many male figures is his father and what happened to Mother Bechan? You will find yourself working to solve the puzzle and feeling the deep drama and jubilee as the story unfolds.

It is impossible to read *The Orphans' Nine Commandments* without comparing the state of child-care and adoption practices of today with Bill Holman's experience. The most startling observation to me was Bill's report of being totally happy with his life only to suddenly experience a darkness that came over him. After years of working with children who have unsuccessful, as well as successful, lives after foster care and adoption, I know that a vast majority report the same darkness. It seems with all of our sciences, we have yet to fill that emptiness of a breech in our family relations and contacts. I am struck that with all of our knowledge today, the greatest hope for a child is the significant relationships with adoptive and foster parents who give unconditional love and acceptance.

The love and acceptance given to Bill by Barbara Louise Switzer became Bill's hope, anchor, and belief that he was loveable. To this day Bill fully banks on his love of Barbara and her love of him.

While there have been extensive studies of medications, evidence, and best practices, the two critical issues facing children in out-of-home care is their sense of great loss of family and their need for a significant adult to believe in, love, and accept them. What has changed is a greater expectation of transparency and accountability with accredited state licensing oversight. The current system would not tolerate a Mr. Wheeler. Safeguards include court ad litems for each child as well as court-appointed child advocates to assure the child's rights are respected.

Today ninety percent of adoptions in the United States are open, meaning the adoptive parents and the biological parents are known to one another. More often than not, the adopted child comes to know the biological parent in childhood and some play a significant role in the child's life. Open adoptions take much of the mystery out of a child's life, creating a greater completeness and understanding about the family. As one child shared with me in counseling, "I just want to see my dad once, so I will know what I will look like when I'm old."

The Orphans' Nine Commandments will provoke deep thoughts and warm laughter that will stay with you as a story remembered and often quoted.

TED BLEVINS, Director
The Lena Pope Home
Fort Worth, Texas

The Orphans'
Nine Commandments

Part One

The Red & White Trolley

Bethany, Oklahoma

1932

❧

If one is to record
one's life truthfully, one must aim
at getting into the record of it something
of the disorderly discontinuity which
makes it so absurd, unpredictable, but bearable.

LEONARD WOOLF
The Journey Not the Arrival Matters

~ 1 ~

My father was an elusive fellow. He and my mother, Anna Bechan, fell in love and were close for several years, gave birth to me, and wove a covenant of secrecy that took over six decades to unravel. Because he was a prominent citizen, already with a wife and children, it was necessary to invent a myth about the birth of their child. A petition filed with the Oklahoma County Juvenile Court reported that my parents were separated and divorced before I was born. This gave me a legitimate beginning and let Momma save face. In the 1930s, there was no greater sin than to have a child outside a marriage.

Momma was tall with gentle hands and a loving nature, but she suffered from weak lungs and hard times. One lady recalled her as an attractive woman with a heap of blonde hair turning gray, blue eyes under light brows, a finely shaped nose, and rosy cheeks. She smelled of rose water and Ivory soap.

Momma and I lived in a small prairie town where by the middle of May, the cumulus clouds ghosted across the sky like fluffs of spun candy, and the fields were strewn with bluebonnets and blankets of daisies and yellow buttercups. My earliest childhood memories encompass hours of running barefooted, catching grasshoppers and roly-poly bugs, playing hide-and-seek, driving my yellow dump truck, and riding the trolley into Oklahoma City. All was right with the world.

My mind often searches into that lingering past where, on a warm Saturday in May 1932, a fresh breeze ruffled my hair as I stirred from the bliss of a six-year-old boy's nap. I watched sleepily as Momma walked into the room and paused by the chest of drawers. She pulled out a pair of my pants, a shirt, underwear, and socks. Folding them neatly, she packed them into a small cardboard box, closed the lid, and tied it with one of her cloth belts.

I leaned up on one elbow. "Why pack my clothes?"

"Staying overnight in the city."

I hopped out of bed and slipped on my white shirt and long pants, looking forward to visiting with our friend, Uncle Paul.

I followed Momma across the hall and watched as she tossed off her housecoat and put on a yellow summer dress. Turning side to side, she adjusted her slip and brushed her hair. She sat down and looked into a hand mirror, powdered her face and put on lipstick. Appearing rushed, she stood up and tied on a white head scarf.

"Come, Roger. It's growing late." She handed me my box of clothes.

Under the warm but descending sun, we walked a block up College Avenue to Main Street, purchased our tickets, and took a seat outside the Bethany Interurban Station. From around a stand of trees the red-and-white trolley clanged into view. I loved the colorful machine that flashed blue and yellow sparks and smelled of hot iron. Within minutes the car squealed to a halt, and the blue-suited motorman looked down at us.

We stepped aboard and handed our tickets to the cigar-puffing gentleman. He doffed his cap in greeting and shoved a lever forward. Clutching the handrails, we stumbled to our seats. With her head tilted to one side, Momma held a silent conversation with herself, from time to time pressing my hand into hers. The trolley clattered and swayed from side to side as we sped down the nine miles of track, but the rattling didn't quiet the noisy children who scuffled in the rear.

As we sped through green fields, other trolleys flashed past, and, on each side, small wooden houses with open windows looked out on us. I strained to see the skyscrapers as the city loomed ahead. With the bell ringing, we skirted the tall buildings and rushed through a canyon of shadows. Within a few blocks, we approached Hudson Street and screeched to a stop in the Oklahoma City terminal, an arched metal structure open at both ends.

"Hurry along," Momma said as we swung down, scattering a flock of pigeons, and boarded a waiting streetcar.

The car rumbled northward, block after block, leaving the tall buildings behind. Finally, we approached a wide avenue. With a hiss of air, the streetcar jolted to a stop and the door sprang open. We stepped down and entered the full growth of summer. Leafy elms arched overhead. Rows of sweet smelling honeysuckle, intertwined with red roses, crowded the street.

Swinging my box to and fro, I hopped and skipped down the side-walk in my Buster Brown shoes. For good luck, I avoided every joint in the walk as I hummed, "Jumping jack, if you step on a crack, you'll break your mother's back." On the second corner I tugged on Momma's skirt. "Where are we going?"

She grasped my hand. "Be patient. We'll soon be there."

In the next block we walked alongside a rock wall and paused before an opening. I looked through an iron gate and saw a path leading to a brick mansion with tall windows and an ivy-covered tower on each side. From the distance, it beckoned like a gingerbread house.

Maybe we will visit here for a bit before we go see Uncle Paul. In the approaching twilight, Momma unlatched the gate and we walked down the path and onto the front porch where a woman in a white dress greeted us. She possessed a narrow face heightened by a stiff manner, a mop of gray hair, and wore black-rimmed glasses resting on the tip of her nose.

"I'm sorry for being late," Momma said.

"It doesn't matter." The woman opened the screen door and ushered us into the house, down a carpeted hallway, and into a lofty room lighted by a round chandelier. She closed the door behind us. I looked up into Momma's face, startled to see tears flowing down her cheeks.

"What's wrong?" I tugged on her skirt.

Instead of replying, Momma slipped off her scarf and blotted her face. Then she knelt down and ran her fingers through my hair. She kissed me—soft brush of her warm lips on my forehead. "Give me a hug." She held out her hands.

I set my clothes down and stretched my arms up around her but only for a moment. Without a word, the woman in white spun me around and grabbed my box. I turned to Momma for help, but she rushed out, her yellow skirt brushing the wall. The door banged behind her.

"Momma! Wait! Wait for me!" I dashed forward and pounded on the door, my heart hammering against my chest. This couldn't be true! Momma had never left me before. My knees gave way and I slumped on the floor, sobbing. Why had she left? What was happening? Panic and despair flooded in as my strength ebbed.

The woman stepped to where I crouched near the door. "You're staying here. Get up."

I looked up at her through tears. She yanked me onto my feet and as I pulled away, she slapped me. I kicked back. She grabbed my collar and marched me upstairs. We entered a sweltering chamber with three windows at each end. Under a beamed ceiling, a row of baby cribs, several iron beds, and a couple of rocking chairs stood on a bare wood floor.

The woman shoved me onto one of the beds. Dim lightbulbs dangled from above. The cries and sniffles of babies filled the air. Several

4

black oscillating fans stood before the windows, swinging from side to side like angry doodlebugs, whirring and clicking, straining to clear the stench of soiled diapers from the long room.

I lay in disbelief, clenching the edge of the sheet between my teeth as the onrush of night, like a giant bogeyman, grasped me and tossed me into a dungeon. It is black now. I am trembling and wrapped in a blanket of fear. The darkness has no corners, no shape, no movement. My mind quivers with the thought of Momma leaving me behind. Why didn't she take me along? Had I done something wrong?

The hours crept by and I dozed off, only to awaken in the midst of a horrifying nightmare, entrapped by a wall of fire. The flames spread across the bed. I jumped up and screamed. Only silence. I screamed again. And again. But no one came to ease my mind. I laid there for hours talking to Momma. Tears slid down my cheeks as I prayed for her to rescue me in the morning. Sometime during the night, I drifted into a restless sleep.

I woke in a smelly puddle. During the dark hours, someone had moved me from the iron bed into a large crib in the middle of the room. A soggy baby lay on each side of me. I jumped up and rattled the headboard. The babies screamed and bawled. Fans clicked and droned. I crawled over the side rail in the half-light of morning to look for Momma.

Grasping a banister, I tiptoed down the wooden stairs and paused on a landing. A splinter of light came from below. I slipped down the last flight of stairs and entered the kitchen to the sound of pots and pans clattering. A teenage girl wearing a dirty apron stirred a kettle of oatmeal under the hood of a stove. Mingled with the scent of breakfast, a rich aroma percolated from a blue enameled pot. Yesterday's gray-haired stranger sat at a long table. She spooned oats into her mouth and washed them down with coffee. Her dark eyes looked out from a hardened face smothered in powder. A smudge of rouge gave a glint of life to her cheeks.

"Mornin' Roger," she said around her cigarette. "I'm Tillie Banks, your matron."

"Where's Momma?" I'd never heard of a matron.

She paused, glanced at the girl filling bowls from the kettle, then turned back. "Your momma left you here. I take in children for William Wheeler. He's head of the Home for the Friendless."

No! I didn't want to live with strangers. Momma wouldn't leave me for long. I rubbed the tears from my eyes.

Bound within the walls of an unwanted home, I began my struggle to cope with the daily routines. I was the tallest boy. The other older kids were small tykes still in diapers. They couldn't even play checkers. Bawling babies filled the cribs. Despite the noise, there were no more than a dozen children in the home.

Every night I prayed for Momma to return. In the morning, to speed up the Lord's work, I crawled out at dawn, slipped on my clothes and sat on the windowsill where a garden of skyscrapers glimmered in the distance. I knew that one morning, any day now, Momma would come rushing up the front walk. I pictured her hand grasping mine as we caught the trolley home to Bethany.

Day after day, I yearned for her to return. I prayed with more fervor. With all of my efforts, surely the Lord would hear my pleas. Perhaps Momma had run out of money for the trolley.

A day or so after I arrived, Tillie waddled in, jabbering away. "Down for a nap." Fumbling with a stack of blocks, I hesitated. She twisted my ear. I squealed. She clapped her hand over my mouth. My teeth caught her finger and blood spurted onto her dress. I took off running.

She shouted as she chased me around the baby cribs, drops of her blood spotting the wooden floor. I crawled under my iron bed.

"Come outta there, you little devil." I curled into a ball. She turned away.

In a moment of quiet, I felt safe. Then Tillie's legs reappeared. She wore white hose rolled below her knees. I began to sweat. She leaned over and thrust a broom handle under the side rail again and again until she poked me in the nose. The salty taste of blood trickled through my lips. After a few minutes she stomped off moaning about her bloody finger.

No matter how Tillie ruled my hours, I clung to my memory of Momma. She must be missing me by now. She was my warmest love. No father, no brothers or sisters, no grandmothers, grandfathers, aunts or uncles shared my life. Momma said Uncle Paul was merely our friend. While my father's identity remained a mystery, Momma was my teacher and playmate.

Without Momma my life no longer had direction. In the mornings I lived within my daydreams, though these depended on where I was. I usually hid under the bed where I felt safe. There, Tillie could no longer slap me or twist my ears. In the afternoons, I sought the comfort of the warm brick wall on the west side of the building. I'd crouch down and lean back with my knees to my chin, and cry . . . always longing to return home.

*

Momma made our home in the village of Bethany, on the prairie grasslands nine miles west of Oklahoma City. The town rested near the banks of the North Canadian River, a wide but often shallow stream meandering around the settlement like a gigantic horseshoe. Founded by the fathers of the Nazarene Church, Bethany had a pastoral feeling with its towering steeples whose bells beckoned families in from the outlying wheat fields. Evidently the elders envisioned the same biblical village where Jesus raised Lazarus from the dead. Like the early Puritans, they banned alcoholic beverages and wrote laws prohibiting gambling, pool halls, and theaters.

I later learned that Momma moved to this town of 2,000 not because of religious beliefs, but to work as an independent bookkeeper. In 1932 the Depression deepened, and she lost many of her clients.

We moved from a green-shuttered cottage into a small walk-up apartment on College Avenue. We lived one block south of Main Street where the trolley cars, running between El Reno and Oklahoma City, rattled into town.

In the morning hours I played with my yellow dump truck in the side yard, digging ditches, building tunnels, and hauling dirt back to the alley. Near noon Momma called me for lunch and a nap. I opened the screen door and walked up a flight of wooden stairs to a tiled landing. Our bedrooms and bath lay down the hall toward the back. The white walls made the rooms seem as large and bright as summer. Across the windows Momma displayed lace curtains, one of her treasured possessions.

My yellow dump truck was the size of a Radio Flyer wagon. One Saturday morning, in spite of Momma's repeated warnings not to stray, I gripped the steering wheel and placed one foot in the bed as the other pumped the sidewalk, propelling me uptown. No one stopped me because I often went shopping with Momma.

I turned the corner from College Avenue to find boxes of orange fruits and green vegetables in front of the Square Deal Grocery. Farther down I entered a front door wrapped in red and white paper, the Davis Confectionery store. The small room smelled of chocolate and peppermint. This day, I handed Mrs. Davis a nickel and dashed out with an all-day sucker.

Momma looked angry when I trotted home pulling my truck with a small rope, the juicy caramel confection clenched in my teeth. "My Lord, your sticky fingers have been in my pocketbook again. What a handful! Like your father, always up to something."

I was tall and long-legged with freckles from ear to ear. The neighborhood kids said I was quick-fisted, always ready to fight. One day when we boys were playing marbles, one kid snatched my red agate out of the ring and took off. I chased him down the alley and busted him in the nose. "That temper comes from your father," Momma said.

I don't remember ever seeing my father, but another neighbor kid always jabbered about his dad. He claimed that his old man could whip mine with one hand tied behind his back. I told him I didn't mind, but he'd have to find my dad first.

One afternoon, while playing on the floor, I looked up to see Momma sitting in a rocker. She whispered to herself and brushed away tears with the tip of her apron. I asked her what was wrong.

"I'm praying that your father will return." She paused and with a smile, "I want him to live with us again. Perhaps before your summer haircut."

To keep me from repeating my trip uptown, Momma stored my truck in the closet. We sat at the dining table, and my daily lessons began. She cut pictures from *The Saturday Evening Post*, labeled them, and stuck them on a deck of old playing cards with flour paste.

With flash cards flying through her hands, Momma taught me numbers and my ABCs. She added airplanes, dinosaurs, caterpillars, mockingbirds, oil wells, skyscrapers, President Hoover, and one of my favorite loves—trolley cars—to my vocabulary. "You're my golden-haired boy," she often said when I learned a new word or read from one of my books.

Each night after I climbed into bed, Momma read books about rabbits, the three little pigs and a mean fox, and told me a grown-up story about a jumping frog. Momma said he had lead in his pants. When I laughed, she kissed me and I was happy. After story time, I stood beside my bed and prayed. "Now, I lay me down to sleep. . . ." Momma tucked me in, and I drifted off.

Momma—warm, accommodating Momma—crowded my small bedroom with an array of toys, furniture, and animals. My furniture consisted of a single wood-framed bed, a chest of drawers, and three apple crates to house my animals and toys. No doubt with my father providing the money, she bought me a giant dump truck, a bag of marbles, a box of dominoes, a brown rat in a wire cage, and a white rabbit in a wooden hutch.

On steamy afternoons when the temperature soared, Momma's blue eyes gleamed as she served Kool-Aid to the pigeons who flocked to the window ledge. She often spent time on the back porch in the evening and read the stars. Perhaps her mind wandered with flights of fancy; she appeared to be a dreamy soul who talked to herself.

Some afternoons she rested on the divan worrying about her lack of money. She believed President Hoover took her job away. We listened to our round-topped Philco radio as the president spoke: "Prosperity is just around the corner." But around the corner, Momma found little work and only snippets of food. On Saturdays, we received sacks of groceries from the Nazarene Church. For breakfast, I stood on a chair in front of the stove and heated up a bowl of cornmeal. Momma fried mush for lunch, and for supper, we often shared a boiled potato.

Occasionally, she would say with a smile, "Your father has sent money."

On those days, we strode up to the Square Deal Grocery and bought bacon and eggs, apples, tomatoes, bread, and several cans of Pet milk.

*

Despite Momma's money worries, we rode the red-and-white trolley into the city every few weeks to see our friend, Uncle Paul, about business. One afternoon we stepped off the streetcar, walked up a couple of blocks, and entered a three-storied building off Hudson Street. His secretary greeted us with a warm welcome. Several carpeted rooms made up his office. His adjoining dental laboratory overflowed with mixing bowls and small molds.

Laughing and tousling my hair, Uncle Paul boosted me in the air. He was a short man with a bald head ringed by a wreath of blonde hair. When he sat down, I crawled onto his lap, leaned my face into his brown suit and sniffed the scent of cigars. His blue eyes squinted through thick glasses as he showed me a monstrous set of Plaster of Paris teeth with pink gums that he opened and closed with one hand. I played with the funny teeth until he handed me a comic book and ushered me into another room.

For some reason he and Momma argued about our staying and then talked in hushed tones. Finally Uncle Paul closed the door. I read my book. Mother decided we wouldn't stay overnight. Before we left, he slipped a penny into my pocket. He handed Momma an envelope.

Momma and I walked out into the glaring sun, seeming to leave her worries behind. We hurried up the street listening to honking horns. Yellow cabs and white buses belched gray clouds of smoke into the air. I dashed to the side of a building where a man wearing a suit and tie held a small box of apples. "Golden Delicious. Only a Nickel today," a sign on the box read.

Momma rushed over and grasped my hand, explaining that the man was down and out, but we didn't have money to spend. "Now settle down if you want to get a treat from our doctor."

We turned and walked up Robinson Avenue through a tunnel of skyscrapers to Second Street. Momma looked skyward and pointed to an oil derrick perched on top of a tall building. "It's the Petroleum Building. Remember, Dr. Dardis is a tease, so don't act up."

We walked through the marbled lobby and past a shoeshine stand. The elevator operator, dressed in a blue uniform with a yellow stripe on each pant leg, whizzed us up to the tenth floor. As we emerged from the speedy lift, a red-haired nurse walked us to the doctor's office.

There Dr. Dardis, a large bear of a man wearing a gray-vested suit and gold-rimmed glasses, greeted us. He guided Momma to a chair next to his rolltop desk. Then he bent over and shook my hand.

"Young man, I'm glad to see you again." He gave me a smile that lifted his big ears. His office glowed with natural light heralded into the room by a wall of tall windows. Beyond the desk stood an examining table and shelves of pharmaceutical bottles. Through the window I saw a distant trolley heading toward a large stone building.

Questions popped out. "Why didn't they build it downtown?"

"That's the state capital," my doctor said, "where the governor works."

"Momma, let's ride the trolley out to the big house." She smiled.

My doctor put his hand on my cheek and examined where a bumblebee stung me below the eye last month. "I see no swelling or scar. Whoops," he smiled, "I mean where did you get those big blue eyes?"

"From Momma." I reached over and touched her sleeve.

I liked to be quizzed and spoke right up. He was a funny man, and I wanted to know him better. I stared at his tiepin, a golden lion with long hair, ruby eyes, and a diamond in its mouth. It looked like a great toy. I asked to see the lion, and he pulled it out and let me hold it. Then he placed his hand on my head. "You've shot up like a giant this month."

"Momma says I'm going to be taller than Uncle Paul."

"Your doctor's a teasing Irishman." Momma giggled and tucked in my shirt.

He took back his pin, peeked into my ears, poked a stick down my throat, and said I would live. Handing me a package of gumdrops and a wire puzzle, he ushered me out to sit in his waiting room under the supervision of his nurse. Now Momma's turn came.

Within a few minutes, she strode out of the office holding a new bottle of medicine. Her hand grasped mine, and we walked to the streetcar. Mother bragged on our doctor, saying he prepared his own medicines.

Every month I looked forward to riding the trolley into the city. I enjoyed visiting Uncle Paul and having checkups by our friendly doctor. They always gave me treats.

On Friday morning, May 20, 1932, the day following our last visit with Uncle Paul and our doctor, Momma said she needed to attend to business in the city. We rode the trolley downtown to a tall whitestoned building. We walked down echoing hallways and entered a

12

large room where we met a man wearing a black robe. As I stood to one side and played with my wire puzzle, I never realized what transpired. Years later I learned that the Honorable Cicero Christison, Judge of the Oklahoma County Juvenile Court, wrote in a red ledger with pen and ink that he was committing me to the care and custody of Mr. W. C. Wheeler for the purposes of finding me a suitable home. William Wheeler was the superintendent of The Oklahoma Society for the Friendless.[1]

Within three months of my seventh birthday, Momma walked gently in my mind, and each night, in the depths of my dreams, we rode the trolley to our apartment in Bethany where we played checkers before going to bed.

But in the stark morning light, Momma's caring voice no longer called to me. "Roger, you're my golden-haired boy. Stay close to home. Come here, sweetheart, and let me tell you a story." Her voice faded into the past as matron Tillie Banks introduced me to my legal guardian.

2

I didn't know it at the time, but Mr. William Wheeler, the superintendent of The Oklahoma Society for the Friendless, made his living by soliciting donations and pocketing fees from brokering abandoned children into adoptive homes. His benevolence also provided guidance for state prisoners and released felons, placing their children with more stable families, again garnering income for his services.

Mr. Wheeler levied a commission of several hundred dollars from each adoptive family. He usually required money down with the balance due in monthly payments spread over the year. During the Great Depression these funds provided a sizable income. A new Ford or a modest two-bedroom house could often be purchased for less.

*

One morning, after I had been at Tillie's for nearly a week, I slipped through the kitchen and out the screen door. I pushed open the rear gate and trotted down an alley to a sidewalk. Within two blocks, I stopped in front of a grocery displaying boxes of colorful fruit. A man wearing a white apron tossed me an apple. I sat on the curb, curled up my legs, and enjoyed my breakfast. Within a few minutes the gentleman asked me, "Where's your mother?"

I stood up and added lying to my human equation. "She's going to meet me at the trolley stop."

He paused, looked me up and down, and told me to come along. Hand in hand, we walked inside and back to an office. I sat in a chair and looked at the calendars hanging on the wall. Contentment filled me until Tillie's shadow loomed at the doorway. "What in God's name are you up to?"

"Looking for the trolley. Goin' home."

She grabbed me by the arm and marched me back to the home. We entered the warm kitchen where she shoved me into a chair. "Your momma's gone. Won't be back. Get that in your head." She paced back and forth thumping my hand with her hair brush. I pushed her arm aside and whacked her knee.

Tillie shrieked. "You devilish brat. Your guardian is in the office today. He'll straighten you out!"

My heart filled with panic. The word guardian aroused the image of a policeman. She latched onto my left ear and led me down the hall. Opening a door, she shoved me into the office. I saw a gray-haired man sitting in a swivel chair near a long table. A whirling ceiling fan stirred the hot air.

"Here's that bratty kid. Just busted my knee."

"Well, well. So this is Roger," Mr. Wheeler said in cheerful voice, ignoring Tillie's complaints. With a friendly smile he stood up and shook my hand. My guardian filled the room, a clean-shaven,ruddy-faced, man. He looked like a proper gentleman, dressed in a blue suit and a tie. He held out a soft-looking hand, dropping a yellow wrapped ball of chewing gum into my palm.

"Miss Tillie says you bit her." Mr. Wheeler towered over me.

"Don't like her. She's mean." I stood fingering the wrapped treat.

Despite Mr. Wheeler's smile and his gift, I didn't know what to make of him. I had never seen a man wearing a red bow tie.

He sat down, opened a black briefcase, and pulled out a folder of papers. "We'll need your best behavior if the Lord is to find you a new mother. You'll soon be adopted."

Earlier, Momma had told me the Lord brought new babies, but I didn't believe He could bring me a new mother. It didn't seem possible. The idea scooted around in my mind. If the Lord could provide me with a new mother, perhaps He could find my father. I scratched my head. "What is adoption anyway?" My guardian didn't answer.

Though Momma was gone and my father had never appeared, I still longed for my only love. I stood before my guardian. "I wanna go home!" I said.

"Home." His face turned red. "Your mother no longer wants you."

"Yes, she does. Momma loves me."

He reached down and twisted my arm. "Your mother's gone. Will never return."

His threatening stance did not sway me.

"She will. She will." I pushed his hand aside.

But my protector paid little heed to my plea. I longed for freedom so one day I might return to Momma and find my mysterious father. If she didn't return, a new mother might take me in. I was an only child, and I didn't care to live with a bunch of other kids. Either way, I didn't wish to remain in an institution, as one child among many.

Because of this turmoil, Mr. Wheeler whisked me on a journey filled with warm hellos and crushing good-byes. With the howling winds spiraling the arid earth into a dust-bowl sky, I became a tumbleweed kid. My guardian uprooted and tossed me like unsalvageable debris across the prairie fields. Life whirled by in a rush of packing, unpacking, and tearful repacking as my heart was parceled out along the way.

My memories of my first three homes are like a series of faded snapshots, covered with water stains and aged with creases and torn edges. They form anxious days of longing to find a loving mother in a new home. Outside of court documents, these fragments form the only record I have.

It is late summer, 1932. In the long room, I am sweltering in the summer heat.

First came an elderly family who made a first payment to my guardian. The couple lived several hours from the city. Tall hills rose in the distance behind their two-story house surrounded by other new homes. I recall a room with a window overlooking a green lawn. After I got into a fight with one of the neighbor kids, the mother said she was unable to care for an active boy. The father returned me to Mr. Wheeler and, I imagine, he asked for his money back.

Within a month my guardian escorted me into an interview with a preacher and his wife. After a few questions, they wrote Mr. Wheeler a check and took me home. They lived in a white-framed house next to a small brick church near downtown Oklahoma City. He was a funny-looking man with wrinkled ears, who never smiled. I enjoyed singing about the Lord's work in Sunday school. But I grew bored with the reverend's long-winded sermons and stuck my tongue out at him to show my displeasure.

The reverend said I was a rebellious child and had the devil in me. Apparently I did, but neither he nor his wife wanted to take on Satan. The reverend returned me to the orphanage and ushered me into the office.

My guardian sprang up from his desk. His toothy smile vanished. He said if I didn't learn to mind and stay put, he'd never receive his full fee. He complained about bills coming due. Perhaps I felt sorry for Mr. Wheeler when he moaned about his hardships. I don't know. But if I felt any concerns they vanished when he put me to bed without supper. There I lay, humming "On-ward Christian soldiers . . . Marching as to war. . . ." under the covers.

Within a few days, Mr. Wheeler whipped out his handy smile, shuffled papers in his briefcase, and introduced me to prospective parents. Though I brushed my hair, smiled, and answered all their questions about my longing for a home, I failed one interview after another.

The couples always left with a bundle in their arms. The babies bawled all the time. Why wouldn't they take a grown-up boy? After each couple left, Mr. Wheeler urged me to be polite and more personable. "Perk up. Look happy. Be friendly." But I continued to fail.

Regardless of being shut away in the long room, I spent hours living in a private world of my own. On the closet floor below the shelves of diapers, I found a basket of items. I built houses and skyscrapers with stacks of dominoes, and made airplanes out of wooden clothespins using magazine covers for wings. I flew them across the baby cribs. Sometimes I pushed open the screen and tossed my birds out the window, watching them glide over the back fence.

Like Momma had taught me, I made a wondrous machine from one of the discarded sewing spools: I pushed a rubber band through the hole, inserted a matchstick in the rubber loops at each end and wound them tight. I built several more and placed them down. They sped across the floor and crashed, then climbed over each other and bumped along the wall. I saw these constructions as rocket-powered racers, and I kept them close by.

I learned to explore small ventures; even the trifling objects close at hand became important. I have no idea why I loved my marvelous spools, except they sang a soothing whirr and felt so magical to the touch. To me they were the grandest of toys.

It is early April 1933. Over ten months have passed and we are into a new year. Warmer weather ushered in prospective parents: Mr. and Mrs. Leonard Bascom. They lived in Nichols Hills, a township of stately mansions adjoining Oklahoma City to the northwest.

Mr. Bascom, stocky and bald-headed, greeted me with a firm

handshake. His wife, Mary, dressed in black and wearing high heels, looked taller than her husband. Mrs. Bascom led with a question.

"How old are you, young man?"

"Seven. Be eight in September."

"Have your parents passed away?"

"Oh, no! Momma's somewhere. Don't have a father."

"Well, let's talk about happier things. Would you like to live with us? We have a swimming pool."

"Yes, ma'am. I love water. I'll learn to swim."

The interview was a success. I had apparently said all the right things. The Bascoms signed the papers, and Mr. Wheeler thanked them with his brightest smile.

He warned me: "None of your foolishness. Better keep this home." I packed my cardboard box and tied it with Momma's belt. The following morning, a Cadillac, long and black, came gliding into the driveway. Out stepped the driver, dressed in a gray uniform with a funny cap perched on his head. I dashed out to the car. I looked forward to playing in the water. We drove north on Classen Boulevard for several miles, turned onto a curvy road, and parked in the driveway of a red-brick mansion with four white pillars. The lawn ran on for a block.

The driver led me to the back door and knocked. Mrs. Bascom greeted me with a hug. She said her husband would come in after work. She took my box of clothes and I tiptoed down a hall past a living room crowded with divans, tables, and lounge chairs. The place looked like a furniture store, not a family home. I entered a green-carpeted bedroom, and she put my box of clothes down.

Mr. Bascom returned in the evenings, and we often played checkers in the sunroom. Day after day Mother Bascom taught me to dog paddle in the pool. Other days we went shopping in the afternoon. She read scary stories at bedtime. But we had a couple of conflicts. For lunch one day, she served an onion sandwich. I pinched my nose and shoved it back.

"Now, look here, young man. Eat what's placed before you." She didn't smile.

"Onions stink. Not goin' to eat 'em."

"I'm not putting up with a sassy kid." She shoved me down the hall and locked me in my bedroom. I crawled out a window. She caught me near the garage and led me back inside. I stomped on her toe. She spanked my bottom and put me to bed.

I calmed down, and Mother Bascom smiled. We were soon on good terms again, making me a happy boy playing with my toy boat at the shallow end of the pool. Within a few minutes the phone rang. She rushed into the house.

A whirling noise caught my attention. Curious, I entered a small shed with one window that spread a dusty light across several metal tanks, motors, and red levers. I pushed a couple of the handles. Mother Bascom called for supper, and I hurried inside.

Mr. Bascom, having been out of the city on business, returned in the evening to see a rippling stream flowing down their driveway. The empty pool showed its tiled bottom, and I was in trouble. The following day, while I cried and pleaded with Mr. Bascom for another chance, their chauffeur ushered me into the car and we headed south. I began to sweat. My hands shook. I hated to face Mr. Wheeler. I knew he wouldn't want to see me again. We pulled up in front of the orphanage.

My guardian stood on the front porch. The chauffeur opened the door, and I stepped through the iron gate. Mr. Wheeler took a puff on his cigarette and flipped it onto the lawn. He grabbed me by the arm and shoved me into the office.

"It . . . wasn't my . . . fault." I tried to pull free.

His eyes were red; his voice had a thunderous growl. "My Lord, what's your problem? I get you a home. You're back in a couple of months. What's a man to do with a brat like you?"

He yanked off his belt and snapped it in the air. "I'll teach you to get along with your elders." With one hand he held me upright and lashed me from my ankles to my rump. His pumping arms never seemed to tire. I threw both arms around his legs which helped to soften the blows. Finally, he tossed me down.

I groped my way up the steps to the long room and crawled into bed. I cried as my legs throbbed throughout the night. Blue and red welts appeared in the morning, and pus oozed through the festered stripes. I could no longer chase after my racing cars or airplanes. Miss Tillie, with unusual kindness, rubbed a soothing ointment on my wounds, and I remained in bed for several days.

Many evenings, before I dozed off, I imagined the sound of Mr. Wheeler's belt exploding in my ear. I grabbed my pillow and crawled under the bed. My heart raced as I waited for my mind to ease. On other nights, I stood before the window with my forehead pressed against the glass, still looking for Momma to return. As the darkness blackened, I feared the monsters outside.

In the Oklahoma Society for the Friendless, I changed. I wised up to the world. My belief in grown-ups turned to disbelief. With their explosive tempers, their harsh words, their put-on smiles, they became my natural enemies. A smoldering anger settled into the corner of my heart.

Since no family wanted me, I told my guardian I would wait for Momma to return.

"She's your problem. Spoiled you rotten." Mr. Wheeler said I was a failure, an outcast whom no one wanted, not even my own mother.

Doubt swarmed through my mind. No. It couldn't be true. I believed Momma longed for me as I longed for her.

The weeks drifted into months and into an endless year, and I still harbored a deep longing for Momma. In the evenings, I often caught myself talking to her. Why would you leave? You said I was your golden-haired boy. I still couldn't believe she had abandoned me, knowingly and willingly. Thinking she no longer loved me gnawed at my soul.

It felt as if I were caught up in a whirlwind. No matter which direction I turned, dust clouded my eyes, breathing became difficult, and my legs were bound together like a bundle of weeds. Only when I looked to Heaven did life seem real. High in the sky the orange glow of the sun filtered through the clouds. I dreamed of crawling upward into that warm light and living as a child again. I couldn't understand the confusion and reality of it all.

One May day in 1933, a few months before my eighth birthday, and after being confined in the Oklahoma Society for the Friendless for a year, the saddest of feelings came over me. I no longer believed that the Lord could hear my prayers. I no longer ran downstairs on hearing a voice that could be, might be, Momma's. I realized she and I would never ride our red-and-white trolley into the city together again, and I quit looking out the window to see if she might come walking back into my life.

~ 3 ~

"Roger, get down here. A young man is here to see you," Tillie shouted. It was a sun-filled morning in late May, 1933.

I was upstairs building a fort with a box of dominoes. Could it be Uncle Paul? I pushed the dominoes aside and scrambled down the stairs. A tall, stout-looking teenager with wavy black hair and large, dark eyes stood in the entry holding a piece of paper out to Tillie. She took it and read it, looking confused.

"Who's this?" I stepped toward the stranger.

"Roger, this is Jay Cole Minter. He's unable to talk, but this paper says that he's to take you to a new home." The young man looked at me with the quiet lips and searching eyes of the very deaf.

Tillie paused, fingering her glasses. "I shouldn't let him go. Mr. Wheeler needs . . . But he's outta town." Jay Cole handed her an envelope. She wet her thumb on her tongue, opened the flap and looked inside. Finally, Tillie agreed to let me go.

I tore upstairs and pitched my clothes into my cardboard box. Scampering down the steps, I breathed with excitement. I felt forever free; I would never have to face Mr. Wheeler again.

Without speaking, Jay Cole guided me out the door. I asked him where we were headed. He only smiled as he tied my box on his bicycle rack, then lifted me onto the handlebars of his blue racing bike. We peddled down elm-lined streets with large homes sitting on green lawns. We rode for several miles, turned a corner, wheeled into a driveway at 324 North East 12th, and skidded to a stop in front of a white-frame house shaded by two towering oaks.

Jay Cole untied my possessions and, as we approached the front steps, the screen door opened and a woman, wearing a pink sweater, strode out. She embraced me with a kiss and a comforting hug, like an old friend who knew my history better than I did myself. Then she took both of my hands in hers and introduced herself.

"Good morning, Roger. My name's Helen. You'll meet my husband, Will Minter, later. Come in and have a glass of lemonade."

We entered the front door, walked through a walnut paneled foyer furnished with a bench and a hat rack, and into a bright sunlit living room. Floor-to-ceiling windows lined one side. A rock fireplace formed another wall, and a divan with fluffy cushions and several lounge chairs filled the room. The corner shelves contained wooden models of oil-drilling rigs. Helen walked over and turned off the Zenith radio.

Tall and willowy like a blade of bluestem grass, Helen had a tendency to curve her chest forward when she spoke, giving her voice a commanding tone. "Society for the Friendless! Nonsense. You have true friends now, Will and me." Her throaty but comforting voice promised the kind of love I yearned for—a love that would ease my turmoil. I had no idea how or why I had been saved, but I was truly grateful.

She looked me over with her large brown eyes. Her dark lashes contrasted with her fair skin. Helen looked young at fifty; a small-boned but graceful lady with abundant energy. She kneeled down and looked at my legs.

"How come the welts?"

"Don't hurt anymore."

Helen sighed. "I'll doctor you up."

Helen served a ham sandwich for lunch, but the morning's excitement had tired me. I yawned.

"You could use a nap."

We walked down a hallway and paused before a room with framed pictures on the walls. A divan and a desk stood to one side, and a long piano sat in the center. Further down the hall we entered a disheveled bedroom that smelled of dust. Magazines lay strewn across a colorful quilt. Helen scooped off the litter and tossed it onto a chair.

Pleased to have a room of my own again, I crawled up on the mattress, grabbed a fluffy comforter, and laid back. But Helen pursed her lips and looked serious. She told me to roll over. I turned onto my side and she slipped the large pillow from under my head and handed me a thin one. "Big pillows make curved backs. Remember that." This was the first of her many wisdoms.

The kitchen radio stirred me from my sleep. Helen called for supper. I hopped out of bed and walked up the hall and into the dining room. It was a spacious area with chairs around a long table. She and Jay Cole talked to me with a mixture of words, smiles, and sign language, explaining how they rescued me from my guardian's care. Helen claimed she had ransomed me into freedom by giving Mr. Wheeler a promissory note as a partial fee. Her throaty laughter brightened the room as she talked with her hands. She spread her palms up, then down, her fingers moving in curves, touching her thumbs, her diamond rings glistening in the light. Once Jay Cole clamped his hands over his ears. Helen smiled. She explained it was his way of not wanting to learn anything that might upset him.

That night, after Helen soothed my legs with black salve, she read a story and kissed me good night. I closed my eyes, but when she flipped the light off I sat up.

"Please, Helen, kiss me again."

She returned to my side. "Another hug and you'll nod away." I craved one more story, one more kiss, before I drifted off.

In the morning I woke up crying and gasping for air.

"Try to forget your days with Mr. Wheeler." Helen looked concerned.

"Oh Helen, he beat me."

"I know. But he says you hit your matron."

"I don't like Tillie either."

"Yes. Mr. Wheeler's a do-gooder." Helen said my guardian at one time was an upstanding minister. "Now he longs to get custody of another child. Then he will hound some couple for adoption fees."

Mr. Wheeler and my previous families, with their hard hands and harsh voices, had darkened my heart. I didn't want to cry, but the tears flowed.

"Has Mr. Blues come to visit?" Helen brushed my cheeks with her apron.

I covered my eyes.

"It's okay to cry. But it's not good, it's not healthy to live with the blues. They'll turn dark." Helen encouraged me to run outside and play with other kids. Make friends. Laugh, have fun, and chase the gray clouds away.

Despite my efforts to be happy, Mr. Blues now lived like a forlorn creature in my imagination. His tall frame looked like a sack of rags stretched over the grieving hulk of a weeping man. Tears ran down his face, dripped from his pointed nose, and wet the front of his torn shirt. There was a darkness about him—in his skin, his eyes, his crushed felt hat, and the tattered suit that covered him. His bony hands hung to his knees while he stood next to me, moaning and sobbing. Then we became one anguished heap; his scrawny fingers entwined with mine and he led me down the hall as he whispered woeful words.

I tried to reason with my inner voice, but these episodic periods of depression, without warning or reason, continued, year after year, to be a burden.

A week soon passed. Helen woke me from my nap. "Roger, quit dreaming. Will's home from the oil lease." With the sun glowing through the window, her apron smelled of steaks and onions. The radio talked from the kitchen. "While I fix your plate, go see Will on the sun porch."

I first saw Will Minter as he looked over a stack of papers, a cup of coffee close at hand. He pushed everything aside and stood up, jostling the ceiling's dangling light fixture. Will had a pleasant way about him, a quiet reserve, and a winning smile that brightened with his handshake.

He reached down and boosted me onto a chair. He smelled of oil and White Owl cigars. Now standing level with his eye, he asked if I could play cards.

"I like checkers and dominoes."

"I'll teach you slapjack. Then a hand of blackjack followed by a game of poker." He turned his mind to Helen, saying she loved children, but I shouldn't let her spoil me. I climbed on his lap as soon as he sat back down. He looked like an outdoorsman with his hands large, tan, and steady.

Helen Minter served fried potatoes and onions, and steak with iced tea. What a feast! I dug into the tasty meal, but I couldn't clean my plate. I glanced at Helen to see her reaction.

"I see that look. Don't worry. Eat what you can."

I finished my plate.

Later, after outfitting me in long pants, Helen began sharing her apron full of maxims to shape this youngster into a man. To emphasize her approval of my meager eating habits, she said, "Slim people outlive fat ones. Put that in your mind." This was one of Helen's favorite sayings, one which fit her slim frame and reflected her interest in personal health. "Look at Jay Cole. He's trim as an athlete."

"Is Jay Cole your boy?"

"No, he's Will's nephew. He's leaving tomorrow, heading back to the School for the Deaf in Sulphur to study for exams. He is a star on their track team, and we're so proud of him." Helen expressed concern in matters of family, health, and politics, and wised me up to a crafty world.

Helen, with her love of jewelry, fancy shoes, and fine furs, kept a chaotic house: she filled closets with galleries of feathered hats, left last year's calender on the Frigidaire refrigerator, and stacked old theatre programs on the Victrola record player. Dust accumulated on the piano, and the floors saw the broom and Eureka vacuum on a skimpy schedule.

Newspapers covered the coffee table, stacked for "later reading," and the beds were made with a slap and a dash and needed remaking. But she always had time for me. I was her prime project, and she gave me the best of her energies.

Will and I played slapjack as he smiled and talked about Helen. "She keeps house while wearing pearls. It's her way." Perhaps he felt that a messy house could be fun and relaxing. Will sometimes rolled out the sweeper and tried to clean the rugs while I picked up newspapers and emptied the trash. We two worked out a cleaning routine, but the chaos was too complicated for our hasty hands.

A month slipped by. One afternoon, a vision shocked me from out of the past. Stumbling onto the sun porch, Uncle Paul lugged a box filled with my toys. My mind rattled with questions. How did he know I was here? Is he a friend of Helen's? The room turned quiet. I asked him, "Where has Momma gone?"

"She's taken a long trip." Uncle Paul curled his arm around my shoulders. He refused to talk about Momma, but he promised to visit every few weeks. Though it had been over a year since I'd seen my toys, they had weathered the time well. That evening I played with my yellow truck, box of bugs, and homemade flashcards.

Near bedtime I asked Helen, "How did you meet Uncle Paul?"

"Why, Paul is Will's brother. I thought you knew."

"How did he find my toys?"

"Let's not worry about how your things arrived." Helen smoothed my hair. She told a story twice, tucked the covers in, and kissed me. I drifted off into a quiet sleep realizing that Paul Minter, my so-called Uncle Paul, had come through for me.

Helen's bedroom possessed the attractions of a secret hideaway. One rainy morning while she was in the kitchen talking on the phone, I snuck into her chamber to play among her possessions. I found a pleasant room with furniture smelling of wax, lipstick, and ladies powder. The best smells came from her dresser.

In the bottom drawer I rummaged through silk nightgowns and several slips. A scarf fell onto the floor. I shoved the drawer partially closed to search the middle one. Her pearl necklaces, small boxes of diamond rings, pins, and a gold watch were neatly stored there. The top drawer slid out under my curious fingers. I found her makeup powder, lipstick, her combs and brushes. And there to the back, in the far corner, I spied a gun and pulled it out.

The black pistol shined blue and smelled of fresh oil on metal. It appeared similar to the black gun Dick Tracy used in the funnies. I palmed the cold metal and rotated the cylinder, listening to a curious click, click, click. I lugged it down the hall, and stuffed it under my mattress.

After making a mess in Helen's room, I returned to put things in order. Just as I straightened a few items in the top drawer, Helen's shadow loomed in the doorway. She slipped on her glasses. "My dresser. What are you up to?"

"Just playing."

Helen leaned over and looked among her things. Her faced stiffened. "My Colt!" Helen shouted. "It's gone. What have you done with it?"

"You won't spank me?"

"I have other means." Helen stood before me, arms crossed and the blue veins in her neck swelled.

"It's . . . ah . . . in the . . . bed-r-room," I stammered.

We walked into my room. "Ok, where is it?" She placed her hand on my shoulder. Finally I walked around the bed and pulled the pistol from under the mattress.

"Damnit, Roger, use your noggin. This is a Colt .38. You could have blown your head off." I cried and Helen wiped my face with her skirt. That weekend she limited my play to the living room, the sun porch, and the backyard. From then on, Helen kept her blue-steeled pistol elsewhere.

The middle years drew lines in Helen's face, but her vitality and friendly eyes remained from her spirited youth. She was as vigorous as Uncle Paul, who drove an Oldsmobile convertible when he came to visit. He and Helen smoked, played the piano, drank coffee, played cards, and talked about Alfalfa Bill Murray's efforts to control the flow of oil.

"Hell no, the governor shouldn't use the army to shut down the oil fields," Helen said. "He'll run every wildcatter out of the state."

"Helen, don't be so hard," Uncle Paul said. "He's only trying to pump up the price of gas."

Will always said that Helen was smart. She didn't mince words. "Will, don't hand over those oil leases until I record them at the courthouse. You'd better get some new tires for the Packard. Those on the front look mighty bald."

Will smiled.

Then she looked him over. "Get a haircut. And while you're at it, have them shine your shoes. You're looking rather seedy."

Like a confident queen, she ruled her court with gaiety and directness. She lived by her own laws of honesty, warmth, and a lofty will—all wrapped with laughter. Pretension and sham weren't part of her life. Helen never threatened or ordered me around; she led me with a mother's insight. Like a sovereign, she watched over her home, sparked my imagination at bedtime, and instilled me with a feeling of love.

"Tomorrow," Helen said one night with a glimmer in her eye, "Will may take you out on his oil lease where you will see the Mighty Oil Mouse."

"Oh, Helen!" My curiosity leaped. "Tell me about the Mighty Mouse."

Lit by a night lamp, her veined hands glowing with sparkling rings, she weaved the story of the mysterious mouse. She said that Jay Cole had brought the mouse home from school, and fed it bowl after bowl of buttermilk till she grew to twice the length of Will's big foot. "Since the giant mouse could no longer live at home, Will drove her out to the oil lease where she makes her nest near his drilling rig."

"Is she safe?"

"The roustabouts keep the cats away with slingshots." Her voice followed her animated gestures as she embroidered the tale with the mouse's three children.

"Does she have brown fur?"

"Oh, no. The Oil Mouse wears a gold coat and has six feet. She can dig down a mile a day." She gathered up her pencils and water-color box. In a swirling hand, she drew a picture of a gigantic mouse with big ears, a curled tail, and six long legs. She colored the oil mouse with quick brushstrokes of yellow-gold, painting the nose and toes a soft brown. A fancy red ribbon graced her neck.

She said that when Will decided where to sink a new well, the mouse would sneak into the field and burrow a hole to the center of the earth. Her children would scoop out the tunnel. Then the workers spun pipes in the hole, spewing oil into the air.

With her lean gazelle grace and fierce intensity, Helen engaged life with a passion that seemed much stronger than Momma's. I now looked at Helen as my mother. Who else knows about the Mighty Oil Mouse? Oh, my marvelous Helen. I believed her then and honor her still.

31

One morning I was in my room reading a comic book when I heard footsteps on the front porch. The doorbell rang. Couldn't be the mailman. He came in the afternoon. I tossed the comic down and ran back to kitchen to tell Helen. But she was outside near the back steps working in the flower garden. Then a bang on the front door echoed through the house.

"Mr. Wheeler," Helen whispered, tugging my sleeve. Helen slipped off her apron and hurried toward the living room. I dashed down the hall, entered the music room, and crawled under the piano. Like Jay Cole, I clamped my hands over my ears, not wanting to hear any news from my guardian. His words only brought trouble. After a few minutes Helen stood near me, and I crawled out and stood up.

She reported that my guardian had left an envelope. After reading the letter, she told Will that Mr. Wheeler was going to court about his custody rights.

"I know his type," Will said. "Perhaps I'll take Roger out to the oil rig with me."

Occasionally, Helen and Will talked at once. "Around those men of yours?" Helen asked. "They'll have him cussing like a roughneck." Will started to answer, but she interrupted. "I don't know. If Wheeler hears of it, he'll make trouble."

Though Helen made her point, Will won. "I'll keep the boy in hand."

*

The bright chrome and white-walled tires of Will's Packard gleamed as we floated over the rolling hills southeast of the city. We were on our way to sign drilling leases and work on his oil rigs. When we climbed in, he tossed his briefcase beside me. I kicked it on the floor. "Wheeler! Wheeler's bag," I said. Even today when I see a briefcase I think of my guardian's wily ways.

"Now, calm down." He pulled his briefcase back onto the seat. "Needn't worry about the old man. You're my new roustabout."

"I'm a roustabout?" I asked, fiddling with the lock on his leather case.

"We'll live a week or two out on the oil lease. Just the two of us. See if we can help the crew bring in a new gusher." He told me that I was to carry his files and polish the car like Jay Cole Minter did before he left for school.

I loved the deep-throated sound of the Packard, a smooth lumbering machine, that floated alongside fields of corn and over the dusty road stretching out to the giant oil derricks reaching up to the sky. After a dozen miles we turned onto a narrow lane and parked in front of a boxcar-shaped structure. Will crawled out of the Packard and led the way across a wooden walk to a bright blue building, welded together using large sheets of steel.

With an iron entry door at one end, the twelve-by-thirty-foot building looked unlike any house I had ever seen. Bare lightbulbs dangled from the curved ceiling, providing the only light for the windowless home. The furniture consisted of three bunk beds and a pine table with eight chairs. The room smelled of kerosene mixed with coffee. A blue coffeepot sat on the two-burner kerosene stove. Fresh air came in through a ventilator toward the back of the roof.

The oilmen called our new home a doghouse. Will said that I would love the oil patch and claimed our steel home was safer than living in the city. Inside the door, Will kept a wooden slingshot which the men used to scare away the cats. He said they protected the mice who lived under the floor. Will lit a White Owl cigar, pulled up a chair, and leaned over the table to study his notebook.

During the summer of 1933 and on into the spring of 1934, we lived out on the leases for a few days or a week at a time. "Boys need to brush shoulders with roustabouts and roughnecks. You'll grow up tough." Each morning, before daylight, we'd crawl out of our bunks. Will made coffee in a blue pot and fried bacon and eggs—which never tasted as good anywhere else. He let me take sips of his black coffee out of a saucer. He claimed it would grow hair on my chest.

33

I now lived among hardworking drillers and roustabouts, who gambled and drank whisky like oil-soaked giants. The workers took their breaks and slept in steel houses next to ours. Will explained that the buildings sheltered them from flying timbers and the rain of crude oil when a gusher blew in. Some of the other men lived further away in canvas tents with board sides, and I was fascinated by the drowsy dogs that guarded each door. The men lived close to the earth but many drove shiny new cars.

In the evenings, Will taught me to play blackjack with stacks of pennies while the drillers, roustabouts, and a couple of wildcatters shared their dreams. Story followed story of black gold buying new Ford convertibles, Chevrolets, Cadillacs, Hudsons, and Packards. Stories spun among the men like the rotary drilling rigs.

We often walked the fields checkered with oil derricks, giant steel towers surrounded by oil pits, and stacks of rusted pipe. Will Minter talked, shook hands, and signed papers with farmers and oilmen. I jogged along toting his leather briefcase. When my legs wobbled, he boosted me up on his shoulders and I eyed the men on their level.

In the mornings, I prowled around catching grasshoppers, crickets, and roly-poly bugs and tossed a handful under the edge of the dog-house for the mighty Oil Mouse and her children. On many afternoons, when the sun warmed the field, I took a bucket of suds and washed Will's Packard. One day I would scrub the bumpers, the next day the radiator grill, and other hours were devoted to polishing the wheels. Then I emptied the ashtrays and swept the seats and floorboards clean. A few lines of dust streaked across the hood, but Will smiled and paid me a penny a day. He claimed to the men that he had hired a good hand.

Working on Will's Packard helped to calm my Wheeler anxieties. I enjoyed living among the dozens of tall drilling rigs draped like Christmas trees, ablaze day and night with electric lights. They rose out of the ground in every direction. The producing wells made a rhythmic sound. *Chug-a-chug-Sput! Chug-a-chug-Sput!* The steel rods drove down and up, sucking oil from the earth.

My heart thumped with excitement as I thrived in this world of lights and rumbling sounds.

One night the bed shook me awake. I climbed down from the bunk as the table danced across the steel floor. I dashed out the door, my stomach churning with fear. The earth growled. A rumbling roar shook the ground, followed by an explosion that shot a gusher of oil through several derricks. "Roger, get back. Back inside. Turn off the stove," Will shouted.

Shivering with fright, I rushed in, turned off the oil burner, and jumped back in bed. I spent several hours listening to the rain of oil on the roof. *Wham!* A timber crashed across the doghouse. The building shuddered, the table tumbled over as the coffeepot clattered across the metal floor. I pulled a blanket over my head.

Will worked through the following day and into the night without supper. Early the next day, the men capped the flow of oil from the damaged wells. But the explosion destroyed Will's two producing wells and burned his steel drilling rig beyond repair.

The tragedy of losing his income left Will sad and unsmiling. His red eyes and shaky voice reflected his worries. We returned to the city and entered a house already shrouded in despair.

~4~

When we arrived, the darkened house and drawn blinds made us apprehensive. Will fumbled in his pockets for his keys. Not finding them, he rang the bell. After a long delay, Helen cracked the door enough to let us in. We struggled through the half-opened door, shutting it quietly behind us. Obviously, skulduggery was afoot. Helen ushered us down the hall and through the swinging door into the kitchen where she fixed a pot of coffee, lit a Lucky, and told of being surprised by a visit from the sheriff. It seemed Mr. Wheeler had accused Helen of threatening him over the beating he had given me. The sheriff had delivered a warning on that bit of business along with a summons for Will and Helen to appear before Judge Christison, the very judge Momma had used to sign me into my guardian's care. Now having lived with the Minters for over nine months, I realized we three were in the same hellish boat. Helen faced threats from the sheriff and the judge. Will's money was running thin from his oil-field fire, and I was sitting on the edge of a cliff, hoping not to lose this loving home.

When Helen and Will returned from their meeting with the

36

judge, I felt uneasy. Seeing my worried face, Helen shrugged my concerns aside, assuring me she could resolve any problem that might arise.

"Don't worry, Will's brother will help him sink another well. And I'll find a way to keep your Mr. Wheeler at bay. A few dollars will make him smile." She assured me I would be her boy forever and ever. Helen treated me as if I were something rare and special. She now called me Bill Minter in honor of Will. "If times get better, you'll become our adopted son."

The following day, Uncle Paul arrived unannounced and brought me a pal named Tippy, a street dog with black hair and a white tip on his tail.

Helen wrinkled her nose. "Your mutt smells to high heaven."

I picked up my new friend, dashed into the bathroom, filled the tub, and jumped in with Tippy. I scrubbed, rinsed, and dried him with one of Helen's towels. That evening, my bed partner curled up under my blanket.

Helen joined in celebrating the arrival of Tippy. She threw her arms around me and mentioned a new word which captured my imagination. "I have arranged for you to receive an allowance of seven cents a week."

I had a penny a day, but one penny had to be set aside each week for St. Luke's Methodist Church. This new situation gave me the freedom to shop, forget my troubles with the court, and enjoy Helen's buoyant spirit. During the Depression, a dime or a quarter seemed like a fortune. I never understood Helen's generous nature, because Momma never gave me an allowance.

One day I rushed into the music room and sat down at the piano in high glee to plunk out the one song Helen had taught me upon Tippy's arrival, "I Dropped my Doggie in the Dirt," which was played with the index finger of each hand, but ended with full-knuckle acoustics. (We always said "Doggie" for Dolly and I didn't know it was anything else until years later.)

Helen threw up her hands with a "whoopee," and we danced a jig side by side while Tippy circled us, snapping at our heels. I felt the spirit of liberation.

I let my pennies accumulate during that first week while I basked in Helen's wondrous personality. This southern lady, born in an oil patch, was worldly and wickedly funny. She shared spicy stories with her neighbors, prayed to the Lord regularly, kept a blue revolver handy, played the piano and sang a varied repertoire, and loved me without reservation.

Who wouldn't be happy? And I was, unless I overheard conversations concerning judges, lawyers, guardians, orphanages, or missing mothers. It was then I remembered Mr. Wheeler's sneaky smile. My heart thundered as I felt that trouble might come. And surely no one but Helen would want to adopt me.

If I heard Mr. Wheeler's name, I crawled under the grand piano, hugged Tippy between my knees, and clamped my hands over my ears, wishing I was deaf like Jay Cole. Then I couldn't hear bad news. Deafness could drive away my guardian and all the strange parents.

When Helen saw me in this glum state, she lifted my spirit with double games of penny-ante checkers. She set up two card tables in the music room, laid out two checkerboards and chips, and giggled at the absurdity of the world outside. Her lively nature drew me in, and before long we'd be squealing over each game.

Sometimes my pilfering fingers dug into her cup of coppers, but she'd slap my hand with a caution: "Nobody likes a cheater." This maxim hung in the air to caution me for years to come—along with many others issuing from this feisty life-lover: "small pillows for straight backs," "skinny ones outlast the fat ones," "look before you leap," "busy fingers, busy minds," "sorry is as sorry does," and "a little dirt is good for you."

One day, Helen handed me an extra nickel along with my pennies. She wanted to take me on her daily errands so I could learn to be a smart shopper. "Dress up now. Look alert."

I took a bath with Tippy, dressed in my Sunday clothes, and slicked my hair with a splash of water.

Talk of dressing up enlivened Helen. She darkened her eyelashes with mascara, dusted her cheeks with rouge, and brightened her lips with lipstick before checking my clothing and hair style.

A pair of black slacks draped her thin legs, and she slipped on a blue blouse covering her sinewy arms. A row of glistening pearls peeked out from her silk collar. She highlighted her graying hair with a brown velvet hat, a purple feather slanting back over her ear.

Helen looked like a female Robin Hood as she click-clicked down the walk in her high heels with open toes and ankle straps. Her tilting feather glowed like a colorful bird in the morning sun. But unlike Robin, she wore a fox fur slung over one shoulder. Helen didn't follow any style, she created her own.

We strolled out of the house with the goal of walking to the Peerless Drugstore located three blocks down and around the corner. Her entrance through the store's double-hung doors was so beguiling that everyone turned in awe. We sat at a marble-topped table, and she laid her fur piece over the back of the chair and placed her purse on the table. Smiling like a lady in a newspaper ad, she tore the cellophane from a fresh pack of Lucky Strikes with her long fingers. I was fascinated as she tapped out a cigarette, inserted it into a silver holder, and lit up. Helen squinted her eyes and inhaled slowly, blew a gray cloud upward, then waved her hand for a breath of fresh air. The owner, in a white apron, approached. "Good morning, Mrs. Minter. Who's your young friend?"

She smiled. "Mr. Cunningham, meet my boy. He will be shopping today."

While Helen sipped her hot coffee, I drank a Hires root beer. She watched as I turned to explore a table filled with watercolor boxes, rulers, Big Chief writing tablets, and yellow pencils. She saw me eyeing a receipt book interleaved with carbon paper. I hesitated over spending a nickel.

I thought it would be swell to own a writing book and make copies of Helen's art lessons. Helen caught my eye to give me a negative shake of her head on the receipt book. But when she turned to talk with a neighbor, I plopped the precious nickel on the counter, and sidled back to face Helen. She soon spied the book.

"My Lord! You've been taken." She tapped the cigarette in an ashtray. "Run back and tell Mr. Cunningham you want your money back!"

"Gee whiz, this is a book of magic. Don't you see? It's mine. I bought it. Don't wanna give it up."

Helen sighed and looked bewildered. "All right, all right, keep your book. But later I'm going to give Mr. Cunningham a piece of my mind."

"Boy, oh, boy!" I hugged Helen, pulled out my book, and drew pictures of an oil well and Tippy, my happy pal. Later, Helen and I strolled back to the house hand in hand. In my eyes, our outing had been a success.

Uncle Paul now took to visiting me once a month. I always asked him about Momma.

"Sadly, I haven't heard from your mother," he would say.

We pitched horseshoes and played catch in the backyard. Later he often sat at the dining table and drank coffee with Helen. She smoked Luckies, he smoked Camels. I collected their empty packages, and they whispered and sent me outside to play.

One afternoon, I found a fresh Lucky in a discarded wrapper. I pocketed a couple of matches from the box near the stove and moseyed out behind the garage. I lit up, drawing in the warm air, but the smoke floated upward, burning my nose. I stomped the cigarette out. I would have to grow up to smoke Luckies.

By the spring of 1934, Momma had been gone two years. I often heard Helen and Will talk about my guardian but never about my momma or father. I felt they must have known them. Was Will or

Uncle Paul my father? I asked these questions of myself, not daring to voice them aloud.

In May 1934, I felt happy because I hadn't seen or heard from Mr. Wheeler for several months. But on the drizzly morning of the fifteenth, the doorbell rang longer than usual. Helen freed the security chain and opened the front door while I looked past her in all innocence. There stood my guardian, filling the doorway and looking proper in his red bow tie and blue suit. A man and a woman I had never seen before stood beside him.

I ran and hid, clamping my hands over my ears. No, I didn't want to hear any of their conversation. If only I were deaf.

Helen found me crying and shaking under my bed.

"Oh! My pet, my darling. I have bad news. Bad news for Will and me. Maybe good news for you."

"I hate Mr. Wheeler."

"Now. Now. Perk up. Your guardian wants to place you with a younger family. The husband holds a steady job. And they have two young boys." She talked about a city farm. "You'll have pigs to play with, and you love pigeons. Maybe milk a cow." She said that they lived in Sulphur, the same town where Jay Cole attended school.

My mind jumped in one direction and another, searching for a corner in which to hide. But seeing Helen with her defeated posture, her tears, her pleading, I crawled out and stood up. She brushed my hair, wiped my tears, and steered me into the living room to meet my fate.

Mr. Wheeler called me over, but my feet couldn't navigate. With a cheery "Never mind," he introduced me to Mr. and Mrs. Warren Hardt, a sunburnt-looking couple—the tall husband rather calm in appearance, the attractive lady looking at me with a friendly smile. They both dressed in dark suits as if they were going to church.

I clung to Helen, who took my limp right hand and extended it to Mr. Hardt's. My rebellious behavior didn't escape his scrutiny. He exchanged worried glances with his wife. "We'll need to put meat on his bones."

"The boy is a bundle of energy." Mr. Wheeler laid his hand on my shoulder. "He will thrive at your place."

Mrs. Hardt walked over and kneeled beside me. She grasped my hands in hers and looked into my eyes. "Young man," she said in a soft voice, "I am longing to have a boy your age."

I loved animals. Perhaps, if I gave it a chance, Mrs. Hardt would be a loving mother, and I would have two brothers to play with.

Mr. Wheeler tut-tutted that the Hardts must be getting on down the road. And, yes, they told Mr. Wheeler they wanted me to go with them.

"Wait one moment." Helen's eyes widened. "May the boy take his pal, Tippy?"

"We no longer want a dog," Mrs. Hardt replied in a distant voice.

Why didn't they understand that Tippy needed me as much as I needed Tippy? And they already had two sons. Why did they want a boy my age? Grown-ups were a puzzle.

I stood with a small box of belongings strapped together with Momma's belt, once more saying good-bye to the one woman who loved me now and forever.

"Be brave for me, my boy. I'll write; I'll be in your life as best I can." Helen hugged me. "When we come to pick up Jay Cole, we'll take you with us for a picnic. You'll see. I love you."

Mr. Wheeler put his finger to his lips, motioning for silence. I crawled into the backseat of the Plymouth. Mrs. Hardt slipped behind the steering wheel. Her husband sat by her side. A steady drizzle washed across the driveway.

I looked out the rear window to catch one last glimpse of Helen. She stood with a sorrowful look on her face as she held Tippy. I couldn't understand why Mr. Wheeler would tear me away from Helen. She had replaced Momma and made me her boy in loving ways.

I clutched my box of clothes to my chest and tried to remain upright as the car lurched and rolled down the street.

~5~

The purring Plymouth, shrouded in fog and swirling rain, headed south from Oklahoma City. Mrs. Hardt steadied the steering wheel against the swings and sways of the rain-dancing car as we sped down Highway 77. The windshield wipers thumped as the lights of the oncoming cars bled through the mist. The tail lights ahead, like blinking fireflies, guided us around the curves. Over an hour later, as we turned from the main highway and drove east on a narrower road, the storm slackened and the world glistened after its dramatic scrubbing.

Mr. Hardt, a hefty man of about fifty with blue eyes and a bronzed face, looked out over the rolling land. He swept his gray-suited arm across the window and talked about the Chickasaw Indians who once roamed the prairie fields after they were forced into Indian Territory from Mississippi in the 1830s.

"Hope you'll join Scout Troop 65," he said. "I'll teach you to make an Indian headdress with wild turkey feathers."

I looked forward to being a Boy Scout.

Mrs. Hardt glanced back and talked about the fun I would have helping her two sons take care of their livestock. She said they owned a couple of cows, a sow with a litter of pigs, a flock of chickens, and a loft full of pigeons.

"By the way," Mr. Hardt turned in his seat, "We will call you Billy. You're a member of the Hardt family now."

"No, no," I protested. "My name's Roger." But Mr. Hardt ignored my plea.

The car slowed and stopped at 1600 West Broadway, the main street leading into Sulphur. There, on a busy corner under a towering pine, I saw a grand two-story white house with a red barn to one side. "We have three acres," Dad Hardt said, "and a comfortable house."

Mother Hardt tooted the horn and two boys bounded out to the car. She laughed at their enthusiastic response as she stepped out and reached to open my door. The taller one walked over and introduced himself as James, saying he was sixteen. His broad shoulders made him look like a football player.

The younger brother, quiet as a morning prayer, offered a friendly hand. "Call me Edward. I'm eleven."

I stood to my full height. "I'll be nine in September."

"Easy boys, Billy needs to catch his breath before you scare him away with your eagerness. James, you take his things, and Edward, you show him upstairs." We entered the front door, climbed an oak stairway, and walked down a carpeted hallway.

In Edward's room, James dropped my box inside the door. He told me that the bed in the near corner was mine. "The sounds are better. Like Mother calling for meals." He tapped me on the shoulder as he walked out, and the scent of Brilliantine hair oil floated in the air.

I felt a sense of relief when James left. His red hair and brusque manner intimidated me. Edward was more my size and, with a friendly smile, welcomed me to share his room.

Two single beds, a mahogany chest of drawers, and one oak desk with two chairs constituted the furniture. The walls were bare except for two bulletin boards, one displaying a collection of butterflies. A

44

pine bookcase along the wall held a stack of comic books and a shelf of magazines. Next to the bookcase was a table filled with model cars and sailboats.

"Would you like to pin anything above my desk?" He pointed to a snapshot tacked on his bulletin board.

"Not really. Is that James wearing a football helmet?"

"Yeah, he's a tackle for Sulphur High."

Outside, Edward spent an hour showing me around the place, across the back pasture and through the barn; we paused by the pig pen and he introduced me to Peggy, the friendly piglet who squealed when I scratched her belly.

We returned to his room where he let me handle a couple of his sailboats. Then he thumbed through a stack of *Popular Mechanics* magazines showing me plans for several more. "Tomorrow, after church, I'll teach you how to build a boat."

That evening, after serving a fried chicken supper, Mother Hardt asked the brothers to do the dishes. She guided me into the living room. We sat on a tan leather divan as she interlocked her arm in mine, and with her large, expressive hands she brought Tom Sawyer alive with words and gestures.

She was a short, attractive lady who wore a black dress trimmed with white lace at the neck and sleeves. Her hair was black, interwoven with strands of gray, and she swept it back over her ears. Her face was round and full, with high cheekbones, and tanned from the sun, but smooth and without a blemish. Her eyes were soft brown, overshadowed with a quiet sadness.

The next day was Sunday, church day. The house bustled with activity as everyone rushed about, checking wardrobes, polishing shoes, and spiffing up. I went about my preparation with a heavy heart. I didn't want my new family to find out I had a hard time sitting through long-winded sermons.

Just before we left for the Calvary Baptist Church, Edward talked about his favorite meal. "Mom's making apple pie for dinner. And she fries beef so good that the steers don't even mind."

The first hour of Sunday school comforted my restlessness. A motherly teacher read a booklet about Moses and the Red Sea, the kind of story I liked. We finished the hour with the familiar song. I sang and clapped my hands. "Je-sus loves me, this I know. For the Bible tells me so!" I felt uplifted as I tapped my foot and swayed to the comforting melody. But for the life of me, even when I repeated the chorus, I still couldn't swallow the message. If Jesus loved me, why did he let Momma leave, and why hadn't my father showed up? But neither the sermon nor the songs offered answers.

Back home, we trooped in and seated ourselves in great expectation of the feast. Dad Hardt quieted us, then said grace. Mother Hardt had prepared a perfect meal of vegetables and meats, mashed potatoes topped with a puddle of butter, and a white pool of gravy in a blue bowl. I dug in, but before I could finish, Dad Hardt ladled a monstrous serving of spinach onto my plate.

"Make you strong like Popeye!" He smiled.

"I hate greens!" Perhaps, with a small taste, I could walk out of this spinach patch. I nibbled on one of the leaves.

"These are hard times," Dad Hardt said. "We don't waste anything in this house."

I slipped half of a turnip in my pocket and stirred in some gravy in the spinach. I finally swallowed a spoonful. But a mess of the green weeds remained.

Having eaten all the food on my plate except the spinach, I picked up my plate and walked out to the pig pen that housed the sow and her litter of pigs. My friend Peggy was asleep on her side, all four feet in the air, her head resting on a bundle of straw. A sunken washtub, used as a trough, looked empty. I reached through the fence and scratched her stomach. She squealed to life. "You like greens?" Her corkscrew tail twitched as she cleaned the plate. I returned the empty dish to the kitchen sink. Mother Hardt smiled and patted me on the back, but Mr. Hardt refused to serve me a slice of apple pie.

Edward and I spent the afternoon working in the barn. Using a band saw we cut out a couple of boat hulls from a pine board. We each sharpened a bow on one end, and set a dowel mast in one hull and two masts in the other. For sails we cut pieces of starched cloth from one of his dad's old shirts.

Edward held up his two-masted schooner and my small sloop. "Tomorrow, I'm goin' down to the pond at Bellview Park to try out my new boat, if you'd like to come." That night I could scarcely sleep, thinking of playing on the water.

On Monday morning after Edward and I fed the chickens and slopped the sow and piglets, we walked back of the barn and down a leafy lane and entered Bellview Park. Oh, what a wonderful duck pond! The water covered a couple of city blocks with a shallow end sloping deeper to the other side. A small island rose in the middle. Upon hearing our voices, several gray-feathered ducks glided into the water, quacking to the bobbing turtles to stay clear. We lined up our sailboats and raced them back and forth across the shallow end of the pond. We played until it turned time for supper.

Several weeks flew by, punctuated by Sundays. Thinking about Mother Hardt's cooking and her comforting hugs made me feel secure about my new home.

*

The most disturbing moments in the family didn't involve Mother or Dad Hardt, but our big brother James. Every few days he harassed Edward and me about doing barnyard chores: "Get busy you lazy dumbbells. There's work to do."

"Dad has appointed James as our straw boss," Edward said.

"What's that?"

"You know. A lazy cuss who orders everyone around."

On the following Monday, waving his dad's cane from side to side,

James ordered Edward and me to clean the chicken house. We shoveled the black-and-white droppings into a couple of wheelbarrows and spread the stinky goo over the back field. We finished the job and yanked off our overalls. We hosed each other off and washed our hair in vinegar to reduce the smell.

Several days later, James forced us to haul bales of alfalfa out of the loft and spread them over the floor of the chicken house. Edward and I struggled with the heavy bundles. James stood looking over us. "Come on, give us a hand," I said. He refused. I kicked him on the shin, and he punched me in the mouth. Blood trickled from my lips as I headed for the hydrant.

After supper Edward and I gathered a sack of cockleburs out of the back field. Wishing James a good night's rest, I spread the sticky burrs between his sheets.

"I'm going to tell Dad about you devils," James screamed.

Where Edward spoke with a soft voice, James shouted orders like a carnival barker. Where Edward soothed over differences, his big brother instigated trouble. I found myself growing skeptical whenever I overheard Dad Hardt boasting about James. He talked about how his eldest son had a good head on his shoulders, saved his allowance to purchase a new Remington rifle, and how he would soon become an Eagle Scout. "Someday, James will make something of himself."

Never a week went by, except when James took the bus over to Ardmore to visit with his cousins, that he didn't shout out a new order. Edward and I resented the idea of having a straw boss, and we looked forward to the days when he left town.

I felt joy within the family when we gathered in the living room and listened to Jack Benny and Mary Livingston on the radio. They made us laugh. We grew quiet when Will Rogers delivered his weekly radio talk. Mother Hardt claimed that he was the most famous person in the world, more beloved than President Roosevelt. Will

JUVENILE DOCKET No. 8

TIMES-JOURNAL PUB. CO., OKLA. CITY

Title of Cause   Attorneys

STATE OF OKLAHOMA

7128

Bechan. Roger.
vs.

Defendant

DATE
1932

May 20th Filing Petition.

" 20th Filing Journal entry wherein the said Roger Bechan was declared to be a dependent child and made a ward of this Court and committed into the care and custody of W. C. Wheeler living in Oklahoma City, Oklahoma for the purpose of finding a suitable home into which home said child may be adopted.

Oklahoma County Juvenile Court Petition placing Roger Bechan
into the custody of William C. Wheeler who was Superintendent of
The Oklahoma Society for the Friendless. May 20, 1932.

OKLAHOMA SOCIETY FOR THE FRIENDLESS

Oklahoma City, Oklahoma

W. C. WHEELER, Supt.

Number of pieces of literature distributed 6790
Letters sent 1185
Letters received 920
CASE WORK:
Number of cases handled 208

RELIEF WORK:

Number of families relieved 136
Number of children in families 231
Number of transportations given 89
Number of meals given 1160
Number of lodgings given 280
No. of men and women placed and replaced 95

INSTRUCTIONAL WORK:

Number of audiences addressed 130
Number of persons in audiences 35,600

ANNUAL FINANCIAL STATEMENT FOR 1929

RECEIPTS:

Balance on hand December 1, 1928 ....$ 14.15
Total cash received Dec. 1, 1928 to Dec. 1, 1929...............$5,736.04

    Total for the work of the year $5,750.19

EXPENDITURES (ACCORDING TO USE)

Administrative and publicity 615.10
Office expense 760.40
Travel expense 510.10
Material relief 1,812.35

CONSTRUCTIVE RELIEF:

A: Employment finding, investigation, consulation and
    follow- up work $1,208.30
B: Education and field work   831.94

Total expense for year $5,738.19
Balance December 1, 1929 ,.............................   12.00

Oklahoma Society for the Friendless. Annual Report, 1929
William C. Wheeler, Superintendent (One state commissioner stated:
"We do not feel justified in approving [their] work.")

Mr. & Mrs. Warren Hardt's home, Sulphur, Oklahoma

RICHARD HARDT'S OBITUARY

The Hardt family brought
Roger Bechan into their home
as a boy to replace their son
who had died of rabies.

Sulphur Times Democrat
April 21, 1932

RICHARD BUDDEN HARDT

Richard Budden Hardt, seven year
old son of Mr. and Mrs. W. N. Hardt
of West Tishomingo avenue, passed
away in the Durant hospital last Saturday night near twelve o'clock, after a brief and sudden illness. He
was confined for less than a week.

Richard was a student of the second grade at Washington ward school
under Mrs. Gordon Alexander. His
entire student body was lost in grief
at his passing.

Funeral services were held Tuesday afternoon at the Presbyterian
church, Rev. Hoyt Wakefield and
Rev. George Quarterman, pastor of
the Episcopalean church of Ardmore,
officiated. A large group of family
friends, chums and classmates attended the services. Interment was held
at Oaklawn cemetery.

Dunn Funeral Home handled the
arrangements in Sulphur.

Second Grade. Washington School. Sulphur, Oklahoma, 1934-35
Roger Bechan is sitting in bottom row, third from left.

Rogers often talked about the United States Congress and its foolishness. I believe the Hardts saw him as an Oklahoma cowboy who had made it big. But the friendly evenings didn't carry over into the following day when big James harassed Edward and me about being lazy.

Edward hated the drudgery of work as much as I did. Every day there were nothing but blistered hands left over from yesterday's chores. We thought alike: playtime is now! Through play we celebrated freedom, fantasy, and high adventure, where our imaginations created a world apart from their city farm. When allowed the time, we built slingshots, wooden cars, model boats, and played in Bellview Park. We were becoming fast friends.

Even Mother Hardt nourished our comradeship. "Tomorrow, I am going into the city. Billy, you and Edward can ride along. We'll have lunch at the Belle Isle Lake." This sparked a joyous whoop from Edward who vowed, "We'll catch a perch or two." With that he dug up a can of worms and packed his fishing tackle.

Saturday morning, September 7, 1934, Mother Hardt prepared a picnic basket and we hopped in the car and drove north on Highway 77. Edward and I played cards in the backseat as the rolling fields ran on, holding herds of cattle. We crossed the North Canadian River and entered the outskirts of Oklahoma City, heading toward the smokestack near the power plant where we picked up a box of electrical parts. From there we turned into a tree-lined park with picnic tables bordering a beautiful lake.

Then, "surprise!" Mother Hardt hadn't forgotten my birthday. She unpacked a chocolate cake which she brightened with nine glowing candles. I took a deep breath and blew them out, feeling grand about her thoughtfulness.

Edward and I tossed our lines in the water but failed to get a bite. So we walked the shore tossing our worms to the ducks. Near dusk, we piled into the car and headed home. Edward and I both looked forward to our next trip into the city.

49

As the heat of summer waned, I longed for Helen Minter to pay me a visit, but she never appeared. Perhaps Jay Cole no longer attended school in Sulphur. But the beginning of autumn held the promise of fewer chores and a new semester of school. Whenever Edward and I played together or attended school—and James wasn't around—I was happy.

But the world stirred in turmoil. The Atwater radio announced the news: President Roosevelt signed bills to relieve unemployment; the FBI gunned down John Dillinger in Chicago when he walked out of a Clark Gable gangster film; Al Capone was locked in Alcatraz; and the latest news from Europe reported that Adolf Hitler won the election and became president of Germany. These reports from distant places were the talk at the dinner table.

But other times, all Dad Hardt wanted was to settle our arguments over chores, and Mother Hardt said school would calm us down. When the second week of September arrived in 1934, I prepared to enter the second semester of the second grade. Mother Hardt reminded Edward and me, in her schoolmarm way, "Scrub up and wear your bow ties."

"Oh no, not a sissy tie," we chorused.

"Only today. Don't dawdle. Get to class. " We obeyed her orders.

Edward and I took turns kicking a coffee can down Muskogee Avenue to Washington School, a flat-roofed, red-bricked building. The school's flag waved over the rocky playground where Edward and I parted. He struck out for the fifth grade classroom, and I walked down the hall into the second grade room.

The boys razzed us about our jaunty ties, but I forgot about my attire when I met Miss Opal Hartsell, my new teacher. She was a tall, round-faced lady with black hair and friendly eyes, and all the kids prized her as a teacher. She listed me on her roster as one of her thirty-nine students, nineteen girls and twenty boys.

Fresh odors and new sights filled the classroom. A basket of yellow wildflowers welcomed us at the door. Rows of wooden desks with blue ink wells filled the room, and a large Oklahoma map hung on the front wall. I saw newly sharpened cedar pencils and white chalked lines on black slate. In the cloakroom, brown paper sacks gave off the twelve o'clock aroma of peanut butter sandwiches.

Children filed in, overgrown bullish boys with stout chests and black-haired Indian girls with shy brown eyes who sat alongside blonde girls with teasing smiles. Most were two generations removed from Europe, but two of the students were pure Chickasaw. I loved my new classmates.

Each week, Miss Hartsell flashed cards with dozens of new words. "Pronounce them, spell them, write them anew," she said to the class. She admonished me, "Billy, write with your arm, glide your elbow, don't squeeze your pen to death." We grasped new words, totalled small numbers, and mastered the alphabet in script.

In Miss Hartsell's class, I found a refuge from the turmoil with James. I flourished like a newborn robin. When I walked out of school with new books, my spirit flew to the top of the flagpole, beaming with Miss Hartsell's recognition.

One October day, when the summer sun returned for a few days, Edward encouraged, "Let's hide from James after class. If we don't, he'll force us to work." So we hot-footed up to the back pasture where we played with our model cars.

Soon James strutted into the field, the dry stubble crunching under his boots. "Get your tails in the barn. Billy, I want you to milk the brown Jersey."

Edward had warned me. "Tina gives rich milk, but she's mean as a bull." I pulled up the three-legged stool, slid the bucket in place and yanked on two of Tina's teats. Suddenly she pawed the ground. Terrified, I took off, but James grabbed my arm and whacked my bottom.

"For God's sake. You'll never amount to a hill of beans."

That evening, Edward and I were walking down the upstairs hallway when we heard James talking to his mother in the living room.

"That kid is scared of a damn cow." James' voice faded.

"Be patient," Mother Hardt said. "You're a man now, you'll soon be in college."

The following day, James stole my sloop and cut it into a dozen pieces with his dad's band saw. He broke the dowel mast and ripped apart a set of starched white sails. He placed all the scraps in a paper sack and left his cowardly deed under my pillow.

A week later, after my temper calmed, Edward and I decided to teach big James a lesson. I sneaked his Remington .22 rifle out of his room. Edward shoved several pieces of buckshot down the barrel and packed in wad after wad of cotton. A week later, James went out in the back pasture for target practice. He pulled the trigger and the end of his barrel warped into a new shape.

The daily battle of wills continued. I wouldn't sway and James wouldn't bend. Either I slopped the pigs, milked the cow, scooped the manure, and followed his orders, or James complained to his dad.

In late November, after I had defied his order to clean the pigeon nests out of the barn loft, he let me have it.

"Billy, you're a pain in the rear. Little Richard was a lotta fun."

"Never heard of him."

"He's the brother we lost."

"What! He's gone?"

"That's right. Our old dog Jack bit him. Rabies took him over a year ago. Mother worshiped that boy. You're nothing like him."

"Thanks a lot, James. So, I'm suppose to take your dead brother's place, huh? What an insult!"

James tossed me a look that could have killed. I shouldn't have taken the cheap shot, but I wanted to strike out at the lunacy of my situation. "So, that's why your folks wouldn't let me bring my dog." I started to see another part of the picture.

James, sniffling, said, "My mother wanted a boy your age. Last May, she drove to Oklahoma City and brought you into the family." James let out a deep breath. "You were the boy who was to replace her lost son."

I stared at James' bloodshot eyes as a dark cloud swept over me. I was torn between an urge to run in and comfort Mother Hardt and a desire to get away from the wretchedness of it all. I walked down to the duck pond where I sat beside my shadow, and I cried. That evening Edward showed me the clipping. I read the newspaper account of his brother's death. I now understood how Mother Hardt lived in pain.

Throughout the month of December, I kept a distance from James, and did my share of the work. I dried the supper dishes, fed Peggy three times a day, built new nests for the chicken house, and helped Edward clean the cow lot.

A few days after Christmas, James and Edward took a bus over to Ardmore for a visit with their cousin. Without the brothers around things were boring.

On a Monday morning in late December, the towering elm outside my bedroom window jittered with the swirling winds, orchestrating a melody of winter sounds. I snuggled under a blanket examining a rusted Elgin pocket watch and a pocketknife which Edward had traded for my yo-yo and two model boats. "It's a genuine black-handled Barlow, a single blader," he had claimed. "Like the one Tom Sawyer carried."

Just then, Dad Hardt peeked in the doorway. "Billy, it's a pleasant day. We're driving into the city. We'll have a picnic at Belle Isle Lake."

"Oh, great!" I shouted, bouncing out of bed. It would be fun to play near the water. I dressed, combed my hair, and rushed down the stairs to a breakfast of Wheaties, toast, and jelly. Mother Hardt left the table to put our picnic basket in the trunk of the Plymouth. I crawled in the backseat.

Without Edward to play cards with, the drive proved dull. Low white clouds lay over the sea of buffalo grass as we crossed the spreading North Canadian River and entered Oklahoma City. A forest of tall buildings gleamed in the distance. We traveled north on Classen Boulevard where a red-and-white streetcar clanged toward town. I thought of Momma and Helen Minter. Every time I thought about them—and I thought about them often—I wondered if Momma still lived in Bethany and why Helen hadn't come to see me in Sulphur.

I wiped my cheeks as the generating plant powering the city's street cars came into view. Its smokestack spewed a fine sliver of smoke across the sky. We turned into the park at Belle Isle Lake, a picnic area with tables and tree-covered lanes leading to the water. Chilly air drifted through the trees, but the sun soon warmed the earth. I grabbed a slice of bread and dashed down to the water to toss crumbs to the ducks. I returned to see Mother Hardt brush tears from her cheeks as she served ham sandwiches with a thermos of hot cocoa. My mind questioned the sad arrangement: A picnic on a cold day; no words being spoken; tears for no reason. What's happening here?

Before I could fathom this strange scene we crawled back in the car. Dad Hardt drove north on Western Avenue and turned west on 63rd Street. After a mile, we turned into a driveway. A weathered sign, with white and black paint peeling at the edges, the BAPTIST ORPHANAGE, stared down at us. A monstrous brick building stood in the background.

My heart quivered with terror. No! Not another orphanage. I looked at Dad Hardt. "Is Mr. Wheeler inside?"

"We're fed up with Mr. Wheeler. This is a Baptist home."

I wanted to scream, but my voice fell silent with disbelief. We bumped down the pothole-pitted driveway and parked near the old building.

"Give me a minute." Dad Hardt stepped out of the car. My eyes filled with tears as I watched him walk up the front steps and enter the brick fortress. In the front seat, Mother Hardt blotted her eyes. Within a few minutes, he returned with an older lady dressed in a housedress. The lady reached in and comforted Mother Hardt with consoling pats on the shoulder. She was suffering. I was suffering. But Dad Hardt was not. He jerked open the back door and leaned in.

"Billy, this is your new home." His words cut through my heart.

"Damnit, I'm not getting out."

"Don't give me any lip." His hands began to shake.

Children yelled across the playground. A few boys drifted down the driveway and peeked in the window. I scooted to the passenger side of the car.

"I'm sorry, Billy." Mother Hardt twisted around in her seat with tears running down her cheeks. "You'll be free. James won't push you around anymore."

"I want to stay with you and Edward." I sat trembling with anger. "I've been tricked. I hate Dad Hardt."

"My Lord," she said. "I only wanted the best."

"Stand back, I'll get the kid out." Dad Hardt paused, loosened his tie and unbuttoned his collar. I stood up in the backseat and leaned against the passenger door. He lunged in and snatched me by the cuff of my pants. I shook him off. He reached in again. I kicked his hand aside. He paused and wiped his brow.

"Damn, you long-legged devil." He latched onto my left ankle. Standing on one leg, I grabbed the hand strap on the passenger side. Dad Hardt jerked me with all of his might. The strap popped off and fell on the floor. I reached above for anything to hold on to.

Finally, my fingers dug into the soft lining of the roof. He yanked again and a ripping sound of cloth zipped the air. Then, a strip of the dusty headliner came off in my hand. I glanced up and saw the bare metal of the roof with steel ridges running across. Another bell clanged from across the driveway.

Dad Hardt stood in the doorway, red-faced and puffed up with rage. His mouth spat whiffs of cotton lint that floated out the door, settling like white moths over his blue suit.

He kept licking the white specks off his lips and stomping up and down, looking like a clown dancing to wild music. His words tumbled out as I reached for another strip of cloth. "God almighty. Get outta there! You're tearing up my car!"

It felt good to see his car torn up. The dirty traitor. He deserved what he got.

He grabbed my leg again and gave a final jerk, dumping me on the driveway as a galaxy of stars floated before my eyes. I struggled to my feet, looked into the car, and saw Mother Hardt bent forward with her hands covering her eyes. Suddenly the starter whirred, and the Plymouth sped away.

The older lady placed her arm around my shoulder. "Young man, let's get you into the dormitory."

She led me up upstairs and into a large room. I crawled onto an iron bed, exhausted and heartbroken. Rolling my head back and forth, my mind spun with the disaster of having been born into this miserable world, of being abandoned in yet another orphanage. I sank into a state of despair.

The lady sat down on the edge of the bed and took my hands into hers. "Son, let us talk to the Lord. He will calm your mind."

"Every night I ask the one on High to watch over me," I said. "But if Momma doesn't return, and no family wants me, what am I to do?"

The lady tucked my blanket tighter and patted my trembling hands, but requested no other thing from me than to have hope. Even as I was drifting off, turning from side to side, I was still conscious of a lonely, unsleeping heartache. Would I ever see Edward Hardt again?

After a night of fitful dreams, a clanging bell jarred me awake.

Part Two

❧

Please!

Don't Call Me Will Rogers

Baptist Orphanage
1935-1936

~6~

I was crowded between two other kids on a narrow mattress that smelled of urine. One boy, wiggling like a worm, lay at the head of the bed, and another coiled his body around my feet. Squashed between them, I struggled to comprehend these new surroundings.

In the twilight, I looked up at naked lightbulbs dangling from a high ceiling. Streaks of yellow light streamed across the barn-sized dormitory crowded with iron beds laden with sleepy children. Steam radiators hissed and rattled, struggling to heat the lofty room.

At 5:30 in the morning, on Tuesday, January 1, 1935, I was once again adrift in a sea of strangers, nursing a lonely heart. My arms and legs ached from the bruises of the day before. Wintery thoughts warned me I was worse off than when I lived with the Hardt family.

Experience had shaped me into a skeptical nine-year-old. I believed that grown-ups were a troublesome lot. If they offered smiles, I eyed them with caution. Promises made and broken had strengthened my mistrust.

I slipped on my clothes and walked down the oak wainscotted hallway, hoping to shed the memory of my embattled arrival. I

59

glanced ahead and saw a round, full-bosomed woman waddling toward me. Her white dress sported a lace collar, and she wore pink socks with white leather shoes. One hand rested on a long wooden paddle attached to her belt and the other held a clipboard. She paused next to me and looked down.

I was frightened by the large paddle even as I looked up into a friendly Baptist face.

"Good morning, good morning." She brushed back a ringlet of grey hair, and smiled. "I'm Bessie Riney, your matron. The kids call me Bessie. And how are you, Will?"

"What? My name's not Will!" I stood erect, looking at her with an unwavering gaze.

She glanced at her clipboard. "I'm sorry but the court placed you here as Will Rogers."

"I've heard Will Rogers on the radio, but he isn't me."

Bessie didn't argue. She settled the matter, "Your name's Will. Yes, Will Rogers, just like the court says."

So now they put Billy Hardt away. A new name, a new game. What was a kid to do?

"Our home is crowded and we must have rules. Don't fight, don't sass, don't wet the bed, and don't wipe your nose on your sleeve." She coughed. "And if you're caught stealing or running away, you'll get tossed in the Dark Room."

A bell rang sharply for breakfast as I wondered where the Dark Room might be. I washed up and walked into the hall. Bessie took my hand and led me onto the front porch, which provided a view of the stadium-shaped campus.

The brick-faced Old North Building featured several white stone arches from the Spanish-mission style architecture. The Baptists had raised funds throughout the state and built the two-story structure with a basement in 1907. A grand staircase at the center led to the first floor. You climbed an interior flight of stairs to the second floor where you entered either the younger boys' or girls' dormitories.

There was a shortage of chairs so on rainy days we would spend dreary hours sitting on the oak stairs leading to the second floor.

The building looked like an ancient ruin resting on a bed of winter-weary grass. The scrawny shrubs, like many of us orphans during that barren winter, looked forward to spring. Snakelike roots poked through cracks in the concrete walk; green paint flaked off walls; shards of window glass sprinkled the earth around the foundation.

We strolled down the west walk as she explained that the older boys lived in the two-story building to the east and the older girls lived in the brick dorm across the way. There beside the girls' dorm, suspended under a wooden "A" frame, hung an iron bell, large as a kettle drum.

Beyond the girls' building, we approached the dining hall. Above it was the chapel for church services and where the rhythm band practiced. She pointed to the west. "The barn back of here is overseen by Pop Hall. You'll meet him later."

We came to the driveway's edge. The space, unbounded by fences, stretched before me. I looked over a meadow and past a weathered shack to a cluster of islands floating like boats on Belle Isle Lake. I felt a desire to dash down to the water. I could imagine catching a frog or rafting out to one of the islands. "Looks like fun," I said.

"Don't get any ideas about the lake. I paddled two Huck Finns who sneaked down and built a tin boat. They nearly drowned."

"Can we play in the field?"

"An old Negro lives in the shanty. He used to take the kids fishing. But Reverend Maxey, the home's new superintendent, doesn't want you boys hanging around his shack."

We turned back and entered the dining hall where Bessie unclipped her paddle and hung it in a locker. She now hovered around the kids like a mother hen. Her lips occasionally formed a quiet smile but seldom broadened into a laugh. But I felt her love for children hidden beneath her quietness. She offered a comforting hand, warm to the touch. From my experience with grown-ups, I learned to trust people by the feel of their hands. And I listened to their voices: words mirrored what they wanted most. Smiles placed me on guard.

She bragged about the home keeping its own pigs and cattle, hoping to become self-sufficient. She said the older children worked on the farm, in the laundry, the dining hall, and around the campus.

She assigned me to a table in the dining hall. We stood behind our chairs until after the blessing. The breakfast bell dinged after we were seated. Then a teenage girl dished up a bowl of corn mush, a dish that brought back memories of breakfasts in old man Wheeler's care. Another bell clanged and the teenage assistants cleaned the tables, while we young ones lined up and marched back to our dorms. I didn't care for the Baptist bells and marching regimen.

In the afternoon, I met Olga. Bessie came marching down the hall with a young lady, tall and lovely, wearing a yellow blouse and a plaid skirt. They paused by my side. "I want you to meet Miss Olga Tuttle, my assistant," Bessie said. "At my age, it's hard to handle sixty boys and girls in two wards."

The bronze-skinned teenager brushed a fluff of blonde hair from her brow and shook my hand. "How are you, young man?" She smiled.

"I'm okay." I didn't smile.

The following Monday, we earned two hours of play for good behavior. I walked to the west side of the building and sat under a mulberry tree. It felt good to be alone. I draped my arms over my knees, placed my head down and mulled over my lot.

Momma lived on the edge of my memory, flitting in and out, and her comforting hugs still warmed my heart. I missed Helen Minter's love, her laughter and kisses, her diamonds and pearls, her bounce and tease. I lived on old love and new dreams as I tried to form a new life.

In the midst of my gloom, a damp nose nuzzled the back of my neck. A large black dog with a wheeling tail introduced himself. My mood lifted when I thought of Tippy. My new friend licked my ear just as a slim freckle-faced kid dashed to my side.

He stuck out his right hand. "I'm Leroy Harris, one of Nick's masters." He was of average height, wiry and thin, with short cropped brown hair. He wore a starched blue shirt and khaki pants. His left hand gripped a rubber ball. With a fierce toss he sent the ball flying. Nick raced to retrieve it.

"Glad to meet you." I stood up.

"Like to know how we got Nick?"

"Just might."

The dog bounded back and dropped the ball near our feet. "He's our Belgian Sheepdog."

Leroy told how the dentist, Dr. G. Nichols, the developer of the Nichols Hills area, had given Nick to the home.

We didn't play under the mulberry tree for long. Bessie shouted, "Time for chores." Today she ordered us to wax the brown linoleum hall connecting the younger boys' and girls' dormitories. Leroy led the crew of a dozen boys. He ribbed the kids, "Hop to it, skinny Tim, hey big foot, J.C., and move your tail faster Johnny." After they mopped and applied paste wax, Leroy introduced me to the three kids who made up our polishing crew.

Tim Curtis, a lanky, long-legged boy of eleven, sauntered over while popping his knuckles. "Clear out guys. I'm first." He looked out from under an unruly mass of blonde hair with distant gray eyes that spoke of sadness. His thin hands and loose-jointed arms gave him a gangly appearance.

The boys nodded, surprised that Tim wanted to be first. He rushed up and jumped onto the middle of an old quilt. We pulled and swirled the weighted buffer up and down the hall until he rolled off, complaining of a dizzy spell.

"I'm next," shouted Johnny Henshall, a mature, good-looking ten-year-old with friendly brown eyes. He eased Tim aside.

"Johnny's father passed away and his mother left him here at five," Leroy said. "He has a twelve-year-old sister named Bertha May, and a younger sister, Betty Joyce. He's sharp at dominoes. Great at kickball, too. He's one of Bessie's favorites." We spun Johnny up and down the hall until he, too, complained of dizziness.

The third helper looked healthier than any of the boys. "Now it's my turn." J.C. Watson, a sturdy youngster who looked like he belonged in the oil fields, rushed up. He appeared stronger than any two of us, and made a heavier weight for polishing. But he tumbled off when we whipped him into the wall.

Next to J.C., I stood taller than the others, but thin as a stalk of cane. Laughing and kicking my feet, the kids yanked me up and down the hall, then with one jerk they tossed me off.

Before I could stand up, J.C. crawled back onto the quilt.

We spent two hours pulling, pushing, and spinning in circles.

Several quarts of floor wax and a few weeks later, Bessie came waddling down the hall humming "Home on the Range." She paused, saying that a Mrs. Minter wished to see me in the reception room. I dashed downstairs.

"Oh Helen, I'm so glad to see you." Tears ran down my cheeks as I kissed her. She was simply dressed in black, no longer wearing pearls. "How did you find me?"

She paused a second, then her words came out quietly, like she was revealing a secret. "Anna Rice, secretary at the courthouse phoned and reported you here. It seems the Hardts went to court and changed your name."

"Yeah, they call me Will Rogers now."

For a moment I stood silent as my mind rattled with confusion. "I'm not goin' back to Wheeler. I hate him."

"Calm down. He might show up, but let's not worry about him now." Helen led me over to a comfortable divan.

I told her about having to sleep with two other kids. "But Bessie says I'll soon get a bed of my own."

"You will rest better then." Helen brushed back my hair.

Baptist Orphanage. July 28, 1935. Will Rogers (Roger Bechan) and Leroy Harris, right to left, fifth row up, peaking over the shoulder of the girl wearing gingham dress. Matron Bessie Riney, 6th row up, third from right.

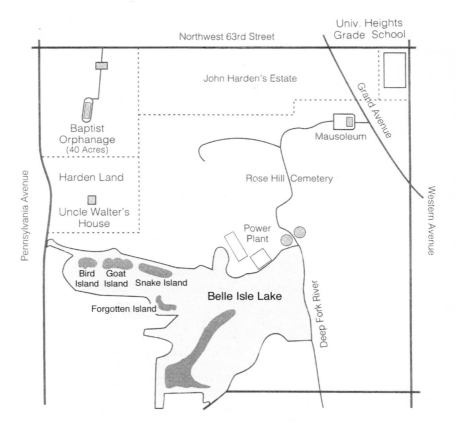

BELLE ISLE LAKE AND SURROUNDINGS

From U.S. Government Aerial Survey, 1940

Map of area where Will and his friends loved to escape.

THE DAILY OKLAHOMAN

Sunday, August 18, 1935, p. 14.

Will's Namesake, An Orphan, Sad Before Portrait

An orphan boy stood heart-broken Saturday before a large autographed portrait of Will Rogers, given him last winter by the humorist.

Nameless when he entered the Baptist Orphans' home here, officials of the institution called him Will Rogers. He wrote Will about it last January, and in reply got a letter from Rogers, together with two autographed portraits. One of these the 7-year-old boy gave to the University Heights school, where he is a pupil.

Mrs. J. H. Lucas, matron of the home, found the boy standing in front of the other picture Saturday.

"Mr. Will, I'll never get to see you," he said. "But anyway, I've still got your picture."

This news article appeared when
Roger Bechan, then known as Will Rogers,
was in the Baptist Orphanage in Oklahoma City.

ABSTRACT OF PUPILS' WORK FOR SEMESTER
Oklahoma City Public Schools

beginning *Jan. 26* , 193*6* and Ending *May 29* , 193*6*

Grade *4th* *Fourth* Class *B* Room _____

U.H. School *Myrtle Critchfield* Principal _____ Teacher

NAME OF PUPILS	Date of Birth	Reading	Arithmetic	Social Science	English	Spelling	Writing	Science	Hygiene	Health Activities		Art	Music	Days Present	Days Absent	Times Tardy	How disposed of
1 Best, Orval	5-17-26													80	9	1	P
2 Rogers, Will	9-7-23													67	2	1	P
3 Wilkerson, Arthur	6-15-26													54	35		C
4																	
5																	
6																	
7																	
8																	
9 Boles, Mary Arline	11-1-26													87	2		P
10 Cartwright, Mildred	2-13-25													81	8		P
11 Gray, Betty Marie	10-11-26													89	-		P
12 Loftin, Betty Jolyne	12-30-25													82	7		P
13 Skaggs, Esther	2-5-25													89			P
14 Penfield, Marjorie	2-15-27													78	11		P

Oklahoma City Public Schools
Official Transcript

Certified by: _____
Record Clerk

Date: _____ 19__

University Heights Grade School, Oklahoma City.
Fourth Grade Class Records, 1936.
Will Rogers (Roger Bechan) is second on the roster.

"But why can't I live with you and Will?"

"Will hit another dry hole." Her voice sounded thin and reedy. Helen said they had lost their home and now lived in a small cottage at 531 N.W. 59th near the Santa Fe tracks, a few blocks east of the University Heights School.

"You'll make it here. I'll visit," Helen said.

"A couple of kids have sneaked off and visited an old Negro down by the lake. He knows all about frogs," I whispered.

"I don't want you sitting around with a glum face. Run down and ask the Negro to take you fishing. Have fun."

Helen stood up to go. Her slim fingers dipped into her purse, and she handed me a quarter. I hugged her, then pocketed the coin as she left me standing alone. I always felt better when I was near Helen. With her warning that Mr. Wheeler might return, I decided that when it looked safe, I'd light outta here and find a home on my own.

*

Bessie Riney had grand plans for our enlightenment. First, she preferred a well-rounded program of higher education. This included enrolling us in the University Heights Grade School for the three Rs, related academics, and a few sports. She also believed in enlarging our minds with reading. In one corner of a storage room, she gathered a few Bible stories, a series of Rover Boy adventure books and a collection of Little Blue Books, ten cent paperbacks published by Haldeman-Julius. There were hundreds of stories to read.

I filched a stack of the paperbacks and stored them under my mattress. In the evenings, these books, printed on cheap newsprint, became my refuge. In their pages I found myself playing with Robin Hood, living on an island with Robinson Crusoe, and exploring Alaska with Jack London. But, during one of her bed checks, Olga hauled off my library.

The University Heights Grade School announced that within a

week the spring semester would begin. Bessie marched into the dorm and outlined her three imperatives for attending class:

GOOD HEALTH, CLEANLINESS, and PROPER DRESS.

In the matter of health, Bessie knew all about the ills of mankind and she explained them to us in detail: chickenpox, where all the kids broke out with spots, mumps, whooping cough, T.B., and polio, which could leave you with a short leg.

She stood tall, her paddle dangling at her side, and informed us little souls, "I don't want any of you kids playing sick to skip school." Perhaps it is to Bessie that I owe my robust health, for she believed that the goal of perfect attendance could be reached only through administration of laxatives and vitamins.

On her oak desk next to her Crosley radio and open Bible stood a gallon jug of castor oil. Bessie considered this the remedy to all ills. She said her oily medicine relieved the most serious of threats—as she put it, "to cure you of worms, my dears!"

One evening, Olga bustled into the dorm, telling us boys to march into the lavatory where she lined us up like a row of stalks in a cane field. When my turn approached, Bessie poured a spoonful of the gooey stuff.

"Quick, Will, hop on the stool."

I sprang onto the seat and sat kicking the cross bar when I observed the puckered mouths of her earlier customers.

Then, yuck! A whiff of her oil floated across the room. It smelled like a family of dead rats. I suddenly had the urge to jump out the window. "Hell, let me outta here!"

"Quit cussin'." Bessie held her monstrous spoon—looked like a shovel to me—over my head. "This medicine will grease your innards."

I squirmed like a grub worm. "Come now, be brave and gulp it down." I refused. Suddenly she poked me in the ribs and I giggled. With a flick of her wrist, she dumped the slimy oil down my throat.

"Attaboy," Bessie nodded. "Now, lick this orange. It'll sweeten you up." I flinched at having to lick the spongy orange that the four boys ahead of me had drooled on. I sat vacillating between throwing up or dashing out the door, but I finally licked the slobbery fruit.

This yellow tinted oil, pressed from castor beans, acted as a wrenching laxative, leaving the sensation of a string of Chinese firecrackers going off in your insides. The resulting trots to our lavatory created toxic fumes that provided the dorm comedians with hours of bathroom humor, comparing our plight to scenes from Tarzan when Cheetah eats green bananas to a Dr. Frankenstein script where the monster gets "Montezuma's revenge."

Bessie also handed out other cures. One morning, I noticed a lump on the knuckle of my right hand. I showed it to Bessie.

"You got a bloody wart." She offered a remedy: "Catch a black cat. Have it lick your hand for three days. Then be patient." Since the townspeople dropped their unwanted pets at our gate, we had plenty to choose from. Olga captured a black cat as it walked down our driveway. "Let's call her Midnight." Olga placed her under my bed.

I fed Midnight leftovers from the table. For dessert, she licked a smudge of butter I smeared on my knuckle. Within a week the wart disappeared. This miracle impressed my classmates. The next week, J.C. Watson needed Midnight's cure, so I swapped her to him for a green agate and a bag of marbles.

After Bessie completed doctoring us, cleanliness consumed her thoughts. "Boys, Olga's going to clean you kids up." She demanded that we be spotless, our hair scrubbed, feet soaked, and our teeth gleaming. To reinforce her message, she handed Olga her ominous paddle.

"Whack any kid who acts up."

On a chilly Saturday the weekend before classes began, Olga ordered us to march into the lavatory. She grinned as we straggled beside her.

The scouring pen smelled of damp plaster, homemade lye soap, and Lysol disinfectant. The stark room, lit by a dim ceiling bulb, featured a concrete floor with a center drain, and two commodes. We flushed one of the toilets by using a leaky can to pour water into the bowl. Two wash basins with dripping faucets, one long urinal, and a cast iron tub perched on four claw feet completed the bathroom fixtures.

Olga, with a rag and a bottle of greasy-looking shampoo, lined us up along the far wall. "Every stitch off. You're in for a scrubbing." We leaned against the wall and stripped, stark naked in the January chill. The room grew quiet. "Now, one at a time, climb in the tub. And no sass." The slap, slap of bare feet resonated upon the cement floor. Olga glowed with sadistic glee.

I stood fourth in line and turned to move to the end. Anything to postpone the scrub down.

"Get back in place." She slapped me on the rear. Olga had her bluff in on us ragamuffins.

All the kids quivered with goose bumps. Finally, Olga knelt by the tub and called, "Will, you're next." I stepped into a murk of gray water that stank like a pig pen.

"For God's sake, let me out of here." I stepped back out onto the floor.

"I'll cure you of cussin'." Olga cut off a chunk of soap and shoved it into my mouth. While I spit and sputtered, she scoured my body until my skin turned red. It felt degrading to stand naked in front of Olga while she removed layers of skin with her watery assaults. Our tormentor stalked us kids with sudsy hands and a mulish will.

The following morning, Tim Curtis and I stood in the hall tempting each other with a trade. I offered my Elgin pocket watch in exchange for a quarter.

His eyes lit up. "How about a dime and three corn-silk cigarettes?" He pulled them out of his shirt pocket. They were slim with wrapped toilet paper twisted at both ends.

"Yeah, I can go for those." I had taken several puffs on one of

Helen's Luckies, so I pictured sharing a couple of smokes with Leroy.

"But it's an old watch," Tim said.

"Specks of rust don't hurt." Holding the end of its chain, I swung it before his eyes.

Tim grasped the Elgin and pressed it to his ear. "Hell, it doesn't work."

"It's a pocket watch, silly. It'll tick as you walk."

"Well, maybe." He paused and fingered the stem. "Okay, it's a deal." We shook hands.

Tim took the watch and handed over the dime and three cigarettes. Olga, in her duties as the hall monitor, walked up displaying her usual smile. I slipped the dime and the corn silks in my shirt pocket. "You boys know better than to trade goods in the dorm."

Neither Tim nor I paid any attention. Without another word, she grabbed the watch and slapped me on the cheek with her open hand. Then she smacked Tim so hard that he slumped against the wall. I jumped up and reached for Olga, but Tim grabbed my arm. A mean heart lurked behind her angelic looks.

The following afternoon, Leroy Harris and I sneaked out behind the apple shed. We lit up. He told me to take in a deep breath, swallow hard, and smoke would ooze out of my nose. With a raw nose I coughed till tears dampened my face.

"Little strong," Leroy said.

"Yeah, stronger than a Lucky."

Leroy and I sealed our a friendship while sharing a smoke, even if it smelled like a stack of burning leaves. Finally, we stomped out the cigarette, and strolled inside feeling mighty grown-up. I asked Leroy, "Why can't the Baptists cure Olga of her mean temper?"

Leroy didn't respond; his heart ached with his own sadness. His father had left for California, leaving his mother with seven children. The family, without resources, abandoned Leroy at the orphanage at eight, along with his six-year-old brother Billy, and his two sisters, Mollie May and Shirley Gene, ages eleven and five. Their mother kept the two older children and her baby girl at home in Chickasha.

Leroy and his brother and sisters, like J.C. Watson and Johnny Henshall and so many of the other children, didn't qualify as true orphans. "Most of the kids," Leroy said, "have either a mother or father still living. Some have both." We represented a collection of discarded waifs, the children of dysfunctional parents who were unable or unwilling to care for their own.

*

After her cleaning ritual, Bessie attended to our clothing. "In school, I want you boys better dressed than the city kids."

"My pants look great." I stood before Bessie wearing blue bib overalls. But Bessie had a mind of her own.

"Now Will, you'd look better in a spiffier outfit. I'll write your church sponsor." She claimed the parishioners would open their hearts for one of her boys.

Sure enough, within two weeks a cardboard box and a brown paper package tied with heavy twine, both addressed to "Master Will Rogers," arrived. Trembling with excitement, I ripped the paper open to find a quilt of a hundred colors. The coverlet brightened the dorm. What a glorious sight. The Ladies' Auxiliary of the Baptist Church in Frederick, Oklahoma, had stitched it together.

The cardboard box remained. Beaming with anticipation, I had visions of impressing my new teacher by wearing low-cut leather shoes, a pair of khaki pants, a new white shirt, and my black bow tie.

I yanked out my pocketknife, cut the string, and opened the lid. I reached in and pulled out a Lindbergh aviator cap with plastic goggles. The clear goggles gleamed. A leather strap snugged it under my chin. It was much like J.C. Watson's, only mine had creases on both sides. I softened the leather with Vaseline and hung the cap at the head of my bed. I wore my Lucky Lindy cap with pride.

Digging to the bottom of the box, I found a starched pair of unionalls, worn shiny at the seat and the knees. I sat on the edge of my bed and slipped them on. Sewn out of striped cloth, the suit looked like a mechanic's uniform but with an added feature: a rear drop-bucket seat, held up by four stubborn buttons. This trap door provided an exit for my most private bodily functions. How could I keep my dignity if I fumbled with the buttons as I rushed to the john with the castor oil blues? But then, on the bright side, they might flesh out my skinny bones.

I buttoned the front. With both hands in my pockets, I walked down to the end of the dorm and looked in the mirror. My smile faded. The unionalls bulged at my rear as if I carried a watermelon on my rump. I glanced to Leroy for reassurance. He walked over and fingered my new outfit. "Wow! Where did you get these duds?"

"Bessie got 'em."

Everyone turned and gazed at me. Several kids hooted and whistled. The dorm shook with laughter.

"Okay, knock it off guys." In an effort to smooth the cloth, I did back bends and ran in place till sweat dripped into my eyes. The suit looked better.

I looked up to see my friend, Tim Curtis, grinning and rubbing his hands together. "Aren't you the dandy? Dressed for school?" The kids stomped the floor like savages.

The whole dorm branded me as an odd spectacle. I rolled up the sleeves, unbuttoned the top button and stuffed a handkerchief in the chest pocket. With hope of a reprieve, I turned back to Leroy. "Now what do you think?"

"Yeah, you look Sunday-school fancy, but don't go outside."

"Why's that?"

"You'll scare our pigeons away." He chuckled and covered his eyes.

Lordy me! How I hated those orphan hand-me-downs. I felt a deep shame. Someday, I'd show 'em. I saw myself as a big-time wildcatter driving a black Packard with a million dollars in the bank. Then, by golly, I'd own a Nichols Hills mansion and I'd wear a new shirt and dress pants every day of the week.

Shaking with humiliation, I rushed down the basement stairs and into the laundry room. I took off the unionalls and pitched them in the corner. I pawed through a basket of clean clothes and swiped some other boy's white shirt and khaki pants. I ripped out the laundry tags, said a grateful Baptist prayer, and slipped them on. Now, though clothed in guilt, and adding thievery to my blossoming lying, I felt properly dressed for school.

～7～

On the opening day of school in January, Leroy and I struggled out of bed at 5:30 a.m. We washed up and marched in line with our classmates to breakfast. We gobbled down our mush, returned to the dorm, and brushed our teeth with soda powder. Then Leroy smoothed his hair with a pat of Bessie's pomade, and he smelled like a rosebush in bloom.

"Don't be a sissie," I said.

"Oh, hush." Leroy tossed me his comb.

Bessie stomped her foot on the floor. "Don't you boys hear the bell?"

Leroy and I jumped to attention.

"Skiddoo, or I'll give you another dose of oil."

We tossed on our coats, grabbed our books, and trudged out the front gate with sleep in our eyes. A sliver of orange stretched across the horizon, a dazzling sight. A marvelous day. We quickened our pace. Within minutes, the sun sprang above the hill, flooding the street with light, draping my classmates with long shadows.

Across 63rd Street the two-story Nichols Hills mansions caught my attention. The red-brick homes with spreading lawns looked mighty grand. One day, I said to myself, I'm going to scout the neighborhood. Possibly I could find the house where I drained the swimming pool.

Leroy and I continued down the mile-long slope to the University Heights Grade School. The stately, brown-brick building stood on the corner of 63rd Street and Western. A flag billowed a welcome.

Miss Kate Specht, our sun-tanned teacher whose brown hair was streaked with gray, greeted us with a commanding voice. "Girls and boys, welcome to the third grade." The boys nicknamed her the "Shaker," because she shook the daylights out of any misbehaving student. But Miss Specht, a grown-up tomboy, loved baseball. This redeeming grace overshadowed her stern discipline.

With my Will Rogers name I became one of her eight students, four boys and four girls. One of the girls, beautiful Daisy Butter, stood tall, slender, but never seemed aware of the cluster of freckles sprinkled across her cheeks. She wore a white blouse and brown skirt with a blue ribbon in her russet hair. During recess she sat cross-legged playing jacks, her hands flying in the air. I wanted to talk to Daisy but couldn't get up the nerve. I decided she'd be my girl when we walked home to the orphanage.

But I forgot about girls when baseball called. On the playground, Miss Specht sprang to life like an over-the-hill coach who had inherited a windfall of superb athletes. She recruited boys from all the classes and scrounged gloves, bats, and a bucket of balls to use in our tryouts. Her voice echoed over the field as she spewed forth orders.

"Will, you're up after Leroy." I grabbed a bat. With my wild energy, I could picture a home run soaring over the back fence.

Orville Best, a rawboned city boy, strolled on the field with a knowing smile. He stared down at me from the pitcher's mound. His cheeks bulged with a wad of bubble gum, a hank of blonde hair flopped over one eye.

With a look of disgust in his eyes, he raised his right clodhopper foot and delivered a screeching fast ball. Swish! I swung the junior Louisville slugger with all my might, but twice I heard the ball pop into the catcher's mitt.

Miss Specht walked over. "Will, choke the bat. Slap the ball to left field."

I gripped the bat as though it were Olga's neck.

"No. No. Don't grip it tighter! Scoot your hands up from the knob."

I shifted my hands and swung harder as another ball zipped by. The catcher called me out. I turned to my coach. "Golly, when Orville sticks his big foot in the air, I lose track of the ball."

"Sharpen up. You'll soon be a hitter." Miss Specht's optimism lifted my spirits.

Though I usually walked with Leroy to school, one morning I lagged behind and crossed 63rd Street, entering Nichols Hills. I moseyed up Briarwood Street where I roamed the area searching for my old home with the swimming pool. I didn't find the house, but in front of one stately mansion, I discovered a balloon-tired Elgin bicycle leaning up against a leafless oak. Since some city kid didn't appreciate his wheels, I hopped on the seat and pedaled block after block through the neighborhood. Riding free on a bike widened my world, speeding my escape from the home. I no longer felt abandoned and lonely, but grown up and free.

Finally I headed down Sherwood Lane through the brisk air, listening to the tires hum on the asphalt. I slid to a stop in front of Andrews Grocery across the street from school. With a bell tinkling above the door, Mr. Andrews, a short round-faced man, called out a hearty welcome. I bought a penny Tootsie Roll and four cents' worth of Double Bubble gum. I relished these pink chewables and kept extras on hand.

I couldn't take the bike up to the orphanage or I would land in trouble, so I parked it under a tree outside the school. For the next few weeks, swiping wheels became a series of adventures. After three

75

unclaimed bikes stood outside our class, Leroy caught on.

"My Lord, stealing bikes. Bessie will be after your tail."

"She's never down at school."

"She has big ears," Leroy slapped me on the back.

"Bessie will never know."

While I suffered with a guilty conscience, back at the orphanage Bessie dug out a folder of newspaper clippings on Will Rogers.

"Here's material on your namesake," she announced. "He was born in Oklahoma, near Oologah. He's part Cherokee."

I opened the folder. Will Rogers' wrinkled face gave life to his popular sayings. His comment, "I have never met a man I didn't like," intrigued me. On Monday, after I read the articles, I knocked on my matron's door. Bessie, in a starched white dress and a red shawl, sat at her desk reading the morning paper with her rimless glasses down on her nose.

"Matron Riney," I said, leaning into her doorway, "would you help me write a letter?"

She placed her paper down. "Honey, what's this?"

"I would like Will Rogers to send me a photograph."

She stood up, then took in a deep breath that fluffed her round chest and sighed. "All right, we'll try."

Bessie appeared happy and her quiet loving ways calmed my uneasy mind. She cleaned her desk top and placed a pencil, a pen, sheets of paper, and an envelope in my hand. I licked and chewed the pencil, and faced a clean sheet of paper. For a moment my thoughts froze. I finally printed the date at the top and scribbled out a gush of words.

Mrs. Riney's pencil flashed over the letter, cutting and correcting. She handed me her Waterman fountain pen. I copied the letter in an awkward hand. Bessie thought it was messy, but I stuck it in an envelope and mailed it in the office.

January 17, 1935

Dear Mr. Rogers:

My name is also Will Rogers and I will soon be ten years old. I live in the Baptist Orphanage in Oklahoma City. I have read your funny stories.

 In school we're studying the Indian tribes. When you return to Oklahoma, would you visit our home? Please send me your photograph. I'll show it to my friends.

     Signed,
     Will Rogers

Days dragged by, but no reply appeared. I became restless. "Have patience," Bessie said, "have patience." The days turned into a week, and I became moody. Perhaps Will Rogers didn't answer letters from strangers.

Finally, on Thursday of the following week, Bessie came lumbering down the hall in a light-hearted mood. "Will, your mail has arrived." I dashed down to the office, picked up a manila envelope, ripped the flap open, and pulled out a typed letter and two photographs.

Will Rogers thanked me for writing, but didn't tell when he might return to Oklahoma for a visit. In both of the photographs, he looked like a happy cowboy as he stepped into the loop of a twirling rope. He had signed both in the lower right corner. I slipped his letter and photographs back into the envelope, and scampered out on the playground.

"Looky here," I bragged to Leroy, "I got two photos from Will Rogers."

"Lemme look at one." Leroy extended his hand.

"You'll get it dirty."

Leroy took a step forward. "Hell, I can't hurt it."

I tightened my hold and tore off to the other end of the field to share my good news with Daisy Butter. She looked beautiful wearing a yellow dress and a blue bow in her hair. She took the photograph in her delicate hands and showed it to a couple of her friends.

On Monday, I gave one of Will Rogers' portraits to Miss Specht at school. She read his letter to the other kids and posted it on the bulletin board. My classmates talked about their love of one of America's most important men, and for an hour or so I was kinda famous in school.

*

Bessie's concern for education reached beyond the public schools. With sin threatening to consume the world, Bessie believed only the Good Lord could save our souls. In her mind, our Baptist fathers would show us the light, leading us to accept Jesus as our savior and become his disciples. Then the preacher would baptize us in holy water, washing away our sins. She believed children were born imperfect; we boys needed two worship services a week to save us from the devil's grasping hands.

Bessie dedicated her days to shaping us orphans into upright characters so that the good Lord, when we approached heaven, would usher us through the pearly gates without an interview.

But for many of us boys, Sunday arrived like a day of torture. We celebrated Monday because we could enjoy six days before we faced the preacher again. When the Sunday bell tolled, we could imagine the dire warnings we'd hear about the nether world on this glorious day of rest.

One Sunday, the church bell rang at 8:30 a.m., all of us donned our Sunday best and we rode a bus into the city where we attended the Mountain Baptist Church. It was a red-bricked Gothic building with stained-glass windows and two white pillars set to each side of the entrance.

I tolerated Sunday school because the teacher told us Bible stories in a gentle voice—a pleasant contrast to Olga's rasping words. She played the piano and we sang: "Jesus wants me for a sunbeam." I sang and swayed and clapped my hands, but one question flooded my mind: "Why doesn't the Lord ship old man Wheeler down to the devil? I no longer need a guardian."

After class, we marched into the auditorium and took seats to the right of the podium with grown-ups sitting to one side. Many sat fanning the clammy air with paper fans provided by the Greater North Side Undertaker.

The Reverend Roscoe Halfred, a man who never missed a meal, stood center stage. He believed all of his flock lived in the state of damnation.

Clasping a Bible to his chest with his left hand and waving his other toward heaven, Reverend Halfred spun across the platform like a heavyweight boxer wearing ballet shoes. Dressed in a blue suit, his pocket handkerchief shining like the Star of Bethlehem, our preacher offered to save our souls.

"The Lord created a caring world. He especially loves you little ones." His face was now pink and wet with perspiration as he looked out over row after row of discarded children who sat like a field of rootless weeds.

"You boys, especially, must avoid stealing and lying and cleanse your minds." He claimed that evil desires lead to evil acts. "You must confess your sins, and if you accept Christ you will be saved from being burned forever in a fiery hell."

"My Lord, the preacher makes my ears ache." I whispered to Leroy. "If hell is hot as he says, the devil would burn us up in a flash. How could we burn forever?"

"You're a damn heathen." Leroy poked me in the ribs.

I found it difficult to sort my misgivings about sin from what the preacher saw as evil. Should I confess to smoking corn silk cigarettes? Must I tell about the rust-filled pocket watch I traded to Tim Curtis because it took a hard shake to make it tick? Should I inform the preacher about the dozen cracked marbles stuffed in the bottom of the sack I swapped to J.C. for a Waterman fountain pen? Would the preacher be interested to learn that I planned to sneak off and meet the old man who lived down by the lake? Would I sizzle in hell if he learned about my borrowing three bikes in Nichols Hills? It seemed best to keep these thoughts to myself.

My morals slipped further as a black-suited deacon approached with a platter overflowing with green and silver. I gently laid a bubble gum wrapper in the collection plate and palmed a dollar bill. I stuffed it into my shirt pocket.

Here in the Lord's temple I became a sinner. The service reached its climax, and Bessie sighed with contentment. The idea of running away always burned in my soul, and I could envision the rich rewards that a dollar would purchase on the streets. I said a quiet hallelujah and strode out into the warm noon air. Cardboard fans rested on the pews, and the church reclaimed its serenity.

The following Sunday, I resolved to live an upright life. This led me to be a careful listener. The preacher must have noted a shortage in last week's offerings because he again proposed to save his flock from a life of sin. I was feeling rather low, so I decided to make Bessie proud. I bowed my head and walked down the red carpeted aisle and claimed my repentance. It was a big word, but I got the drift of the idea. The preacher shook my hand and opened a blue curtain to reveal stairs leading down into a long baptismal tub. But suffering from Olga's weekly scrubbing, I declined to be immersed in water.

A couple of Sundays later, I made an effort to sit through the services without wiggling. But when the stone-faced deacon passed the wooden plate down our row, I was overwhelmed again with temptation. I left a fresh gum wrapper and palmed another dollar.

In the evening, after lights out, my conscience squirmed with guilt. Come morning, I trudged south of the orphanage and sat down on the meadow. In this magnificent refuge, I enjoyed being apart from one hundred and fifty restless children. And, above all else, I could cry or talk to myself without my classmates calling me a sissy.

I sat in the field thinking about my sins and selfishness, battling good against evil. I had walked down the aisle and our preacher had said I was saved. But the collection platter had tempted me twice. I pulled forth both dollars and smoothed them out on my knee. I loved the crisp feel of the green paper.

Then came the creeping feeling that Mr. Wheeler might get custody of me again; I never wanted to go back to his Home for the Friendless. I would sneak out of here before that happened. So I needed getaway money.

But more sober questions floated across the field. Why did I steal from the church? What a dumbhead. Hell appeared like a horrifying reality. Perhaps God kept a grade card for me, just as Miss Specht did at school. Next Sunday, I thought, I'll return one of the dollars to the collection plate. I yawned and stretched out on the grass, feeling lazy. I slipped into daydreaming when suddenly the earth shook.

A clang, clang, clang rolled from over the hill. The infernal iron bell that hung from the wooden tower near the girls' dorm shocked me back into reality.

Smaller bells erupted in the dining hall and the dorm. Bells clapped and clanged through the day; the tyranny of sounds bellowed rules and restrictions. Every hour, morning to night, the bells echoed like fire alarms. Bells . . . bells . . . bells . . . they tolled as bleak as misery. Would they ever end?

The Baptists lived by the clock. They got up on time, ate on time, prayed on time, marched on time, met on time, talked on time, bathed on time, and sent us to bed on time, always at the sound of a damnable bell. I could never enjoy myself without my heart being jolted by another bell.

Many of my orphan friends didn't live by time; they were centered within their world of self. They ached for their mothers' love while they made an effort to live in their own land of fantasy and play. They seldom recognized time because they never felt the onrush of hours. Time is slow to a youngster bound within an institution. We loved wristwatches. We could keep an eye on one for an hour. But nothing ever happened.

The bells continued to echo across the meadow. I wanted to scream in return, but I trudged up the hill with my hands over my ears. A clanging bell still makes me shudder.

*

Olga, on the other hand, loved the noisy bells. They gave her an excuse to check for wet mattresses. She relished this duty above all others. Every morning she arrived early and stood in the hall outside our dorm. When the morning bell rang, she snapped on the lights. With a stern expression, she marched up and down the aisle flipping back covers, holding sheets up to the light, feeling mattresses, and searching for damp pajamas.

One fateful morning before breakfast, while several of us stood outside the dorm, we heard a commotion on the porch. Leroy yanked on my sleeve. "Olga's hassling Tim Curtis again." Hearing her voice, Leroy entered into a state of frozen watchfulness.

We heard her yelling, "Tim, you've wet twice this week. Must I diaper you like a baby?"

Tim's meek response, "My sheets have been dry for a week," only reflected his innocence. He always succumbed to Olga's cruel taunts. This day she forced Tim, with tears steaming down his face, to wear her old red polka-dotted dress which featured a ruffled lace collar. She buckled a white belt around his waist and stuck a red feathered hat on his head. Taking a step back, she smiled. It seemed like a raging devil lived within her.

J.C. Watson leaned on the banister brushing his hair. "Don't worry. Tim will split in a minute."

"Not with that witch on his tail," said Leroy.

J.C. rolled his eyes. Several kids walked off, hurt by Tim's embarrassment.

This scenario shocked us into reality. Leroy and I never wet the bed, but we cringed as she paraded Tim down the front stairs and into the dining hall.

"Tim pee-peed his bed." Olga wore a satisfied grin like a kid holding the remaining king in checkers. But this was only the first move in her perverse punishment.

Tim was the dreamer among us, a wiggly-eared kid, awkwardly thin, a wistful waif. He often played marbles by himself or built secret hideaways in the hay barn. But his anxious face would break into a smile if you gave him a used wad of bubble gum. Tim was a moody boy whom few understood. But he was our friend.

In the dining hall, she sat Tim at the head of a table and served him a bowl of oatmeal. He ate one or two spoonfuls, then flipped his spoon, scattering gluey streaks across the table. He wiped his mouth with his sleeve and stared at Olga.

"Rip the damn dress off," J.C. encouraged.

"Run like hell," Leroy waved his arm.

A sad, desperate look came into Tim's eyes. He stood up and walked around the table, forcing a laugh for a step or two. His comedic ramble pleaded to be left alone.

But Olga heightened her charade. Under an overcast sky, she paraded Tim down the driveway and onto 63rd Street leading to school. He still sported the frilly dress and the feathered hat. With his slow progress, one mile stretched before us like a dozen. He looked like a clown as he shuffled along in his high topped shoes. His skinny legs sported black knee-high stockings, and his dark hair streamed from under the gaudy hat. Several giggling girls followed the procession, holding their hands over their mouths.

Old Nick followed alongside, wagging his tail and occasionally licking Tim's hand. He sensed the need to nurture this innocent boy, but our principal barred pets from school. So J.C. whistled Nick to one side, and ordered him home. Tim opened his mouth, but only a timid laugh came out. His pleading eyes reflected the defeat in his heart.

That evening Olga served Tim a special meal, a tin cup of milk and two biscuits. He broke the biscuits and dipped them in the milk, as small pieces crumbled onto the table. In the evening she denied him anything to drink. She accused him of plotting to suck water out of his toothbrush, and wouldn't let him brush his teeth. Never satisfied, she chirped on, informing Tim that the Lord wouldn't let bed-wetters into heaven.

"Thank God," Tim said. "I'd live with the devil before I'd go to Heaven with you." With that brave outburst, Tim dashed into the dorm. Like an eel, he slithered under his bed, crying with muffled moans.

For a number of orphans, the home served as an asylum between childhood and adulthood. Leroy and I are still close friends. Even today we talk about the torment Tim suffered. We hear his forced laughter and see the dark pain in his eyes. No doubt his hurtful past became a hurtful future and in early adulthood, Tim's bright spirit slipped away. He took his life. We still mourn the loss of our friend.

~⟨8⟩~

By the middle of March, the days lengthened, and around noon the breeze streamed over Red Hill. It came at first as only a breath. Then, after a few hours, the wind blew with gusty freshness. Kite-building days had finally arrived. Leroy and I dreamed of building high flyers that would spread a rainbow of colors across the sky, but we needed building materials. One day, at school one of the older boys told us about a stash of supplies in the ravine behind the Rose Hill Cemetery. Bessie had threatened to give us a thrashing if we hauled any trash up from the graveyard. This just made it that much more attractive.

So as soon as school let out, Leroy and I took a twisty route home, tramping south and then west. We crossed Grand Boulevard and entered the gates of the forbidden cemetery. Sneaking by the creepy mausoleum, we gazed open-mouthed at the stone structure sprawled at the foot of the hill. The stained glass windows looked like watchful eyes.

"Ghosts live here." Leroy grabbed my arm, trying to spook me.
"Don't be goofy." I shook free.
We took off running, cutting across the hilly cemetery till we

reached a ravine running along a sloping tree line. Here we discovered a mountain of discarded treasures.

We found green waxed string, a broken orange crate that transported us to a sunny orchard, colored ribbons, bailing wire, a coil of rope, a broken floor lamp, stacks of paper, gunnysacks, and an old casket with the lining ripped out. I told Leroy that it would make a great boat. He laughed.

To make our kite lines, we unwound yards of the green string from the discarded flower displays, tying length after length together, then winding them to form giant balls of twine. After sticking our loot in a gunnysack, we walked up the path where I spotted four new wreaths on a fresh grave.

"Looky here." I held up a colorful display bright with red and yellow ribbons. "Whatta you think? Kite tails."

"Hell, we'd be stealing." Leroy looked disgusted.

"Lighten up. They'll rot if we don't use them." I pulled out my Barlow knife, slit the ribbons free, and rolled them up.

"Com'on Will, these tombstones give me the heebie-jeebies. Let's head home." Leroy finished packing our sack with supplies, and we struggled uphill past the Rose Hill water tower.

We arrived on campus just as Olga stepped out from behind the boys' dorm. Wearing a mean look and stoking her hot temper, she wielded a red paddle slightly smaller than Bessie's.

"I've told you boys to come straight home after school." She reported that a gentleman with a briefcase had come by to see me. "He was irritated that you were not home. He talked for over an hour with Reverend Maxey."

"Don't wanna see the old man."

Olga, with her mind bent on giving us our just punishment, didn't pay any attention. She made both of us touch our ankles. She paddled our rears till they turned red. Olga's mean spirit heightened our desire to find solace in our kites.

The following day, using pocketknives, we split thin pieces of pine from the salvaged orange crate, savoring the aroma of a distant grove. With these sticks we built several types of kites. "How wide should we make them?" Leroy asked.

I stuck out my arm. "Oh, about like this."

"How tall?"

"About twice an arm's length." I spread my arms.

First, we built two-stick models. But we found the three-stick kites withstood heavy winds better. We covered the frames with brown wrapping paper and used flour paste to secure the edges. If rain clouds appeared, we dropped by the kitchen, begged a small jar of lard from the cook, and coated our kites with a light coat of grease to repel the water.

We tied red, yellow and green lengths of the discarded ribbons together to make the most beautiful kites on the hill. Once they were finished, we joined our friends in the fields abloom with white and purple wildflowers. But from the lake came the distant sound of frogs and the meadow stood silent.

The windless day spelled trouble. No kites flew. The second day, a stiff breeze combed the grass with a steady moan. The bell clanged and, like string from a ball of kite twine, the dormitories strung us out onto the field. With nervous anticipation, Leroy and I cheered as our kites winged into the air. Nick, barking and wagging his tail, dashed between our legs, pawing and snapping at the bright ribbons.

We let our kites soar over the prairie fields. We felt the firm tug on the line; the tingling sensation of the taut strings spread down our arms and stirred juices in our bellies. When a gust pitched our kites into a tailspin, we slacked the strings, then retightened them and jumped with joy. Kite building taught us to be resourceful and make do with little. Our homemade kites flew higher than store-bought ones. Nothing felt better than a dream fulfilled.

*

To gain more possessions, and therefore more status, many of us kids played the game of "Pocket Trash." We kept our most prized items in our pockets where no one could swipe them. We even collected pop lids. Possessions gave us prestige, permitting each boy to stand apart from his classmates. We were happy when our pockets bulged with stuff.

Tim Curtis toted a three-bladed pocketknife, one of his mother's earrings, and a brass whistle. We admired J.C. Watson because he bragged about his Esterbrook lever-filler fountain pen and a comb with half of its teeth missing. Leroy walked taller than any of us because he displayed a silver buckle, a green yo-yo, and an Indian head penny. I prized my black-handled Barlow knife, a red spinning top and several pop lids. And I tucked a wad of Double Bubble gum, wrapped in its original wrapper, in my shirt pocket.

But in all my dreams for goods, I yearned most for a wristwatch, the grandest of all worldly effects. Playing Pocket Trash represented the quickest way of acquiring one. Each contestant placed an item in the circle. We took turns spinning our tops to spike the treasures and flip the desired one out of the ring. The boy who succeeded became the new owner.

One Saturday in May, I stuffed my pockets with a couple of valuables and dashed out to the far edge of the playground to practice. I wrapped my red top and spun it down. After a bit, I crouched down and, using my middle fingers, I scooped the spinning top into the palm of my hand.

I unbent my legs, keeping a steady arm, then stood erect with the top humming its tune. A shadow appeared to my side. I turned to see Neal Lesserman, a chubby, freckled boy with red bushy hair. He claimed he was thirteen, but he looked older because of his thin hair and high forehead.

"Mornin', Will."

"What's up, Neal?"

He was a somber-looking boy. "He's a funny duck," Leroy said.

He had heard him quoting scriptures one night after lights out. Round-shouldered and high-hipped, Neal wore loose-fitting jeans and a stained white shirt with buttons stretched down his stout chest.

The guys razzed him without mercy.

"Hey, baggy pants," taunted J.C.

"Pull up your drawers," called Leroy.

"How did your mother have a kid like you?" another kid said. Neal ignored the guys. His mind seemed to spin with flights of youthful delusions.

"You gotta groovy spiker. Wanna play Pocket Trash?" Neal reflected the look of a boy who hoped that his lucky day had arrived.

"Ah . . . guess so. Whatta you got to put up?" I gave a sly answer to hide my desire to gamble for a big reward.

He hesitated a bit. "I got a Mickey Mouse wristwatch."

"Let's take a look." My heart pounded.

Looking smug, he reached in his left pocket and pulled out an eye-popping watch. "Best one around."

The watch shone like silver. The spring tightened with sweet clicks and Mickey's black paws on the hour and minute hands spoke the time. "Looks okay."

"Whatta you got to put down?" Neal asked.

"Gotta a snazzy pocketknife." I pulled out my most treasured possession.

"Come on. My watch is worth more than a knife."

"This is a genuine Barlow, just like the one Tom Sawyer carried."

"I'd like a nifty three-blader like Tim's."

"Naw! You don't want a triple blader. A single blade doesn't have any side wobble. This is the keenest knife in the dorm, bar none."

He opened the blade and ran his thumb along the sharp edge as a wide grin lifted his ears.

"You game?" I stood ready to play.

With nervous fingers he clicked the blade shut. "Okay, but you gotta put something up to boot."

"I'll throw in a pop lid." I searched my pockets and handed one over. He flipped it in the air. Like a fish, he nibbled at the bait. I held my line taut, ready to set the hook.

"Okay. I'll go for the lot." He handed me the watch.

My heart throbbed with greedy hope as Neal drew a three-foot circle in the dirt. Then we pitched in our pocket trash. He tossed in my knife, and I laid his watch in with care.

"The best spiker wins it all." He stood grinning from ear to ear.

Neal flipped the pop lid. He called it tails. It turned up heads. With nervous hands, I wound my cord, with a button at one end and a knot at the other, keeping each wrap clean.

I stepped back, squared my shoulders, and spun my Red Killer into the ring with a sidearm throw. The spinning top nicked the ground and hopped over the watch. I had failed.

Neal hiked up his pants, wrapped his top with a shaggy cord and spiked it down on the prizes. Somehow he wound his cord with an overlap. The line caught on his top and dragged my Barlow out of the ring. He reached down and picked it up.

"You've pitched a slug! You're cheating."

"Didn't do it on purpose," he said.

"We may have to fight this out." I doubled up my fists.

"Keep your shirt on. Take another turn, then we'll settle up."

I took a deep breath and held it for a bit. I reminded myself to toss my top with a smooth motion whereby it wouldn't bounce over the watch. I wound it again, let out my breath, and launched it with a steady hand. With a crisp ping, it flipped the watch out of the ring.

Wow! I've won. I picked up my Mickey Mouse jewel. Gee whillikers, this will flip Leroy on his ear.

Neal took a step back. Words as nervous as a wobbling top spun out of his mouth. "If you'll return my watch, my dad will bring you a bike."

Was he bragging about his dad? I couldn't tell, but why else would he offer up a bike in exchange for the watch he had lost?

"Is it a new bike?" I plunged the watch deep into my pants pocket.

"No, it's used. But not a scratch." He shifted his weight from one leg to the other as if he felt cold.

Boy, oh boy! I loved the idea of owning a bike. It would feel grander than wearing a Mickey Mouse watch.

I pictured gleaming red fenders, chrome handlebars, and white-walled balloon tires. My mind raced ahead. I could stash it in the bushes by the cemetery and use it to zip out to N.W. 59th Street and visit Helen Minter.

"Okay, see you Monday. Bring the bike. I'll hand over the watch." To avoid a fight, he turned and tossed the Barlow back in the ring. Monday came and went. The bike never appeared.

I told Leroy about my experience. Leroy grinned, and placed both hands on his hips. "You're the third guy he's promised that bike to. Yep, he's bamboozled all you yokels."

Neal never delivered the bike, but I kept the Mickey Mouse watch and my Barlow. Deluded with fantasies of a soft-hearted and bountiful father, Neal walked around the edges of our playground. A sad figure, he seemed unable to deal with the small cruelties of rough-and-tumble orphan boys.

*

Unlike Neal, I learned to deal with my orphan pals, but I had yet to face any bold treachery. But Neal warned where it lurked. "Now Will, don't get on Pop Hall's bad side, or he'll do you in." Old Pop, whom I considered a windbag, supervised the dairy. He often badgered the kids to do his work. He wore black shoes that seldom showed a speck of dust, so we called him "old lazy shoes."

I had watched Pop worm himself up from janitor to our dairy supervisor. His sweet talk with the matrons and older girls didn't go unnoticed by us kids. He strutted around like a big shot, but he looked like a phony with his "aw shucks" manners and tobacco-stained fingers. And his long-winded stories sounded like lies to me.

Neal, who worked in the dairy barn, had told us not to mess around in the barn. Old Pop threatened his helper. "I'm goin' to whip you, if'n you don't clean out the stalls on time."

When Neal failed to finish cleaning the barn one day, Pop said, "Boy, I told you I was going to let you feel this rope if you didn't finish your chores."

"Now, Pop. This is serious. Don't you think we ought to kneel and pray to the Lord before you beat me with a knotted rope?"

"I've prayed." He lit up a Camel. "The Lord told me to give you a good beating."

After Neal recounted the conversation for us, he pulled down his pants and showed us his bruised rear. "My tail's still sore. Stay clear of the old bastard."

On a June afternoon bathed with sunlight, the meadow yellow and white with daisies, Tim Curtis approached me in the carpenter's shed where I was carving another nick in my top.

"Guess what? Yesterday a truck dumped off a fresh load of hay."

Disregarding Neal's warning, Tim and I hightailed it out to the hay barn where we discovered a building sweet with alfalfa. We planned to build tunnels and secret rooms for our games of hide-and-seek. So we set to work. We tugged and grunted, dragging the heavy bales around to make the sidewalls for our cave. Occasionally we ripped off the baling wire and created a mess.

We had stacked one row of bales out from the wall when BANG. The barn doors flew open and through the glare, mixed with flying dust, a figure approached.

"It's old Pop," Tim shrieked. "Let's get the hell outta here." He leaped for the side door. I bolted for the swinging doors, but a hand jerked me to the ground.

"Okay, you hay rat. Let's see how tough you are!"

My teeth clattered. I couldn't breathe, nostrils itchy from the dust.

His boot scuffed the hay and came up with a length of baling wire. He folded it into an accordion shape, a quick weapon. He clenched his teeth as his thrashing arm flogged me.

"Dance you little devil," he said. The pain shot through my rump and into my back. In desperation, I bit him on the leg. He flinched. I twisted free and raced back to the dorm.

"Whatcha cryin' about?" Bessie took hold of my hand.

I pulled down my pants. "Pop Hall beat me with baling wire."

Bessie examined my bleeding rump. "Oh mercy, mercy be. And he would do this to my boy." She grimaced. Bessie rushed to the medicine cabinet and grabbed a jar of black salve. She smeared the soothing ointment on my rear as she fired questions at me.

"How did you tick him off?"

"He caught me playing in the hay barn."

Shaking her head, Bessie put me to bed, but stayed by my side. I lay on my stomach and heard myself moaning, groaning, and cursing. My knees shook, hands quivered, and blood pounded my temples. Whispers in my mind told me to get even.

"Pop Hall's a jackass in overalls!" Bessie said. "He claims to love the Lord, but he parades around campus with a Bible in one hand and a fistful of hatred in the other."

"He's a mean devil," I added.

"My boy, Pop's like a thunderstorm. Rips you apart. But he blows by. In a few days, you'll recover."

My dislike of Pop Hall twisted my mind like knots in a kite line. Mean thoughts rolled in my head. I dreamed of pushing him out of the hay loft. That would fix him. We could play in the barn.

I often wondered about grown-ups like Pop Hall. Did Bessie have hopes that he would one day be happy? Would he have warmer hands and a kinder heart? Would he love us boys as he did the girls? Would the day come when he was more gentle than mean? It bothered me that Reverend Maxey didn't fire old Pop. But the days drifted by as if nothing happened.

In spite of my fear of Pop Hall, old man Wheeler, and Olga, I still loved Momma, and I cared for Bessie, and I appreciated my teachers. I had Leroy and other classmates as friends. And Daisy Butter's teasing smile brightened many days.

The memory of Helen and Will Minter's care still warmed my heart. But I no longer wished to live in an orphanage and dreamed of having a home of my own. I longed for the comforting hugs of a mother and the words, "I love you, my boy."

~9~

One Friday morning in late June, Bessie marched into our dorm. Standing tall and looking official in her white dress, she announced that we boys were to quit straying off the grounds. "The Rose Hill Cemetery, Belle Isle Lake, and Uncle Walter's shack are off limits." But Bessie's declarations fell on deaf ears.

From the crest of Red Hill I could see a fresh stream wandering to the east around four small islands and flooding into the main body of the lake. These waters cooled the generating plant before flowing downstream to form the Deep Fork River.

The blue lake waters drew us dreamy-eyed boys like a magnet with their dragonflies, tadpoles, frogs, crawdads, minnows, and catfish. We envisioned skinny-dipping and the greatest of all adventures: sailing a boat out to explore the islands.

From all the talk, I wanted to play near the water and possibly meet Uncle Walter, whom the older boys were always talking about. Reverend Maxey said he was a former slave who rode his mule-drawn wagon into Oklahoma before the land rush of 1889.

"There's a lotta talk," Leroy said.

"Com'on, be a good sport. Let's head for the lake." I lured Leroy toward an adventure.

"Hold up. Bessie will blister our tails."

"I'm tired of beans. I'd like a mess of fish for supper." Finally, after dawdling around the dorm for a bit, Leroy agreed to come along.

On a Saturday morning, warm and bright, with a clear, blue sky without a cloud in sight, we slipped down the back steps and headed for the lake. Near the older boys' dorm, I paused and looked over my shoulder to see if Olga might be following. I froze. There in front of the Old North Building, Mr. Wheeler stepped out of his Buick looking as if he expected to meet someone. He reached into the backseat, pulled out his briefcase, and walked up the front steps.

My stomach knotted up, and my hands began to sweat. I stood staring at my guardian in somewhat of a daze until I became aware of Leroy tugging on my sleeve. "What's up, Will?"

"Holy cow, old man Wheeler is after me again. He's heading up to Reverend Maxey's office. Let's get outta here."

We struck out for the lake, my heart pounding with fear. The grass stood summer high and patches of weeds hummed with game and insects. I stuffed a fistful of grasshoppers into my pocket. A rabbit sprang from her burrow, and a covey of quail fluttered into flight. Farther down, we entered a ravine and joined a path. A sign read, "KEEP OUT." Being true scalawags, to us this meant: "Fun ahead."

Finally we reached the water's edge, and after stomping the tall grass aside, Goat Island came into view. We slipped off our shoes and walked along the shore. I relished the smell of wet clay rising from the banks. Then a muffled croak, croak, broke the silence. A brown bullfrog, a jumbo creature with knobby eyes, squatted on a stump. "Stay calm, froggy. I'm your friend." I reached out to touch him. He didn't move. Thinking he was sick and needed help, I picked him up. His quivering throat rippled across my fingers, and I tucked his clammy body in the fold of my shirt. I left my thoughts of Mr. Wheeler up on the hill.

Leroy and I walked up the path to find Uncle Walter who might doctor Louie, a name we both thought suited the bullfrog. We approached a shack that sat a few feet from the cane field, flipped up a loop of baling wire, and unlocked the wooden gate. His place, built with sun-bleached lumber and covered with a rusted tin roof, stood before us.

All appeared quiet except for two whirligigs—red wooden roosters with spinning wings—clattering in the breeze. Across the wind-swept yard, a cedar pole barn sheltered a weathered wagon, two bony-hipped mules, and a flock of chickens. A dozen rabbit hides hung on the side fence, and a path led to the porch.

A thin rail of a man, bent like a plow handle from age and hard labor, stood in the doorway. He raised an arm, shielding eyes narrowed by the sun, while he shuffled onto the wooden porch. Under bib overalls he wore a clean but rumpled white shirt with rolled up sleeves, revealing sinewy arms. His gnarled hands held a pipe.

He motioned for us to come up on the porch. "The kids call me Uncle Walter," he smiled.

Lying near him, a brown dog sniffed the air. The hound stood up and growled. My legs tightened. Leroy stepped back.

Uncle Walter looked us over from head to foot, then patted his dog. "Down, Blossom." The hound stretched out and put his nose between his paws. "Are you young'uns looking for that old tin boat?" He went on to say that a couple of older boys had abandoned one last summer.

Our ears perked up with the mention of a boat. "I'm Leroy Harris and my friend here is Will Rogers. He came in several months back." Leroy leaned over, eyeing the dog.

"Sho-nuff." He slapped his thigh. "You hear that, Blossom? This boy's totin' a big name. Be quiet now so's I can learn 'bout this Will Rogers."

"The judge tagged me."

"No reason? Just handed out a big name?"

"That's right. One day my name was Roger Bechan, and the next day it's Will Rogers."

"That's shore something," Walter wiped his forehead with the back of his hand. "Well, what can I do fo' you young'uns?"

"Louie needs doctoring up," Leroy pointed to our frog. "And our friends up at the home would like some catfish."

Uncle Walter slipped his corncob pipe into his mouth, freeing his hands. "I knows about frogs. An' they's fish on my trotline." He took Louie and stroked his underbelly. "He's an old one. No tender legs on this'un." He turned, and with the frog in hand, entered his house.

"Don' mine me young'uns, my place is a plum mess." We followed Uncle Walter into a small room hazy with smoke. A kerosene lamp hissed a soft glow. He turned up the wick, lightening the shadows that crowded the furniture. I saw an iron bed and a bare wood table. On the far side of the room, a ribbon of steam spewed from a black kettle atop a potbellied stove. The smell of coffee mixed with the oily scent of kerosene spread a strange odor. To our surprise, the floor of his home was bare earth, worn smooth with time.

In the middle of the room, a brown bearskin rug rested on the red clay floor. I kneeled down to feel the fur.

"You can set on the grizzly bear." As a city boy, I didn't take to playing with a wild animal. But the luxury of owning a bearskin lent an air of dignity to his modest home.

Leroy told me that Uncle Walter's few dollars and the bearskin rug came from John Harden, who owned the land to the south and east of the orphanage's forty acres.

Uncle Walter plowed Harden's fields of cane, corn, and hay, but he spent many of his hours trapping rabbits and running trotlines.

Uncle Walter walked back to the porch carrying a tin can smelling of soda, kerosene, and lard. He rubbed the potion on Louie's stomach. "He'll be jumpin fo' you knows it."

Leroy placed Louie in a paper sack and handed him to me. Walter led us down to the lake, and he unhooked several catfish from his

98

trotline. He skinned a mess and rolled them up in an old newspaper. We shook his hand with thanks.

Leroy said we should head home and sneak our catch into the kitchen's icebox. I thought it was a good idea, so we lit up and shared a corn silk. When we eased around the dining hall building, we saw Olga approaching. We stomped out our smoke.

"You boys smell mighty strong." She wrinkled her nose. "And what's wrapped in the paper?" Leroy, with the fish in hand, struck out for the kitchen. Our cook, ignoring any words from Bessie, granted any kid's request to prepare fish or frog legs hauled in.

I pulled a couple of grasshoppers out of my pocket and tossed them at Olga. She squealed and jumped back. I lit off for the dorm.

Leroy placed Louie under my bed. We listened to his croaking until lights out. Then Leroy carried him down the hall and slipped him into the girls' dorm. In the night, we heard shrieks and giggles. In the morning, Bessie marched through our dorm with Louie in a shoe box.

"I'm tossing this noisy frog out the back door. I don't want to see his ugly face again."

Leroy and I peeked out the window as Louie hopped away into the open field. We never saw him again, but we felt Uncle Walter had performed a miracle. To our thinking, he saved Louie's life.

From then on Leroy loved trash and wild creatures. He often kept a frog, a horny toad, a yellow snake, a sack of grasshoppers, or a ball of old string under his bed.

After breakfast, Bessie stopped me in the hall. "Your Mr. Wheeler dropped by yesterday and talked to Reverend Maxey."

I felt a knot in my stomach. "Don't wanna see him. Ever again."

"You needn't worry." She laid her hand on my arm. "Mr. Wheeler is no longer in your life. The Baptist Orphanage has custody of you now." I still felt apprehensive.

In spite of the warnings, Leroy and I returned often to Uncle Walter's home with its whirly birds, bare hides, and pots of boiling stew. We lived freely there, without a thought of my guardian. And, strangely enough, neither Olga nor Bessie ever walked down the winding path to the tin-covered shack.

"Let's share a healthy lunch," Uncle Walter said one day. "Old Blossom treed a possum last night."

"Uh . . . well . . . all right," Leroy said.

Uncle Walter served possum and sweet potato stew, spiced with pepper and onions and colored with carrots from a black pot. He offered a large pan of corn bread slathered with sorghum. The stew smelled wild but sweet potatoes and a few sips of dandelion wine mellowed the gamy concoction. To our surprise, Uncle Walter fixed mighty good eats.

When our stomachs were full, Uncle Walter lugged out his guitar. He curved his weathered fingers around the neck of it and strummed the strings as though stroking a friendly hound. In a voice scratchy with time, he sang "Old Uncle Ned."

Old Uncle Ned.
Have no teeth fo' to eat the whole cake,
and then he had to let the whole cake be.
One cold morning Old Ned died
and the tears came down like the rain.

Hang up the shovel,
Hang up the hoe,
Hang up the fiddle and the bow.
They's no mo work fo'r po' ol' Ned . . .
He's gone where all the good darkies go.

As his tune floated in the air, mournfully and touchingly, the tears flowed down his cheeks. I can still hear Uncle Walter's doleful voice rolling across the prairie field: "One cold morning Old Ned died . . . and the tears came down like rain."

That day, saying that good luck would always follow us, he gave Leroy and me a rabbit's foot. We admired our friend and his zest for life. He gave us the rarest gift—a heart that never condemned, moralized, or tried to convert us to any cause. He taught us boys to judge a person by his character.

*

Several weeks later in August, Leroy and I lay on our backs smelling the crushed playground grasses burned brown by the August heat. We sat up to dreamily peer down at the waters of the lake shimmering a silver-blue under the intense sun. I was painting pictures myself, having read old copies of *National Geographic* magazines and imagined myself as a pirate, sailing ships into exotic ports where palm trees and parrots abounded. Like hearing a siren song, I dreamed of distant islands, even exploring the river below the dam.

"Let's drag the old coffin down from the dump. We can pour tar in the cracks."

"Naw, let's find the old boat Uncle Walter talked about." Leroy fumbled with his pencil over a piece of paper.

On a warm August morning, after we completed our chores and the fog lifted, we stepped onto our favorite meadow and tramped south. We never discussed our plans with friends because too many boys leaving the grounds would attract attention and bring an end to our adventures.

A footpath crossed a small ditch, beyond which the prairie field sloped to the water's edge.

"If we find a boat, let's sail out to Forgotten Island." Leroy pointed to a spot on a penciled map he had drawn of the lake.

"Let's see what you got."

He handed over his sketch. His penciled marks faded away near the dam. I told Leroy I had studied the wall map at school. The Deep Fork River ran below the dam. "Perhaps it'll flow to the Mississippi and out to the ocean." I told him we could find a deserted island. We could live on fish and coconuts.

"You've lost yer marbles."

"Naw, just thinkin' ahead," I said.

The thistles and milkweeds brushed our pants as we rustled through them, then trotted, zigzagging around ruts and gopher holes. We lengthened our strides as we sped down a path that led to a ravine guarding our safe passage. We stomped a path through the high grass and walked to the edge of our favorite cove across from Goat Island.

A rush of smells flowed over us. Damp weeds, dead fish, and when the wind shifted, a whiff of burning gas settled over the water. The vapors came from the smokestack towering above the power plant on the north edge of the lake.

We scrambled down the embankment and kicked off our shoes. Waves slapped the shore, reflecting the scudding clouds. We split up; Leroy walked east, and I wandered in the opposite direction.

Before I explored an area the length of a baseball field, Leroy shouted. "Hey, Will!" His call came from a distance. I walked toward his voice. "Will!" He called again, waving both hands above the brush. "Get over here. I've found her."

I dashed up the bank hoping to see a handsome craft waiting to be discovered. Boy, what a disappointment. "Hell, that's not a boat," I said.

"'Tis too." Leroy's voice sounded confident.

Floating a few inches below the water, I saw a large canoe-shaped object made of corrugated tin and pointed at both ends. Someone had pounded the sheet metal together to form a sharp bow and stern. Baling wire held it together and splotches of black tar filled a good number of holes.

"Gee whiz, Leroy. It's ugly. The old coffin would be better."

"We'll patch her up. Make a dandy rowboat." Leroy looked exasperated with my doubts.

We jumped into the water and dragged the odd contraption deeper into the cove. We covered it with branches so no one else could poach our prize. Then we tramped back toward home. Leroy talked about our good luck and insisted I go along with his idea of rebuilding the craft. I finally agreed.

"We can snatch some tar, wood, and nails from Mr. Drummand's workshop." Our dreams of owning a boat invigorated our tired legs as we climbed the hill.

During the next few days, we worked on our project near the edge of the lake. We made a platform from the abandoned casket we had dragged down from the cemetery dump. Leroy hammered the metal bow into a sharp point. We fitted a board from a packing crate as a new stern. Leroy nailed her firm. We stuffed the joints and nail holes with roofing tar. From a length of lath we fashioned two oars.

We created a new boat. To a grown-up, our craft probably looked like a grungy creature—holes stuffed with tar, and the tin bent out of shape. A weathered Nehi soda sign remained on the metal shell. In celebration, we sprinkled a bit of water over her bow and christened her *Miss Daisy*, after my favorite of all the girls.

On a breezy mid-August morning, we took a fruit jar of water, pocketed two biscuits and a couple balls of Double Bubble, and a coffee can. We skipped our chores, and slipped away as we had done all summer. This time, as before, chance favored us.

From the top of the hill, we looked to the far shore where the sun glistened off the choppy waves kicked up by the wind. We stepped into the field, filled with eagerness and hope. The summer day, warm yet comfortable, with a scattering of puffy clouds hovering above a sunny day fog, was a dreamy boy's kind of day.

As we approached the hidden cove, Goat Island appeared. We kicked off our shoes, hopped into the water, and yanked back the branches to uncover our prize. To keep from cutting ourselves on the sharp edges, we tossed gunnysacks over the rails. Leroy tumbled in as I shoved off and jumped aboard. *Daisy* slipped ahead.

I tried to look like a salty sea captain as we swung out into the lake. We took a bearing and headed south, steering to pass between Bird and Goat islands. Our final destination was a sandy cove on Forgotten Island, located much further south and somewhat east from where we left the shore.

Leroy looked out over the wind-tossed whitecaps and grimaced. "Looks wild today."

I twisted about for a moment, looking northward and searching the horizon, gaining a glimpse of the buildings on campus. The moving waters washed away my fear of the Dark Room and drowned my memories of Mr. Wheeler, Olga, and Pop Hall. I could no longer taste Bessie's castor oil.

Daisy began to rock back and forth, tossed about by the choppy waves and our clumsy rowing. If Leroy moved, she tilted to one side, then bobbed up and down.

"C'mon, sit still," I said while trying to keep my balance. "We're dead in the water."

Leroy glanced back. "Watch my strokes." He raised the rough-hewn oar in his right hand and dug it low in the water, and pulled through in a smooth circle. I timed my stroke with his, and *Daisy* sped forward. Halfway to Goat Island, pieces of tar popped out and she sprang a leak. Now I had to split time between paddling and bailing water with our coffee can.

From far atop the hill, we heard the mournful bell calling for lunch. Leroy glanced back with a splash of worry on his face. "I hope Bessie doesn't hear about us being out here."

"Naw. She's got both ears glued to her radio."

Leroy paused, and using his oar, pointed to a tip of irregular earth. Forgotten Island lay like a land of enchantment, silent and sandy, with a scattering of low-lying bushes. The wind tossed my hair, yet sweat dripped off my arms. I could hardly contain my excitement as we struggled to hold a steady course.

My heart thumped in my chest and my lungs burned. Bessie's

vision of a drowning boy swept through my mind. I began to pray, "Lord, save us."

"It's too late to pray." Leroy wasn't sympathetic to my worries.

At last, through sweat-clouded eyes, I saw the island. Its low, sandy beach glistened in the sun, and as we came closer, a small cove appeared. I didn't feel easy till the final stab of our oars sped us up the channel. *Daisy* finally touched the shore.

We jumped out and yanked on our bowline, which Leroy had made from an old jump rope. The tin bottom scrunched as she skidded onto the sandy beach. We spread out our gunnysacks. Exhausted, we laid back to catch our breath, gasping and wheezing for air. After a bit we wolfed down our soggy biscuits. Leroy said he felt mighty proud that we had reached Forgotten Island and talked of building a secret island hideaway.

But there was no one to cheer about our accomplishments; only the blackbirds flew out from the prickly brush and soared above. They sang a melody of sounds; then one by one zoomed down to pick off water bugs and mosquitoes. Several frogs croaked in chorus.

"We'd better head for home." Leroy said after we had finished our evening meal. In preparation for our return trip, we turned *Daisy* over and dried her out. We filled a couple of the leaky nail holes with wads of Double Bubble. As we paddled out of the channel into deeper water, we talked about necessary repairs.

"We need to recaulk and build a rudder," Leroy said.

We headed northward, then steered to the east end of Snake Island where we tacked west, hugging the shoreline. We wished to avoid the current swirling out toward the center of the lake. Exhausted, with stiff backs and tired arms, we slipped into our favorite cove across from Goat Island. After camouflaging *Daisy* with branches, we stepped ashore dazed with success. As the sun touched the water, we slapped each other on the back with congratulations but quickly sobered up.

We experienced sailors climbed the hill and slipped up the back stairs into our dorm. We would have been smarter to remain on the outlawed waters than to have returned to land and faced the sadness that waited us in the dorm.

On that late Friday afternoon, August 16, 1935, Leroy and I entered the dorm to find Bessie pacing back and forth in the hallway. We thought we were in deep trouble. On closer observation, we didn't see angry retribution in her face. Instead, tears of grief flowed down her cheeks.

We froze, waiting to hear that a classmate or a beloved teacher had had an accident. Then she motioned with an outstretched hand. "Will, I have dreadful news." With trepidation, I walked to her side expecting word that Mr. Wheeler was coming to take me back to his home. But she said, "The radio has reported that Will Rogers and his pilot, Wiley Post, were killed yesterday in Alaska."

On that bright summer day, I couldn't believe death was possible. "Oh, no! It can't be!" Why did I face another loss? Someone I cared about—my Oklahoma cowboy, a philosopher, a movie star, a teller of funny stories—died on a snow-covered land in the middle of August. I had written Will Rogers a note. He replied with a letter and two photographs. He couldn't disappear from the canvas of my life.

This loss of Will Rogers was my first experience with human mortality. Outside of James Hardt telling me about his brother, death had been the small dove found in the field, a dried-up frog, a rabbit given to our table, or a possum taken as game by Uncle Walter. These were small happenings.

The following day, a Saturday, Bessie Riney together with Jenny Lucas, her supervisor matron, brought in a packet of newspaper articles on Will Rogers. For a person without rank or title, it is doubtful that any man received so many tributes, and they came from all over the world. Spencer Tracy, the movie star, said it best: "Will Rogers cannot die any more than Mark Twain could."

From my locker, I pulled out Will Rogers' letter and glossy photograph. He looked so vital and alive. My fingers brushed his rugged face and felt his hurried signature. He had brought the precious gift of laughter into my life. In my mind, Will Rogers would live forever. I would always have his autographed portrait.

Much to my surprise, in the Sunday morning issue of *The Daily Oklahoman* (August 18, 1935, p. 14) appeared a three-inch news story with the heading: "Will's Namesake, An Orphan, Sad Before Portrait." The newspaper told the story of "An orphan boy [who] stood heart-broken before a large autographed portrait of Will Rogers, given him last winter by the humorist."

"Mrs. J. H. Lucas, matron of the home, found the boy standing in front of the other picture Saturday."

The newspaper quoted me: "Mr. Will. I'll never get to see you. . . . But anyway, I've still got your picture."[2]

The news article should have reported that I was nine years of age.

＊

Unlike the Society for the Friendless where they brokered children into adoptive families, the Baptist Orphanage saw few couples seeking a child. In mid-September of 1935, the Great Depression lingered, and many couples couldn't support a larger family. Many of my class-mates had either a mother or father still living. But the remaining parent often refused to place his or her child up for adoption.

One of the public school teachers asked Johnny Henshall's sister if she would like to be their daughter. Betty Joyce said she would love to have a family of her own. Superintendent Maxey contacted her mother for permission, but Mrs. Henshall replied, "I'm sorry, none of my children is available for adoption."

No one threw this obstacle in my path. Bessie knew I longed to have a mother and father. On a warm afternoon with a soft wind flowing up from Bell Isle Lake, Bessie met me coming in from the playground. "Will, I've signed you and a younger boy up for interviews. A couple is seeking a son."

"Great, I'll get ready."

Bessie drew in her breath. "Wash your ears and dress up. A tie maybe."

This would be my first interview since entering the Baptist Orphanage, but I didn't like the idea of having to face competition from a younger kid. Would a couple want an older boy with freckles and big feet?

Perhaps a family like the Minters will come. They'll live out on an oil lease and would want an older boy. Wouldn't that be great. My mind turned over with ideas as to how I could gain approval. I'll light up the room with my brightest smile. I couldn't sleep because my heart pounded with anticipation of gaining a new home.

On Saturday morning, I hopped out of bed, rushed over to the dining hall, and devoured a bowl of oatmeal, returned to the dorm, took a shower, brushed my teeth with soda, and slipped on my khaki pants and white shirt.

Near ten o'clock Bessie walked in. "Will, where's your tie?"

"Naw, it pinches my neck."

"Have it your way." Bessie ushered me downstairs to the reception room where the Reverend Truman Maxey, our dedicated superintendent, conducted the interview. I entered the meeting with trepidation, feeling like an animal in a zoo.

Reverend Maxey introduced me to Mr. and Mrs. Alan Moore, a young couple who owned a hardware store in Muskogee. The reverend said it was a historic city, proud of being the center of the Creek Indian Agency dating back into the 1800s. The couple invited me to sit on a lounge chair near them.

"How old are you, young man?" The husband looked important in his blue suit.

"I'll soon be ten." From my early interviews, I knew this would be the first question.

"You're tall for your age." The lady smiled. Then looked to her husband.

"How long have you been in the home?"

"Since January."

"How many families have you lived with?" The lady laid her hand on my arm.

My heart raced. How do they want me to answer, I asked myself. "About five, but I would like a new home."

"We have a place on the Verdigris River," the husband said. "Do you like to swim?"

"Yes, sir. And I'd love to build a fishing boat." I gave him a big smile.

"What about your parents?" The lady leaned forward.

"My mother left when I was six."

"Where is your father?" The husband glanced at Reverend Maxey, then faced me.

"I don't know who he is."

They seemed rather upset. I wiped the sweat from my forehead. The Reverend Maxey concluded the meeting. The couple shook my hand. As I left the room, Bessie ushered in a young baby-faced kid who slept in the nursery.

I felt awkward about a couple of their questions, but I felt confident. I walked out onto the sun-filled playground and played capture the flag with Leroy and our friends.

Several days drifted by, and no one offered any information. I had learned earlier that rejection often arrives silently and without warning or news. A week later, I asked Bessie. She said the young couple had returned and taken the three-year-old boy.

My heart sank to my toes. I had failed again. Grown-ups remained a puzzle. The couple had acted as if they were interested. Would I always be an unwanted boy? Perhaps I was too old to woo a family.

Leroy approached me in the dorm. "C'mon, Will, buck up. Let's play some basketball."

"I don't get it. Why did they take that little squirt?"

Leroy bounced the ball on the floor. "He's a good-looking boy, but you wouldn't wanna live a hundred miles down the road without me."

Many of the kids had accepted their fate at the orphanage. I feared my friends would call me a sissy if I cried about another rejection. So I held back the tears, but my heart was filled with sadness.

*

Before the end of August, a more lighthearted adventure picked up my spirits. One evening Tim Curtis, Neal Lesserman, and I were playing Chinese checkers when two older boys from across the campus sauntered in.

"Hey, guys," the taller of the two said. "Wanna see some brown puppies?"

"You betcha," Tim said.

"Follow us." The shorter fellow grinned.

We walked out of the dorm and tramped down the path in the misty light of a rising moon. A light wind blew from the direction of the lake. From below the school, the evening train wailed its lonely cry. The sweet smell of clover mixing with the scent of damp grass hung in the air as lightning bugs twinkled brighter than the stars.

"Hold up." The lead boy rested his hand on Neal's shoulder. We paused on the north side of the older girls' dorm. The open windows glared like a lighted ship gliding through the dark.

The three-story brick building featured a dozen large windows on the bottom two floors; the lower six looked into the basement where a group of scantily clad girls roller-skated while waiting to take their showers. We quickly understood that the older boys had turned an innocent desire to hold newborn puppies into an initiation rite aimed at satisfying our budding lust and male curiosity. A couple of the bigger boys had boosted their smaller brothers on their shoulders, providing them a better view.

We rushed to claim a viewing spot alongside the Devil's disciples already there who were waving their arms with excitement. Behind half-raised window blinds, the girls looked wildly beautiful as they waited to bathe, some wearing only panties.

"My dreams have come true." Neal rolled across the grass.

The taller girls at the far end of the dorm roamed in circles, talking and teasing each other. The younger darlings near the windows were giggling like nervous hens. They tossed their hair and flipped their towels while their round hips and swelling breasts with their brown nipples—brown puppies—pranced before our eyes.

We crouched in the shadows. Neal rested on the ground with his chin in his hands, his eyes glowing like lightbulbs. Tim and I stood up to gain a wider view. One of the older boys, blinking with excitement, squatted beside us.

"What a sight." Tim took a couple of steps closer.

"Stand clear," I said. "Don't block my view."

Neal burst out giggling having recognized several of the older girls. "Look at Jane Sue, Betty Jane, and there's Mary Lou Butter dancing around."

"Quiet, you twerp," said Tim. "Mary Lou is Daisy Butter's big sister. And Will has a crush on Daisy."

"Shouldn't matter."

The boys cracked up, laughing and punching each other and whispering names as they stored memories for long winter nights.

The music from the rhythm band drifted up from the chapel where Leroy was practicing for their next public performance. He'll want to toss his drum in the trash once I tell him about the little brown puppies, I thought.

"God is good." I reflected on the truth our preacher had spoken last Sunday. Two of the older boys scooted even closer when suddenly the last bell clanged for lights out. The front door to the girls' dorm slammed shut, the lights blinked off floor to floor. We lost our view.

Tim hissed, "Jeez, let's get the hell outta here."

Under a blanket of darkness, we scrambled back toward our dorm. The older girls' building loomed black in the dim moonlight.

Now and then the lightning bugs formed a blanket of stars celebrating our night of exotic wonders.

Hopes for repeat performances of the brown puppies filled our evening chatter. But as the weather cooled, the girls donned heavier clothing while they waited to shower. We boys lived on our memories—but they were primeval enough to warm our coldest nights.

If Daisy's sister told her about our evening under the light of a rising moon, what would I say? Could I keep a straight face? Daisy's friendly smile and lively blue eyes brought me out of myself and relieved my loneliness. She had hair the color of a russet rose, a bewitchingly beautiful girl.

Thoughts of Daisy tormented my mind and body with mysterious desires. Neither Bessie nor the church fathers discussed such subjects, and I didn't know what to do about my feelings. During the following months, I walked as close to her as possible when we strolled home from school. My heart thumped with deep feelings. One afternoon she turned and kissed me on the cheek. A fever swept through my body. I longed to press her to me, but I feared my ardor would give me away. I stumbled along with my hands pushed deep into my pockets. Sexual desire had reared its unwelcome self, and I felt embarrassed. Not unhappy, but embarrassed.

~10~

The fall season of 1935 is planted in my mind with colors. Halloween used half of my black crayon and some orange. Thanksgiving blew my black entirely. The other crayons became nubbins as we colored feathered turkeys, pilgrims in black cloaks and hats, and corn stalks. The waxy aroma of Crayolas filled the air as we ringed Miss Specht's classroom with our handiwork. A Thanksgiving dinner of turkey and dressing completed the holiday with a lip-smacking, belly-busting finale.

Within a few weeks, Bessie turned up the boiler and laid out our winter clothes.

Snow blanketed our playground.

Leroy and I thrived on snowball fights and rode cardboard sleds down the hill to school. Classes let out, and with the holidays only days away, Bessie led a Wednesday chapel choir in "Silent Night." The festive spirit of Christmas set in. Leroy and I hoped Santa would know our wishes and dreams and that we would merit his attention.

As the great day approached, Bessie hung up her paddle and took on a lighthearted air. Dressed in a white uniform and sporting a red bow in her hair, she strolled down the halls like a fairy godmother. She hummed snatches of "Santa Claus is Coming to Town," mainly emphasizing, "You'd better watch out, You'd better not cry," as she bestowed a tap of love on one boy's cheek, blessed a young girl with kind words, soothed another child's tears, anointed another with a morning kiss, and hugged all the rest. She was the maestro of warm feelings, tuning her urchins up for the big day.

My classmates came down with Santa Claus fever, an illness which Bessie's castor oil couldn't cure. Our older brothers warned Leroy and me, "The old man in red is a lotta bull."

But Bessie gave us more mature advice. "Don't listen to those Doubting Thomases. There are many Santas. They represent the spirit of giving. Many generous people donate money, clothing, and food to the home."

Leroy and I ignored the naysayers. We became true believers, if not in our preacher, then in Santa. Leroy sneaked the Great Wish Book from the office and carted it to the basement. The marvelous catalog of Sears Roebuck, a couple of inches thick with over a thousand illustrated pages, let us shop our eyes out.

Leroy flipped to the section on toys. Our mouths watered over red wagons, ball-bearing scooters, Silver Flyer roller skates, giant metal Erector kits, Lionel electric trains, Gilbert chemistry sets, and a Buck Rogers Flashing Disintegrator Gun. We drooled over the impossible: an Elgin Bluebird balloon-tired bicycle with head and tail lights and a genuine speedometer. For one glorious month, those catalog pages held all our earthly dreams.

"I got dibs on the Erector set," Leroy said. "You bamboozled Neal out of his Mickey Mouse watch. You can't have everything."

"Don't care. I wanna build a skyscraper."

Bessie told us to pencil out our want lists. "Boys, times are hard. Don't ask for more than one gift."

Leroy dashed off his letter while I sat in the corner and wrote Santa a personal plea: "My name's Will Rogers. I'm ten years old and I'd like a giant Erector set with an electric motor." That would be the grandest of all gifts. After mailing our envelopes, Leroy toted the wish book back into the office. We wouldn't be like the other kids, who would whine when they received a rinky-dink toy because they hadn't mailed their letters to Santa on time.

"Leroy, betcha a nickel I'll get the Erector set."

"Naw, that's my prize. Wait and see."

Bessie decorated our tree, creating a snowlike platform on which colorful packages would soon rest. Leroy borrowed tin snips from the workshop and cut a star from one of our janitor's Prince Albert tobacco cans. This ornament topped our tree.

The days sped by. Day and night, all I could think about was building a model of the Petroleum Building with an oil derrick towering above the top floor. I wanted an Erector set with a motor to power the elevator. Nothing else would do.

On Christmas Eve, Leroy and I joined friends and entered the chapel to await the arrival of Santa. Leroy grinned from ear to ear. I could hardly wait to see his face when I opened the biggest package. Shouts, whistles, and an outburst of cheers bounced off the ceiling.

Amidst the clamor, a red-suited, white-bearded giant entered the main door. A tubby belly with a bag on his back, shiny boots up to his knees and a pinkish face swaggered down the aisle pulling a sled packed with presents.

Leroy eyed the giant and looked to me. "Here's a real Santa! He'll come through for me."

Santa bounded onto the stage, shook Reverend Maxey's hand and placed his bag under the tree. A helper dressed as an elf reached under the tree, pulled out a present and placed it on the table. Santa called out the name listed on the package, then greeted the child as he or she came forth to claim their present.

Santa called Leroy's name. He strutted up and received an ordinary box. He carried it to the back of the room, saying he was going to open it up.

"Great!" I said hastily, too distracted by my own anticipated pleasures to pat my friend on the back. I was dreaming of receiving my own super-duper package. Santa would save the largest set for me.

I eyed each gift because I knew Santa would know Will Rogers, even coming from the North Pole. After what seemed an eternity, the big moment came. "Will Rogers," Santa shouted, waving me forward. I dashed onto the platform. My girlfriend, Daisy Butter, followed close behind and smiled as Santa handed me a whale of a package. It weighed a ton. Wow! This'll get Leroy's goat.

"Looky here, Will. I've already got my Erector set out." Leroy had parts scattered across the floor.

"I've got a bigger one right here." The wrapping alone—three layers encompassed the monster package—demanded attention. My fingers tore away the brown wrapping paper and a second layer of Christmas green, revealing a layer of white. Even a dainty-handed girl could remove the barrier of white tissue paper. My heart thumped in anticipation. At last the box revealed itself, and the flaps opened to reveal the marvelous contents.

But what kind of joke was this? No metal construction kit had pink eyes. Yes, peeking back at me were two button eyes. Did Santa bring the wrong package? I checked the outer wrapping again. Santa had written Will Rogers on the gift tag. It was mine all right.

Perhaps the goofy creature lay on top of Santa's present. But I needed to pull the critter out to see what lay below. I yanked fast and hard, and the last vestiges of my Christmas bubble burst.

Nothing else was in the box. This was my Christmas surprise. "Yikes," I moaned. "It's a ratty pull toy!"

Santa had sent a giant, white wooden rabbit with shoe leather ears. The pink button eyes dripped tears of gummy glue, reflecting the haste of its maker.

I pulled the animal down the floor where I checked out its performance. It swayed and jerked, flipping its tail back and forth. Finally, one leg spun off and the creature crashed onto its side.

What could a big boy do with a wooden rabbit designed for a two year old? My eyes filled with tears. I jammed the rabbit into the box, stuffed in the wrapping paper, carried it out the rear door, and tossed it in the trash. I poked it deep into the can, hoping no one, not even Leroy, would spy it.

Christmas proved as unreal as the silly gift. I now realized that there was no one whom I could count on: no mother, no father, not even Santa could make my Christmas dreams come true. The older boys had spoken the truth. "Santa is a damned grown-up." I didn't let anyone see my tears. They fell inside my heart.

Despite my secretive trashing of the dreadful rabbit, one person had seen my dreams shattered. Leroy walked over with comforting words. "Will, don't feel bad, the Erector set is big enough for the two of us." Leroy said that we could use it to build all sorts of things—bridges, boats, airplanes, skyscrapers. "You know, all the things you're always talking about."

Regardless of our pasts, Leroy Harris had become my best pal. Ready to play? Just ask. Stand up to a bully? Tough as a roustabout. A good sport? You bet. Many of his dreams and mine became one. We shared a common heartache and a tireless energy which spurred each of us to new adventures. Such friendships are rare even among orphans.

*

The Christmas spirit lasted through the following week. It gave me the heart to stroll among the celebrants checking their windfalls without pouring cold water on their good fortune.

Johnny Henshall bragged about his ball-bearing scooter, and Neal Lesserman whizzed by on a new pair of roller skates. I looked up to see my friend, J.C. Watson, swaggering up the sidewalk pulling a spiffy wagon. Big-boned, broad-shouldered, and with the tough hands of a roustabout, J.C. looked like a man, although he was only twelve. The boys liked his easygoing manner, and his friendly smile charmed the girls. But he acted young at heart, still possessed of a refreshing innocence.

I paused to look at his new wagon. "You lucky cuss! How in the devil did you get such a beauty?"

"Dad went into debt again."

J.C.'s mother had died, and his well-intentioned father felt his four children would have a better life in an orphanage. Their father visited the home on holidays and brought gifts.

His Radio Flyer, gleaming red under the golden sun, featured high sides and a sturdy undercarriage, all riding on white-walled rubber tires. The glistening silver hubcaps, the sturdy black tongue, and the sweet smell of fresh-baked enamel turned my dream of escape into reality. J.C.'s wagon presented the magic carpet on which I could fly to freedom.

"Let's see if it'll hold the two of us, eh?" He scooted forward and I crawled in behind him.

J.C. smiled. "Yeah. Deluxe model. Best you can buy."

"Good times are ahead, pal." I patted him on the shoulder.

"Whatta you mean?" J.C. twisted around.

"Oh. We—I mean—you can load it with grub and slip out the front gate, never to return."

"Bessie will beat the devil out of me."

"Naw. She'd say you were brave to head out on your own."

"Yeah, I see. Yeah." J.C appeared more confident.

I hoped to plant the seed for escape in my friend who had probably never thought of leaving the home. My dreams turned to talk, then into plans buzzing like wasps in a coffee can. "How much money you got?"

J.C.'s fingers explored his pockets and fished out four dimes and a penny. "Forty-one cents."

"Great, I've got a dollar and forty-five cents."

"Leroy says you filched two bucks from the church."

"I got saved. Gave one dollar back."

"That was a Christian thing to do." J.C. appeared satisfied.

"Yeah. We now have a dollar and eighty-six cents." I told J.C. we'd take a sack full of supplies and buy hot cocoa and doughnuts for supper.

"Slow down. Let's think this over."

I told him that on the next clear day we'd head out 63rd and turn south toward town. We'd find a family in a big two-story house. It'd be red brick with white trim and would have a genuine fireplace. "No more of Olga's 5:30 mattress checks." Our new mother would serve bacon and eggs and let us sip coffee out of the saucer. Then we'd dash into the playroom, read the funnies, and drink a soda pop. "We haven't had a bottle of orange Nehi for over a year. Now, whatta you think?"

"Maybe so. But . . . what will Dad say about me living with a strange family?"

"Jumpin' Jesus, he'll be happy if a millionaire takes us in. Perhaps our new dad will buy us a Bluebird bicycle with an electric horn. Wouldn't that be swell?"

Finally, after a week of hearing about the glowing future that awaited, J.C. saw the wisdom of our venture. "Okay, okay. On the next clear morning, we'll spring outta here. But don't forget, Will, this is your idea."

After lights out, I went over our plans with Leroy, and asked if he wished to go along. He declined, saying it looked chancy. I patted him on the back and asked him to stuff an extra pillow in each of our beds at night and make them up every morning.

"I'll help. But you two are headed for trouble."

I shook Leroy's hand and said good-bye. My disappointing holiday ended with plans for finding a home where every Christmas would echo with happiness. And once I found a new mother and father, old man Wheeler could never find me.

The clear morning arrived.

"Come on, Will. Let's get outta here!" J.C. whispered.

I didn't answer. He shook me awake before the morning bell. It was a glorious Friday in the first week of January 1936 before classes resumed.

"Oh, no! Go back to sleep." I moaned.

He yanked off my quilt and I rolled out of bed and rubbed my eyes. We stuffed pillows under our blankets and slipped on long underwear, shirts and pants, two pairs of socks and macintosh coats. Finally we pulled on our Lucky Lindy aviator gear and sneaked out the back door. Regardless of the temperature, we never abandoned our leather helmets. The stylish caps impressed the girls even though we stuffed paper in the ear vents to block the chilly winds.

The dawn cast a faint light across our winter playground, and the wind breathed an invitation for flight. The morning was crisp and clear: a quarter moon peeked over the houses in Nichols Hills and the dew glistened on the street.

The night before, J.C. had stashed his Radio Flyer in the bushes behind the front gate. We moseyed down the driveway, tugged the wagon free, and headed west on 63rd Street without attracting attention. Planning to travel in comfort, we had tucked a quilt in the wagon's bed along with a box of Post Toasties, a couple of apples, a bag of peanuts, and a fruit jar of water.

Good luck greeted us as we pulled our wagon up the low hill. When we reached the top we roared down the next grade. The Radio Flyer bumped along the rough road. My bottom took a beating as J.C. pushed on my back like we were riding a Flash Gordon rocket, then jumped into the rear while I steered. By taking turns pushing and steering, we covered the mile to the first major intersection with ease.

We paused for a bit. J.C. opened the fruit jar, took a swig of water, and handed it to me. I quenched my thirst and tucked the jar back in the wagon. We turned south on May Avenue where a few homes lined the street. I sometimes painfully recalled the beautiful brick house in Nichols Hills. I would still live there if I hadn't stomped on the lady's toe and drained the swimming pool. But this day, headed for paradise, I didn't have any neighborhood in mind. We held tight to the present where the perfect family in the perfect house was waiting just for us. We sped along, block after block, past endless rows of small homes, pausing occasionally for water. Near noon we stopped for a lunch of apples and peanuts.

Over each hill the sun arched lower. The clear morning had become a fog-bound afternoon, slowing the traffic. We wove through street signs as darkness swallowed the people, cars, and buildings. We stood in the cold whispering night, hoping that some family might stop and take us in.

But no one offered us a home. Instead, we rubbed our bottoms and gazed at the indifferent world through our Lindy goggles. My stomach growled. We spied a silver-clad diner and huddled under the streetlight to pool our money. "With this nest egg, let's have a hot supper." J.C. spoke through chattering teeth.

"You go in. You're older," I said, rubbing my hands together.

"Naw, you place the order. You're the big talker."

But I wouldn't risk it. So J.C. walked up to the entry, unbuckled his aviator helmet and looked back as if he needed support. I waved him inside.

Within a few minutes he strode out with four doughnuts and two cups of hot cocoa. We pulled our wagon to the side of the building to enjoy our first supper as free spirits. After our stomachs warmed, we crept to the rear of the diner in search of a night's shelter. I spotted a wooden crate. "Let's hole up here."

We squeezed into the box and snuggled under our colorful quilt. But the January air cut us to the bone. We longed for the warmth of a dozen quilts as the night air dampened our spirits.

After tugging the cover back and forth between us, we eventually drifted off.

With the advancing light of day, we scrambled out of our cave and ate handfuls of Post Toasties. J.C. packed our goods in the Radio Flyer and we headed south. We paused on the corner of each block to breathe on our fingers and scout the neighborhood. Some nosy grown-ups could be watching. Goodness knows they might phone the orphanage before we could find a family to take us in.

But beyond a crossroad came a white cloud of smoke spiraling upward from a tall chimney, and then the perfect house appeared. The red brick beauty with white shutters had a circular driveway leading to a black door with a brass door knocker, larger than any I had seen in Nichols Hills. The chimney puffed smoke against the blue sky and lights sparkled from the windows. No doubt the family was worth millions.

"Great guns. They have a Buick." J.C. fancied big cars.

I sat down to catch my breath. "Yep, here's our new home." I envisioned an oil-rich wildcatter and his wife longing to rescue a couple of orphan boys. "We'll have the things we've been dreaming about: fried chicken, pairs of knee-top leather boots, bags of Hershey bars, a couple of racing bikes, and warm feather beds."

"Hell, we'll have it all." J.C. folded our quilt while staring at the house.

"Damn right. We'll have a mother and father who will welcome a couple of smart boys." I hopped out of the wagon, strode onto the front porch, and banged the door knocker. Within a minute, a young lady wearing a gray dress and low-heeled shoes appeared.

"Good morning, Ma'am. My friend here is J.C. Watson and my name's Will Rogers. Would you like to take in a couple of orphans?"

"Well, now . . . I have two daughters. But we could use a couple of helpers to rake the yard. I'll pay."

I yanked the wagon around and headed out to the street. I looked back over my shoulder. "Ma'am, we're looking for a home. Don't need a job." I fingered the smooth dollar in my pocket, feeling fortunate. The woman closed the door.

Suddenly, J.C. grabbed the tail of my coat and yanked me onto the ground. "Will, you're an idiot." He stood above me waving his hands in the air. "Finding a home is another one of your crazy ideas."

I struggled up and brushed my clothes. "Now, J.C., don't get riled up." I spoke with a soothing voice, bucking him up with a golden promise of finding a family with a black Cadillac. We headed toward the next hill.

Our stomachs growled for attention as we approached a small grocery store. J.C. trooped in and bought a quart of milk, sliced meat, cheese, and a loaf of bread. We sat on the curb and devoured our lunch. As we finished our last sandwich, a police car pulled into the parking lot. A blue-uniformed officer slid out of the passenger seat while the driver idled the motor.

"Having a good time, boys?" The officer stood fingering his night stick.

"Yes sir, officer." We both nodded our heads.

"Say, big one, what's your name?"

"My name's J.C. Watson, but I don't live around here."

The officer rubbed his chin. His partner killed the motor and sauntered over. They whispered to one another, then they stuck our wagon in the trunk of the Ford and whisked us off to a police station. The officers ushered us into a large room filled with gray metal desks. A giant city map hung on one wall. The men stood in groups talking and drinking coffee. Several telephones jangled.

We sat on an oak bench for half an hour before the police captain walked in carrying a sack of doughnuts. He lumbered over to where we sat. "Here, boys, have one." He was a heavy-chested man who looked like a boxer but sounded like a kind father.

"Gee, thanks." We eagerly reached for the doughnuts.

Standing erect with both thumbs tucked under his belt, he looked up at the giant city map. "Young men, we need to know where your parents live."

J.C. nudged me in the ribs. We both shook our heads.

The captain looked at J.C., then turned to me. In a gentle voice, he asked, "What's your name, son, and how old are you?"

"My name's Will Rogers. I'm ten." I straightened my back to look as tall as possible.

The captain pulled his thumbs from his belt, looked up at his two patrolmen, and snorted, "Will Rogers, you say. Yeah, my official name's Babe Ruth. Ask the boys." They laughed and slapped each other on the back.

"What you reckon we oughta do?" J.C. whispered with concern. "Think Bessie's missed us?"

"Naw. Leroy's covering."

The captain shrugged his shoulders. "We haven't received a call from any parent. So, boys, until your memories return, we're locking you up for the night."

"Tell you what." J.C. looked up at the officer. "If we talk, will you drop us off at our driveway?"

The captain rubbed his chin and mumbled for a moment but finally agreed. "My men will wait till you've entered your front door."

"The Baptist Orphanage on 63rd. Don't phone or we'll get a licking."

The captain pushed his cap back on his head. "Sergeant, return these young men with as little ruckus as you can."

They stuffed us into the patrol car and roared north on Classen Boulevard. We traveled several blocks when the sergeant stopped at a corner store. "Wait here. I've got business."

He walked inside. He soon returned, whistling under his breath, and tossed a paper sack to his partner as he climbed in. They both smiled as they twisted in their seat and gave J.C. a brass jews-harp and handed me a shiny harmonica.

"Gee whiz! Thanks! We love music." J.C. bragged about playing in the rhythm band.

We drove off. J.C. twanged "Oh Susanna," and I puffed a tune on my instrument. As the raw sounds drifted in the air, the officer parked outside our gate. They popped open the trunk and banged our wagon onto the driveway. With a final salute, we struck out for the Old North Building.

With the gloom of prisoners heading for the gallows, we tugged the Radio Flyer down the long driveway. Bessie stood on the porch, rigid as a tombstone. We stood speechless in the face of her wrath.

She uncrossed her arms. "Well, gentlemen, where in the Sam Hill have you been?" She brushed ringlets of grey hair from her forehead.

I twisted back and forth, placing weight on one foot, then the other. "Well, let's see."

"Quit fidgeting, Will. Speak up."

"Gotta think a minute." Then seeing J.C. grinning, Bessie spoke.

"Only two boys would run away in the depths of winter. Those would be you, Mr. Watson, and your guilty pal, Mr. Rogers."

"It was Will's idea." J.C. pointed his thumb toward me.

"Yeah, but we had a lot of fun." I gave Bessie a big smile.

"Okay, J.C., you'll get off light. Take your wagon to the shop. Mr. Drummond will lock it up."

J.C., hunched over like a kid who had lost his lucky agate in a game of keeps, towed his Radio Flyer down the walk.

Bessie motioned me upstairs. "Now, Mr. Smarty, you have cooked your goose." I glanced at the steps, wishing I had my rabbit's foot. Maybe she will give me a long-winded lecture and put me to bed without supper. We arrived upstairs with Bessie panting for breath. I diverted my mind from the disappointment in her face by counting the openings in my harmonica.

"Will, any foolishness that drifts into that noggin of yours, you do it. The deacon reported that you lifted money from the collection plate. My Lord, stealing from the church is against God's law."

"I gave one dollar back."

"There's no end to your misdeeds. The principal says you left three stolen bikes at school."

"Only borrowed them."

"Doesn't matter. Also, Olga says you have been swiping clean clothes from the laundry room. And what's this smoking and sneaking around the lake?"

"That's all past. I've been saved."

"Now you talked J.C. into running off. If you're not careful, you'll wind up in the reform school."

She stepped forward, unclipped her paddle, and grimaced. "Touch your knees." Then she laid several blows on my sore rump. Her paddle looked fearsome, but her punishment didn't call for tears. She administered her feeble spankings because she needed to keep us in line, not because she wanted to.

I stood up, my bottom warm. Bessie snapped the paddle back onto her belt and walked down the hall. After she entered her room, Olga walked up the steps, wearing the face of a medieval hangman.

She clamped her fingers on my left ear. "I'll teach you."

"Bessie just gave me a licking." She didn't pay attention. With a firm grip, she pulled me sideways up the dimly lit stairs to the attic. She opened the door and shoved me into the dreaded Dark Room. The blackness, deeper than a moonless night, cut off my sight as I slumped on the floor.

"Now, think about the trouble you've caused." Olga banged the door shut.

I heard Olga's shuffling feet and a rattling key flipped the lock. Then, not a sound. I sat church still. The silence felt as heavy as only the quiet moment after a slammed door can be.

I had experienced silence before. The breathless quiets which came with the wet mattress ritual, the abrupt silence following the dinner prayer bell, and the shuffling silence that fell over the dorm when Olga made an unexpected visit. But the louder silence of fear ruled the Dark Room.

Within a few minutes, a rattling anxiety echoed off the plastered walls. First a whiff, next a puff, followed by a gust, and finally a tumultuous maelstrom of despair blew into my soul. An army of rats

126

squealed and scrambled inside the walls. They clawed the plaster and chewed on the wood lathing. I jumped up and pounded the door. "The rats! The goddamned rats! Let me outta here!" No one answered my plea.

My heart hammered. Sweat poured from my forehead. The minutes flowed into hours and the hours spilled into an endless night. Shaking with fright, I felt a warm stream slithering down my pants. I clamped my knees together, but the trickle turned into a puddle. The room reeked of urine.

I screamed again, but to no avail. I collapsed against the wall. Feet cold. Mind awry. I finally drifted into a fitful sleep draped in dried tears and soggy pants.

The morning bell rang as the heat from the second floor's steam radiators slithered through the crevices. I opened my eyes and up popped an image of Olga Tuttle. How could her hate-filled spirit be chased away? I pulled the harmonica from my pocket, rubbed it clean with my sleeve and played "Polly Wolly Doodle," which soothed my mind. I continued this melody until I heard a tap, tap, tap on the door. I paused.

The youngster who fired the boiler spoke. "Will, they forgot. I've come." The door yawned open, and I stepped out into the morning light.

After I shed my smelly clothes and bathed, I slipped on my white shirt and Sunday pants. Olga had tried to break my spirit, but it hadn't worked. The Dark Room had toughened me up.

I longed for the leafy elms of spring when Leroy and I could sneak down to the lake and go fishing with Uncle Walter. Or I could talk J.C. into running away again.

~11~

In the spring of 1936, I still lived on "orphan time," shadowed by Pop Hall, Olga Tuttle, and the damnable bells, and always fearful that my guardian might return and snatch me away. I worked alongside Leroy to finish the first term of the fourth grade at the University Heights Grade School.

Myrtle Critchfield, our favorite teacher, often wore a purple dress with a white silk collar. She was plump, short legged, and small footed like a bird, and her hair was streaked with gray. She drilled us nine students in history and geography, her favorite subjects.

"Just think, boys and girls," she reminded us, "upon Red Hill, the Creek and Kickapoo Indians hunted buffalo not too many years ago. You should be alert for arrowheads or unusual burrows in the soil where the wild herds might have wallowed." This pointer, along with markings on the Oklahoma wall map, inspired us to clip magazine articles and paste them into a class scrapbook illustrating the Indian Territory.

One day in May, after class let out, I walked down Grand Avenue and approached the Rose Hill Cemetery. The mausoleum's stained-glass windows, like watchful eyes, seemed to recognize that I had been that way many times before. I traipsed along the cemetery's winding road and into the meadow below the orphanage. This was my crying field, a secret haven where I sowed my fantasies of being a special child for one special family, not one child among the many in an institution.

I sat down on a blanket of yellow buttercups and looked out over Belle Isle Lake and the forest of trees to six miles away where the sky-scrapers of Oklahoma City glimmered in the fierce sun. I wondered if Momma still rode the trolley in to visit Uncle Paul and have check-ups by our family doctor.

I stretched out and entered my dream world. Including Momma's, this was my eighth home. Though the orphanage provided food, clothing, and a bed, I didn't see a bright future. I cherished tenderness from Bessie, but with so many boys and girls, she could only bestow occasional scraps of attention. I felt slighted when she strolled down the hall without giving me a hug. "Love" was a word never spoken.

I wanted a new beginning. I sought a home uncrowded with chil-dren. I resented the discipline and the frightening hours spent in the Dark Room. And I wanted to live in a far distant town where Mr. Wheeler could never find me.

Several of my friends said they were happy in the orphanage. They accepted the bells, the marching in line, the pinched ears, the endless bed checks, and the lack of freedom. They had learned how to cope with Pop Hall and Olga. One was Johnny Henshall, a handsome twelve-year-old, bright and with an eager zest for life.

"If I have two clean sheets I'm happy," Johnny said. "We are like one happy orphaned family living on a calm lake." Like the level-headed boy he was, he never felt a ripple. "When I leave here, I'll be homesick for the home."

Despite the hours I spent playing on Belle Isle Lake, I didn't see a smooth body of water; I felt a turbulence underneath the surface. I couldn't understand my conflict, but I believed grown-ups were the problem. My yearning to escape and find a loving home never diminished. I had yet to gain the maturity to appreciate the gift of board and room.

"Will, you're one of the rebels," Bessie said.

My rebellious nature must not have been too uncommon because Reverend Maxey, some years later, wrote that the unsettled conditions in the home were the result of the Depression. Not only were there 150 children, but he found an institution in crisis. One hundred and forty-three windowpanes were broken in the buildings. "The children had gravy, sand plums, red beans, and lard. Mrs. Riney couldn't care for so many boys and girls. Just to contain them was almost impossible."

He reported that the orphanage's delivery truck driver was told to pick up a youngster who had been told to stand near a rural mailbox on a certain day. The truck came by, and a total stranger picked up a total stranger and brought him to the home. Reverend Maxey asked if it was any wonder the "orphanage faced so much trauma, homesickness, belligerence and hostility?"[3]

Nevertheless, as to when and how I would realize my desire to find a home, I could only hope to have another interview. And my hopes, like my dreams, remained alive.

Then, miracle of miracles, on May 22nd, 1936, Bessie came down the hall wearing a bright smile. "Bless my soul, you'll have visitors Saturday morning. One is Mrs. Minter."

"Oh! Helen Minter?" I couldn't believe my ears.

"It seems to be quite a to-do! A family is coming to interview a couple of boys. Your Mrs. Minter is on the committee."

The excitement of Helen coming gave me a thrill, but to add to the joy, a new family might enter my life. The evening dragged by. At last I climbed into bed, but sleep escaped me. Thoughts flitted through my mind. This time I didn't mind competing with another kid. I envisioned how I would please a new family.

In the morning, I enjoyed a bowl of oatmeal and a glass of milk. I felt confident. I arranged my clothes and treasures for a quick pack in case I passed the interview. I bathed and dressed in my Sunday pants and white long-sleeved shirt.

I stood like a shining cherub who knew the importance of looking his best, but there was a final touch to my courting finery. I fished out my black bow tie and clipped it into place. The first boy returned from the interview as I sat down at the top of the stairs so Bessie couldn't miss me.

At 11:00 a.m., Mickey Mouse-watch time, Bessie appeared. "Will, you're looking mighty smart. Love your tie."

"I don't wanna fail again. Also, I've tucked a rabbit's foot in my pocket."

We walked downstairs. Bessie smoothed my hair before she tapped on the door. I heard voices. I watched her chubby hand turn the knob and, as I entered, a sudden hush filled the air. Soft light filtered through the lace curtains, and in the center of the room a long oak table rested on a red oriental carpet. Helen Minter, my dearest love, walked over and snuggled me into her white summer dress. Not letting go of her, I found the courage to look around the table at the people. Shocked with disbelief, my hands began to sweat.

There sat my guardian, William Wheeler. I gazed at him, my heart hammering with fear. Bessie had said he was out of my life. But here he was again. He wore a tweed, vested suit with a red tie, and a forced smile on his dull face. My guardian, as on previous meetings, had a way of pretending to be interested without ever really seeing me. His hairy fingers grasped his ever-present briefcase, my life locked under its flap.

To one side of the table stood my good friend, Uncle Paul, holding a file of papers. I dashed over and hugged him. He shook my hand, and pulled out a chair for me to sit on.

Next I met Mr. Arlie Holman, a handsome, middle-aged man who sat at the table with an air of assurance. His gray hair and bright smile, much like a young man's, lit up the room. Greeting me with an accepting expression, he placed his hat to the side of his elbow. His face looked at ease, as though he knew what he wanted.

Everyone stood when his wife, Emma Holman, walked in late with a bouncy air, like the brightness of spring. She looked as round and soft as a powder puff, wearing a flowing blue dress with a white lace collar. Sitting down, she placed her glasses and small pocketbook on the table. Her sweet face and blue eyes held my interest.

Immediately to Mrs. Holman's left sat Mrs. Pearl Blackstock, a thin lady with a calm face, quiet eyes, and brown hair coiled back in a bun; I saw her whisper to Mrs. Holman. She looked to the head of the table as the meeting came to life.

Helen addressed the gathering in a cheerful voice. "I want you to meet a spirited youngster. For a year I cared for him." She went on to say that since she and her husband no longer had the means, she wanted me to be placed with a worthy couple.

"Someday, if given patience and love, I believe this boy will make some family proud." She said that the juvenile court had placed me in the Baptist Orphanage under the name of Will Rogers.

Uncle Paul, leafing through a file of papers, raised his hand. "Wait. We must first address the fact that Mr. Wheeler has filed a petition asking the judge to reinstate his name of Roger Bechan and return the boy to his care." Uncle Paul spoke, carefully choosing his words.

"Now wait a minute." Mr. Holman's face grew red as he pushed back his chair and stood up. "I came here to deal with Reverend Maxey about taking the boy. I agreed to pay the orphanage a commission."

"Let's think this through." Helen looked at Mr. Holman with an understanding expression.

Mr. Holman walked to the head of the table. "With this last bit of news, will the orphanage lose their fee?"

"It looks that way." Something regretful and gruff came into her voice. "Yes, Mr. Wheeler has forced the home to release the boy back to him. The Baptists no longer have any authority over the youngster."

"Must I deal with Mr. Wheeler?" Mr. Holman looked puzzled.

"Yes, and I'm afraid he will require compensation." Helen pushed a document to Mr. Holman.[4]

RELEASE

By authority of the Oklahoma County Court, the Baptist Orphans' Home of Oklahoma City releases Will Rogers to W. C. Wheeler, Oklahoma City, Oklahoma, this 15th day of May, 1936.

Signed: W.C. Wheeler

Signed: Lola Nicholson

[Notarized. Oklahoma County Court]

Mr. Holman, looking confused, slipped on his glasses and read the paper for a bit. "Is Roger Bechan his legal name?"

"Yes," Helen said. She said my name was Roger Bechan, but I had been called Bill Minter, Billy Hardt, and the Hardt family placed me here under the name of Will Rogers.

"Why was that?" Mr. Holman asked.

"We don't know for sure."

"Strange. Very strange," Mr. Holman sat back down.

"I believe he is numb from so many names. If given the chance, the boy will sort it out." Helen looked at the Holmans, then glanced to me and said, "My boy, the Holman family is looking for a son. They live in Drumright, a couple of hours from here."

I smiled shyly at the Holmans as I fingered Uncle Walter's rabbit's foot in my left hand.

Mr. Holman leaned back and clasped his hands behind his head. Then he leaned over the table and spoke.

"What grade are you in?"

"Soon in the fifth." My gaze met his.

133

Putting on her glasses, Mrs. Holman asked with a sprightly air, "Would you be happy in a small town?"

"I like small towns."

"What are your favorite subjects in school?" She stood up and asked to see the folder of papers.

"Geography, history, and arithmetic. I don't like penmanship."

Uncle Paul got up from the table. "Roger, you look well. Have you been sick lately?"

"I'm fine. But I'm full of castor oil!"

Soft laughter rippled down the table. During the next fifteen minutes, lively questions and answers spread about the room. I enjoyed talking with curious adults. As the interview came to an end, Helen led me into the hall. Mrs. Blackstock followed.

Two boys near my age sat on the hall bench. They had come with the Drumright contingent. Mrs. Blackstock introduced her two sons, "Roger, this is Ben and Bob Blackstock. Now run and play till we're ready." We shook hands and dashed down the steps and onto the playground, where we entered into a game of basketball.

Bob told me that his mother, through her lifetime membership in the First Baptist Church, had directed the Holmans to the Baptist Orphanage. The sun shone bright and warm, a light breeze blew, and a white cloud sat along the northern edge of the hill. After we boys finished playing ball, Helen Minter walked out, kneeled down, and placed her arm around my waist.

"The Holmans would like to take you home with them."

"Great. I don't wanna live with Mr. Wheeler."

"Son, I may have spoiled you. But the orphanage has fed, clothed, and kept you in school. That's more than many children receive. Someday you'll appreciate their care."

"Well uh . . . But, I'd like to have my own mother and father."

"You used some foul language when I visited you last."

"Cuss words are handy around the dorm. But I won't need them anymore." I couldn't mention it, but many of my forbidden words came from the weeks I had spent with Will Minter and his crew of roustabouts in the oil field.

Uncle Paul, with a hurried look, walked over and pulled a watch from his vest pocket.

"It's growing late. We must be on our way." He gave me a hug and tucked a dollar bill into my shirt pocket. "My boy, I want you to keep this home. Understand?"

Helen and Uncle Paul climbed into her old Packard, and as they swung by, Helen blew me a kiss. Uncle Paul waved good-bye. I turned and walked to the dorm, brushing tears away with my sleeve.

I stepped onto the front porch to find my guardian standing between Arlie and Emma Holman, shaking Mr. Holman's hand. Mr. Wheeler looked happier than I had ever seen him. His smile stretched from ear to ear. But it would be several years before I learned why he looked so exuberant.

Mr. Holman called from the porch. "Son, pack your things. We need to rush home before dark."

These were welcome words. I took the stairs two at a time. On the landing I met Daisy Butter. "Guess what?" I said. "I'm off to a new home." She squeezed my hand and I dashed on.

The dorm was quiet except for the distant yells of children leaving the playground. Mr. Holman followed me. We found Bessie packing my clothes. I threw my arms around her neck and hugged her.

Her eyes softened. "Will, I'm happy for you." She finished packing my cardboard box. "When you return to the city, come by and visit your Bessie."

"I will, Bessie, I will."

Mr. Holman lugged my possessions downstairs. There, the Holmans and I, together with Bob and Benny Blackstock and their mother, piled into his four-door Pontiac. It glistened with whitewall tires, and a shiny sculpture of Chief Pontiac stood above its chrome grill. The interior featured a custom walnut steering wheel, a compass, and gray upholstery.

When we drove around the inner circle by the playground, I rolled the window down and waved to my friends who stood on the walk.

I called to Leroy, "Take care of Uncle Walter." Leroy saluted. Tim Curtis, my fellow barnyard explorer, J.C. Watson, my runaway artist, and Johnny Henshall, the most friendly of playmates, gave me their thumbs-up signs.

As if to speed my transition from herded conformity to boyhood freedom, Mr. Holman shifted into high, sending the Pontiac speeding east on Highway 66. Hope swept over me. I looked forward to discovering what my new home life would be.

I left the ghost of Will Rogers in the orphanage, standing on the playground with his friends.

~12~

Drumright, Oklahoma. What kind of town would it be? I wrestled
with this thought as the Pontiac cruised east. Mr. Holman said it was
a historic oil town and talked of Mobil Oil, Texaco, and Flying A:
service stations that dotted the highway. He and Emma had moved
from Ohio so he could work as a foreman at John D. Rockefeller's
Tide Water Refinery.

The Holmans must have thought I'd be uneasy all by myself, so
they had brought the Blackstock boys and their mother along with
them. Benny and Bob groaned about the bumpy road. To me, traveling across central Oklahoma meant seeing Kickapoo and Creek
Indian hunting grounds, mysterious legacies from a nomadic time. I
looked forward to a new beginning, speeding across the tall grass
prairie, separated by only a moment in time from its lumbering buffalo past. A new opportunity lay before me.

The sun cast shadows from the scrub oaks and blackjacks as we
approached a steep grade which Bob called Tiger Hill. I looked out
and saw a small village with white houses notched into clay hills
against a blue sky. Pump rigs, like giant bobbing grasshoppers, sput-

tered and chugged, flowing oil into huge silver tanks. The red flares shimmered and danced over a throbbing land as the air, smelling of sulphur, drifted over the hills and through the valleys.

Drumright, a town of three thousand people, lay south of the Cimarron River, not quite midway between Tulsa and Oklahoma City. Mr. Holman said that a wildcatter by the name of Tom Slick brought in the first gusher in March 1912. The news of black gold spread like burning oil, flooding the area with thousands of drillers, roustabouts, and roughnecks. The hard-living riffraff—gamblers, bootleggers, and loose women—soon arrived and a few remained.

During World War I, they pumped more oil from the Drumright field than any other in the world, reaching over 300,000 barrels a day. And the Jackson Barnett No. 11 was the first well in the world to produce a million barrels of oil. Mr. Holman said the production had slackened, but a boomtown spirit still throbbed in the village, filling the people with an exuberant friendliness.

We coasted down East Broadway, the heart of the commercial district, where the businessmen built their stores on the hill running east from Tiger Hill. The town, with a wide main street, had a half dozen grocery stores, three theaters, and no stoplights to slow the traffic.

Hundreds of people crowded the wide sidewalks on this Saturday. A group of oil drillers and roustabouts hung around Nat's hot tamale cart, while farmers in overalls and men in seersucker suits lingered in front of the Citizen's Bank. Many stood in silence, enjoying an afternoon of people watching.

From East Broadway, we turned onto North Ohio, and the brick road turned to dirt covered with crude oil to dampen the dust. After driving a few blocks, we parked in front of my new home. We boys bounded out of the car. After talk of getting together later to play, we said our good-byes and thank yous, and Bob and Benny Blackstock walked with their mother to their home next door.

Under the shade of a giant pecan tree, the Holmans lived in a modest white house, an oil-boom clapboard structure thrown up in the twenties, with a porch swing and planter boxes of pink petunias brightening the entry steps. As we entered, I faced the third member of the household, who sat in a rocker in the living room.

"Please meet my mother, Hattie Shanklin," Mrs. Holman said.

At first glance, the gnarled figure looked like a stuffed ornament, but her fluttery hands brushed her bun of hair as she acknowledged my presence. "You're an orphan, eh? Your folks dead?" Her squeaky voice rose to a whine, and I realized she wasn't happy to see a strange boy enter the house.

I opened my mouth to answer, but Mrs. Holman interrupted, placing her hand on the elderly lady's shoulder. "Mother, we'll talk later."

A comfortable divan and two lounge chairs filled the ivy wallpapered living room. A round coffee table featured a few *Saturday Evening Post* magazines. One picture window, the latest fashion, looked out on the sidewalk. An Emerson console radio sat in one corner. I looked forward to the evening's entertainment of "Jack Armstrong, The All American Boy"; Major Bowes and his amateur hour; and "Amos 'n' Andy" speaking in their slow dialect. The room, although not as large, reminded me of Helen and Will Minter's home.

We enjoyed a warm supper. Near bedtime Mr. Holman asked, "About your name. Do you prefer Roger or Will?"

"I've been thinking about names. The Hardt brothers called me Billy. But I'd like Bill. Roger hasn't been a lucky name."

"If that's your wish, we'll call you Bill. And please call us Mother and Dad."

Bill Holman seemed like an easy name for the kids to remember, and it was great that "Dad" let me make my own choice.

I was excited that night to have my own bedroom. I no longer shared a dorm crowded with noisy kids. The room, freshly wallpapered with floral illustrations, featured a single walnut bed and a brass table lamp on an oak desk next to the north window. A cork bulletin board hung to the right, and good smells came from the cedar closet. That night I slept secure.

The following morning Mother asked me to help with the chores. As a member of the family, I dried the supper dishes, took out the trash, ran the sweeper, and helped with the Monday washing. Mother Holman's legs, often painfully swollen, made it difficult for her to garden, so I weeded flower beds and mowed the lawn.

I adjusted to the chores, but I failed to make friends with Grandma. With a pinched face, beady eyes, and skin the color of a scalded chicken, she wielded power from her rocking chair. She smelled of soured milk and talcum powder. She didn't enjoy the radio soaps and her only interest was grumbling about how the neighbors never came to see her. Her only friend was a bony cat named Baby. And Baby was blind.

Within the second week, after I had sneaked into her room and lifted a dollar from her purse, she leaned forward with her clawlike hands pulling on the arms of her rocker, and asked, "Are all orphans little thieves?"

I thought that if I pestered the old lady, she would return to her home in Indiana. I apologized and handed over the dollar, but I saved my tears. Within a week, Grandma complained about my table manners. "The kid should learn to use a napkin."

Mother's eyes dampened and she tightened her mouth. "For Lord's sake, don't fuss about the boy."

Grandma rattled on. "It's a shame you couldn't have had a child of your own."

Mother's face showed the hurt this comment gave her, but she said nothing. Mrs. Holman possessed too gentle a nature to stand up to her own mother. Whenever this type of showdown erupted, Grandma always won. All this despite their history together when Grandma was the young mother. She abandoned Emma and her brother to a bleak childhood while she escaped to married security with a new husband.

Whenever possible, I avoided the house that Granny ruled and sought out Bob Blackstock and his friend Ray Sebring, a fun-loving football tackle. Bob, a strong, raw-boned boy with glistening black hair, thrived on rough games and bold adventures. One morning, after milking two cows and cleaning his father's barn, Bob took me over to Ray's house, and we three walked back to play with the Cherry Street Gang.

Bob had coined this name for the rowdy kids who gathered on the hill to play with the Sellers twins, James and Hugh. They had an eleven-year-old brother named Jack, and a younger brother, Bill, who was eight. Their father, Coin Sellers, was president of the Citizen's Bank. They lived in a spacious two-story home, and their horse stables looked grander than most of the neighboring houses.

Jack, a lanky kid, walked over and shook my hand. "So you're the new kid from down the hill?"

"Yeah, I'm with the Holmans."

"The Blackstock boys are a lotta fun. But their old man is a grouchy bastard." On this day, Jack stood in the horse lot east of the house, examining a fifteen-gallon barrel. He turned it upside down. A few drops of oil dribbled out.

"What the hell you doin'?" Bob asked.

"I'd like a water can for our new filly. Gotta get rid of the damn oil."

Bob leaned over and peeked in the spout. "Let's burn it out."

"Good idea." Jack pulled out a book of matches.

Bob stood the barrel upside down with the spout sticking to one side. A few more drops of oil trickled out. He struck a match on his shoe. It brightened as he kneeled down and poked it into the spout. Ray Sebring ducked behind a feed trough.

At first the match appeared to have failed, but suddenly the barrel zoomed aloft, hung in the air for a moment and landed on the high voltage lines with a sizzling swooooosh and a BANG like a cannon fired at an Armistice Day celebration. The sky lit up with red sparks rippling down the power lines. The boys rolled with laughter, slapping each other on the back. Bob ran over and picked up the barrel, now rounded like a beer keg. Then we heard the fire truck's siren screaming toward Cherry Street. Bob, Ray, and I dashed downhill with stunned ears.

The Holmans had never raised a child, and they allowed me the run of the neighborhood with little discipline. This proved to be a fertile field for my impulsive nature. One scrape followed another.

The first clash came when Bob and I were scouting Ohio Street and came upon a weathered building, a former grocery. A round Coke sign hung on the front porch. Bob picked up a rock for target practice. He tossed it with fury, only to hear a dull thud as it hit the wall.

"I'll show you!" I picked up a rock and hurled it like a baseball. Instead of hearing the clang of metal, the sound of shattering glass echoed down the street.

After supper, Dad received a call from the lady who lived in the old building. She complained about my breaking her window. Dad shuffled his feet as his hand massaged the telephone receiver. Finally, he agreed to pay for the repair. He held his temper, but his nervous hands revealed his disappointment.

"Damn it, Bill. You know better than to throw rocks."

"I didn't aim at the window."

"No more of your antics. Turn off the radio and get in bed."

"You mustn't rile the neighbors," Mother said.

Dad asked me to play closer to the house and ease Mother's mind. But she seldom appeared content, always worrying over Dad's evening hours. When he arrived late and tired, he usually ate a cold supper and fell asleep listening to the radio. Mother said that Arlie had a weakness for a cold beer and playing poker with his friends out at the Sportsman's Bar. "Sometimes I think Drumright is too small a town for him. He seemed happier when we lived in Akron."

Dad did his best to be a good father, and I loved my new home. One afternoon he drove in from the refinery, quiet and tired, smelling of crude oil and Camels, and greeted me with a boyish smile. "Bill, here's a prize for your good behavior this week." He handed me a pair of Silver Flyer roller skates with steel buckles fastened to leather straps. I leaped on the running board and hugged him.

The next morning, swinging my skates over my shoulder, I found the smoothest sidewalk in town. It was in front of the Blackstock house. But someone had scattered cow dung on the concrete. I dashed home, grabbed Mother's broom, and swept the walk clean. Eager to polish my skills, I buckled on my skates and soared down the hill.

Pleased with my skating finesse, I paused to tighten my shoelaces when a stoop-shouldered man wearing blue overalls blocked my path. With his gnarled hands and humped back he looked like an overgrown pygmy. It was old man Blackstock. His jaw twitched as he yelled in a trumpeting voice, "Get to hell off my walk. Or I'll kick your ass!" He spoke in quick bursts and shouted oaths of damnation.

"How's that?"

"Mind your elders, kid."

"You're not my boss." I kicked off the skates and held them by the straps. "Anyway, it's a public walk."

His mouth sprang open like a trapdoor. "I have a mind to strip the hide off you." With clenched fists, he stepped forward.

I spun around and banged him with the skates. He grabbed his left leg. "My God. You've cut me up. I'm telling Arlie."

I lit out for home and hung my skates in the closet. Then I walked up to the Corner Drug Store and worried over a Coke.

That breathless July evening the katydids and crickets talked across the hills as the lightning bugs sparkled through the screen door. While Grandma rocked and complained about the heat, Mother sat knitting a doilie under the glow of her stained-glass lamp. Dad sat in his overstuffed chair. He snuffed out his cigarette and spun the dial on the radio. After it crackled through a dozen stations, he finally settled on "Amos 'n' Andy," and raised the volume. I sat on the floor, lost in a *Flash Gordon* comic book. Just as the rocket blasted off for the moon, a sharp rap shook the screen door.

"Arlie, we've gotta talk!" I looked out to see old man Blackstock standing on the porch, holding his felt hat in his hand. My stomach felt queasy.

"What is it, my friend?" Dad flipped off the radio, picked up his Camels and a book of matches, and walked out onto the porch in his work clothes. I heard Dad light up. He had a habit of pulling the match head through the closed cover, making it flare with a snap. I walked to the front door.

Mr. Blackstock took in a deep breath and launched into a diatribe about the neighborhood kids who were out to tear up his sidewalk. "Your boy's outta hand. " He raised his pants leg. "Look. He bloodied my leg."

"Aren't sidewalks public?" Dad looked him in the eye, refusing to acknowledge his injury.

"City doesn't own a damned foot of it. I swapped my best heifer to old man Johnson. He poured me a new walk." Mr. Blackstock put his hat back on. "Arlie, you're a good man, but that damn kid is a wild hare."

"I'm doing my best with the boy." Dad's soft tone surprised me as the red arc of his Camel sparkled in the night.

Mr. Blackstock touched the brim of his hat, mumbled about kids being monsters, then turned and limped off the porch.

Dad stepped back into the house, and snubbed out his Camel. Suddenly he slammed his fist into the palm of his hand. "Goddamnit, you should know better than to attack Mr. Blackstock. He's our landlord."

"He threatened me."

"Movies are out for the week, and I'm cutting your allowance for the month."

News in Drumright traveled faster than one of Mr. Sellers' mares. Grandma relished the neighborhood gossip. "It's the truth; Pearl Blackstock says that Bill sent her husband to the doctor. Wants Arlie to pay for the call."

"Settle yourself," Mother said. "Mrs. Blackstock says her husband deserved what he got. Anyway, Bill is her helper." Every week I dropped by and cranked Mrs. Blackstock's cream separator and hauled skim milk out to feed the pigs. She served homemade ice cream and warned me to stay clear of her husband.

A week later, I was reading in the living room when I overheard Mother and Dad's hushed voices at the dining table where Dad played solitaire. Dad started to speak. Mother interrupted, "Arlie, Bill will settle down. I've talked to Dr. Reynolds. He says there's no way to tell the effects that trauma has had on the boy. He needs a mother's love."

I heard Dad scoot back his chair. "The boy may need a mother's love, but he's damned hard on a father."

Mother started to cry.

Dad slammed the back door. The starter whirred and he drove away.

After hearing their argument, I thought I'd better watch my step or old man Blackstock would team up with Grandma and run me outta town. I was happy here, and I didn't want to lose my home.

"Look, Mother, I'll do better. I'm now skating over on Cherry Street. I'll do the dishes, mow the yard, and run errands without an allowance."

"Arlie will be pleased." Mother kissed me on the forehead, and I felt reassured. During the next two weeks, I played basketball with Bob down at the Edison school yard. The days passed without incident.

In late August, Jack Sellers and I pooled our savings and bought a bag of leftover firecrackers. But we got into a fight trying to divvy up the cherry bombs. He clobbered me in the jaw, and I lit after him. He dropped the sack and dashed inside his father's barn. I padlocked the double door, grabbed the bag of fireworks, and bolted for home.

Not content, the following day I sneaked back to avenge my hurt, opened the iron gate to the horse lot, and tossed in a cherry bomb. A clap of thunder echoed over the neighborhood. But none of the horses stirred. So with one hand, I lobbed in three ear busters and they went off with a boom! Boom! Boom! A gray cloud hung in the air. I stood there brushing the smoke out of my eyes as the brown-and-white mare and her filly, whinnying and kicking up their heels, circled the lot and dashed out the gate. Their pounding hoofs sounded like a Model A Ford running on flat tires as they galloped down Cherry Street and streaked toward Oilton.

Jack burst out the back door with his arms flailing. "My old man's going to be after your tail." I didn't pay him any heed as I streaked for home.

Two days later, Dad drove into the driveway and jumped out of the car. "In the name of God, Bill! What's got into you?" He said that Mr. Sellers phoned him at the refinery, claiming I had damaged his barn door and run off two of his horses. The Oilton police chief reported the mare was covered with cockleburs, and the young filly had stumbled into a ravine and was covered with blood. "They called the vet. Now there's a bill."

"For what?"

"Damnit, the vet had to stitch the filly up. He's sending the bill to me. Don't you get it?"

"It shouldn't cost much. Anyway, I got even with ratty Jack."

"If you're not up to one hellish act, you're up to another." Dad stood rubbing the back of his neck. "I was hoping to pay off our note at the bank. Now I'm in a quandary."

I had never seen Dad so mad. His hands shook. He unbuckled his belt. "Go to your room."

Mother grabbed Dad's sleeve. "Oh, Arlie, it must have been an accident."

"Emma, the boy'll turn eleven within a week. He needs a father's firm discipline."

I waited, hoping the spanking wouldn't hurt because the neighbors might hear me cry. Dad came in. His words have faded; I only remember the determined look on his face as he let the blows fly till he made his point.

"I'm sorry it has come to this," he said after my tears turned to sniffles. "You know you're here on a trial basis?"

His words landed like a punch in the stomach. I could hardly breathe. What would become of me? Momma had walked out of my life. Mr. Wheeler had tossed me from one home to another, and my mysterious father had failed to appear. I slumped on the bed.

The days at the beginning of September were anxious ones. After supper on September 6, 1936, I was talking to Mother in the living room when Dad walked in with a grim face, saying that several of the neighbors were still upset about my behavior.

"Son, we believe you need tougher discipline. We're returning you to Mr. Wheeler."

"Oh, no!" I grabbed Mother's arm. "I'm scared of the old man."

"Needn't worry. Mr. Wheeler has gone broke. He's sending you to a state home." Dad looked solemn.

"Not Pauls Valley," I said. "The reform school?"

"No, it's in the town of Helena, northwest of here. Mr. Wheeler has sent papers over, and has asked Emma and me to deliver you there." He unfolded a document.

PETITION 4128 to Juvenile Court, Oklahoma County. September 4, 1936. "W.C. Wheeler hereby petitions to have the said child [Roger Bechan] committed to the State Orphanage located in Helena, Oklahoma."

Signed: W.C. Wheeler

"Why not the Baptist Home? I'll have Leroy Harris and my friends."

"The Baptists won't accept Mr. Wheeler's petition. When we took you in, he did them out of their adoption fee."

"Wheeler's an old goat. I hate him!"

147

"I know you're hurt. But you've got me buffaloed. Go pack your things." I shuffled into my room and kicked my desk repeatedly. Although I desperately sought love, I didn't understand the contradictions working within my mind. Why didn't I see that running off Mr. Sellers' horses might cost me my home?

I brushed the tears away with my sleeve and picked up my skates. I spun the wheels, and hung them on the closet door, listening to the ball bearings clicking a farewell march for another lost home. As a traumatized youngster, I had come to the Holmans with hopes for a new beginning, but now, like a recurring nightmare, I was being sent to another orphanage. I had nothing to prize but failure.

Mother came into the room carrying Dad's old suitcase. I stood silent as she walked back and forth between my closet and chest of drawers, collecting and packing my things.

I didn't sleep that night, haunted by the image of Grandma cackling over my being out of the picture. She'd have Emma back and all would be as she wanted it.

But I couldn't put off the morning. It came and I went. We drove north as rebellious thoughts raged through my mind. Damn old Grandma, the bitter hag. I hoped she would trip over her blind cat and break her neck. I wished old man Blackstock's cow would kick him in the head. To hell with Mr. Sellers and his expensive nags. Within the hour, the oil wells, slush pits, and steep hills disappeared and the land rolled with gentle swells.

The Pontiac lumbered toward the unknown.

My mind buzzed like a hornet's nest damning everything. But no one spoke. Dad, with a stern face, smoked one Camel after another as he drove west.

Mother, her hair unruly and her eyes red, stared out the window.

"Don't Let the Deal Go Down," Bob Wills twanged over the radio. Heading into the Cherokee strip, across the vast sweep of land to the west of Enid, through Lahoma, and past Memo we turned north on state road 58, slowed to ten and idled before a crossroad.

A lone hawk soared overhead as I looked across an endless land-scape with distant fence lines, a few scattered trees, all covered by a blue cupped sky with feathery clouds drifting to the east. This endless country didn't speak back—there were no chugging oil wells, no burning flares to brighten the sky, no hills, no lakes, and no roaring rivers. I listened to a voiceless land. We drove ahead and into the sleepy town of Helena. Several blocks from downtown stood the orphanage—a massive, ornate building with a red-brick cupola rising out of a stubbled field.

I slumped in the seat, steeling myself for the inevitable. The Pontiac pulled to the curb, and Dad opened the door. I grasped Mother's hand and tried to speak to her, but she winced and pulled free with a muffled cry.

I picked up my suitcase and trudged up the stone steps behind Dad. We entered the building and walked into an oak paneled office.

Here we met the incoming superintendent, Mrs. I. L. Huff, an erect, attractive woman looking official in her blue suit. She shook Dad's hand, and he reached inside his coat and handed her an envelope. They appeared to have an understanding.

I never felt so alone as I did that muggy September day. It was as if time stopped. No phones rang, no chairs squeaked, no one spoke. The only sound was the quick, frightened heartbeat that tightened my chest.

Then the clock started ticking again. Dad stepped forward and faced me directly. His long fingers searched his vest pocket and he handed me a dollar. "Bill, take care," his voice faded, his words as thin as paper. "I wish you well."

With awkward steps, he turned and walked out the door without looking back.

Hoping that Dad might change his mind, I dashed to the window where he could see me. But it was a done deal. I pressed my tear-stained cheek against the glass and watched the Pontiac curve out the driveway and head south.

Part Three

❧

Orphans' Nine Commandments

WEST OKLAHOMA
HOME FOR WHITE CHILDREN

1936-1937

~13~

I now lived in the West Oklahoma Home for White Children, located six blocks west of Helena, a small farming town of seven hundred. The home's ninety-acre campus included a weathered main building, three red-brick dormitories, a dining hall, a dairy barn, and a grade school.

After the Holmans drove away, I sat in the waiting room until a teenage girl entered and called, "Roger Beacham. Come along."

Wouldn't you know it? She handed me a new name. I was now a Beacham (pronounced like the beach at the ocean).

We walked across the campus to the boys' dormitory. It was my eleventh birthday, September 7, 1936. Upon entering the dorm, the girl introduced me to matron Myrtle McGoy, a short, pear-shaped woman wearing a black dress and white shoes. Opening a lid of snuff, she placed a pinch under her upper lip and sneezed. Then she assigned me a bed and a locker near a far window.

By the time I put away my clothes, a bell called for supper. I joined a line of classmates and marched to the dining hall located behind the main building. With plaster walls and a low ceiling, shrill voices echoed around the room. Suddenly the dinner bell rang and eight sets of hands snatched up all the bread. Imagine a pack of wild dogs fighting over a plate of bones. My slow hands remained empty hands. I paused in dismay, but with a determined mind. During future meals, using sharp elbows, I planned to snatch a full slice of bread.

So the routine began. They served meals as predictable as the clanging bells. Beans and bells. Bells and beans. When the bell clattered for meals, we ate beans—pinto, butter, or even northern; boiled, baked, and Mexican fried. Occasionally they served wieners with molasses. The state featured a savorless menu.

I trudged back to the dorm to find our matron standing near a bucket and holding out a mop. I refused the chore. Mrs. McGoy's face turned red as she shook her finger in my face. "You're lazy. Another misfit."

Her words floated into the cobwebs of my unconsciousness. I was drowning in a pool of hopelessness, as if suspended in the orphanages and all the foster homes several worlds apart from Helena. I had been tossed aside before, and it would seem that I could handle another rejection without the heartache. But I was beset by a loneliness much deeper than ever before.

Feeling as far down as a boy could go, I trudged outside to the back of the dorm, leaned against the brick wall and sat down, tucking my hands under my legs, and I cried. As the sun began to set, a shadow ran up the wall. The teenage girl who had met me in the morning kneeled down beside me. "Roger, may we talk?"

"No, not now."

Day after day, my restless mind wouldn't let me function. I couldn't read. It took too much concentration to finish a page. I couldn't play ball. I thought of Mother Holman, and every thought of her created an image of Drumright and how I longed to return and play with Ray Sebring, the Blackstock brothers, and the Cherry Street Gang.

A week went by and I remained in the doldrums, often missing lunch. I couldn't understand the mystery of myself.

By the end of the second week I rallied, remembering Helen Minter's advice to stay busy, to run and play, and to lose myself in a game. So, like the miracle of hitting a curve ball, I crawled from under a blanket of gloom and joined in a game of baseball. On the ball field I met a couple of kids who renewed my hopes for a better tomorrow.

The taller of the two—by several inches—was a blue-eyed kid of thirteen, big-boned, freckle-nosed, and gum-chewing, with a broad smile. He wore a red bandanna around his neck, and his eyes looked large behind round steel-rimmed glasses. Benny Button was his name, a long-armed, sure-handed boy admired as a shortstop.

Ned Biddy, a thin, red-haired boy was the shorter of the two. He boasted of being twelve, though he acted older. He looked like a sad-eyed loner, but his glum appearance was made up for by a hearty laugh. He played third and was our leadoff batter. These kids came off of the dust-bowl farms. They looked lost in oversized khaki pants, frayed at the pockets and cuffs, but gained attention through their quick hands on the ball field.

Benny's long legs stood out on the diamond where his blonde hair flowed like a wild colt's mane. He talked up a storm, picking up a glove and tossing the ball in the air while he complained about his last foster home.

"Yeah, last May a farmer and his wife took me in. They lived in a brick house in the middle of a big ranch."

"Sounds like a good life." I was anxious to hear the rest of his story.

"Naw, the old man bitched when I refused to bail hay on Sundays. In September, after the crops were in, he dumped me back in the orphanage."

Bowlegged Ned scuffed his tennis shoe in the dirt. "Yeah, gotta watch those old geezers. They'll skin you." Benny nodded in agreement. You could sense that he wouldn't take any more wooden nickels. I liked his skepticism. We had a lot in common.

On Saturdays, after we completed our barnyard chores and finished wet mopping the dorm, Benny, Ned, and I sneaked downtown to Hoyt's grocery store. Mr. Hoyt was a thin-framed man of average height, a friendly merchant whom all the boys liked, but old fashioned in his dress. He wore gray pants and a white shirt with black sleeve garters and a green visor to shade his eyes. Shopping with our five-finger discounts kept us busy. We started off swiping carrots, a spud or two, and an onion to flavor our beans. But within a week we lifted Butterfingers, Hershey bars, and small packs of Wrigley's Juicy Fruit gum. Mr. Hoyt's good nature was costing him money.

In the dining hall, we received one item I liked—ginger snaps. The same rule applied to cookies that applied to bread. Slow hands remained empty. But unlike most hungry boys, I didn't eat them. I stuffed them in my pockets.

When I trooped back to the dormitory, my pockets bulged with ginger snaps which I stored in my locker. If any classmate wanted a snack before lights out, I traded cookies for a variety of goods, such as marbles, pocketknives, tops, rings, yo-yos, and fountain pens. I swapped a dozen cookies with Ned for an Eveready flashlight, a wondrous invention. Marvelous. Polished like silver. I could flash signals to my friends at night or tuck it under my blanket and read old comic books, escaping to another world within their pages.

My friends introduced me to Faye Kidd, whom the boys called Maggie. She was a fiery young teenager with a wild thatch of auburn hair, high cheekbones, and almond-shaped green eyes that danced with wonder. Maggie looked lovely with bronze skin that shimmered in the light. "Her father was a full-blooded Cherokee," Ned said.

"I've gotta temper," Maggie said. "So the guys stuck me with the name of Maggie from 'Maggie and Jiggs' funny papers. Ain't that a heck of a note?"

I smiled at her impishness and accepted the gift of friendship from my fellow traveler. We had both been tempered by burning bridges behind us.

Maggie, agile as a cat, sure-handed, feisty, and plucky, loved us boys with a girlish delight. On a gusty afternoon in October, she refused to work and called her supervisor an old bitch. The head matron locked her in the dorm. We saw her make her escape by shinnying down a rope made of bedsheets. Then she dashed down Third Street with her skirt bellowing behind her. These blowups happened quite often. We thought she was funnier than the cartoon stories.

As a break in the endless menu of beans, they served cold cereal and water for breakfast. One morning I talked to the cook, a stoop-shouldered man with thinning black hair. He was dressed in blue jeans and a stained white shirt. "Why not a warm breakfast?" I asked. A cockroach scurried across the counter.

He pointed to a sack of corn meal. "It came in last week," he said. "But full of weevils. Anyway, you'll soon be counting your ribs."

When served cold "hot" dogs, we gobbled the blessed meat but shied away from the fungus-ridden buns. Those we tossed on the floor. This sparked Mabel Bassett, State Commissioner of Charities, to say that "The Helena Home was like an orphan's mad house."[5]

Within a few months, the Oklahoma State Planning Board issued a study on the Helena home.

During the past ten years the orphanage's monthly expenditure on food, for each child, had shrunk by 70%; down from a monthly cost of $11.05 in 1925 to a low of $3.31 in 1935. The state now fed each child on approximately 3 1/2¢ per meal.[6]

During breakfast, Benny talked about old Buzz Dorn. Buzz, Ned claimed, began life in a dust-bowl town, so poor he had never attended school. He had slept in a dresser drawer till he was three. His mother finally dropped him off in Helena when he was eight. Now at thirteen, he was the dorm bully who took delight in initiating new recruits.

157

Within a week, Buzz, a big-chested boy with red hair and freckles, walked toward me on the playground. He paused and spit-shined his shoes with the cuff of his shirt. He was a quiet kid. He rarely opened his mouth except in the dining hall to ask for another bowl of beans.

Grinning like he was greeting an old pal, Buzz swaggered up with two of his friends. "Hey, big shot." One of his buddies snickered. The other kid pulled at one of his floppy ears. He looked like a rabbit.

I laughed.

"What's so funny?"

"Your friend's got a rabbit ear."

"You're asking for it." Buzz drew a line in the dirt with the edge of his shoe. "Cross over and I'll teach you a lesson."

I stepped forward and before I could get a lick in, he busted me in the mouth. Blood spurted from my lips.

The kids let out a roar. "A fight! A fight!"

One of his friends shouted, "Knock the stuffing out of him." I hated the tone of his voice.

"Roger, bust the sucker," this from Benny who held the onlookers back.

While I struggled to catch my breath, Will Minter's words flashed into my mind:

"Don't let a big ox humiliate you." I stepped to one side, whirled back, and kicked him on the shin. He bent over and grabbed his leg. I leaped on his back and bit him on his neck.

When we separated, he split for the dorm. Like a stalking tiger, my world and security were all that mattered. I brushed off my pants and started to nurse my wounds when Benny Buttons cupped his hand to his ear. "Ssssh. . . . Pipe down!" I heard a shuffle of feet and a thump, thump, thump on the ground.

Ned breathed words that everyone feared. "It's the Stalker." We looked at each other and froze. Around the corner with a thump of his cane came Mrs. McGoy's husband. Nicknamed "Shaky," he waddled down the path. His bald head featured a ring of fuzzy hair starting at his ears and running around the back of his head like a horse-shoe. He wore a walruslike mustache, and his bulging eyes peered out from behind thick-lensed glasses.

The previous week, Benny and I had watched him take his pocket-knife and punch a hole in a raw egg, tilt his head back, and suck it dry. Then he gulped down another egg, wiped his lips on his sleeve, and tossed the shells on the ground. The sun picked up the gleam on his gold-tipped cane. Benny claimed he was a political appointee who lived off the state.

Shaky now confronted me. "Tut-tut, young man," he said in a voice as sweet as a red jelly bean and as sour as a black one. "We have rules against fighting. Palms up." I stretched my hands for the blows as far out in front as I could reach. With a series of whacks the punishment came, and I danced a wild screaming ballet. I had met other men just like him. A child hater. A child berater. These men were total failures.

After that, I vowed to stay out of Shaky's path, but I couldn't avoid his wife. One night after lights out, Ned, Benny, and I were jabbering about Maggie and her girl friends. The door banged open and Mrs. McGoy, looking like a bulldog wearing red lipstick, burst into the room.

"Hey, you rowdies! Who's been yapping their big mouths?" Her eyes roamed the dorm for the culprits. Heads shaking with denial popped up like a field of prairie dogs.

"Okay, I'll lay it on all of you." With that warning, I shoved two comic books in the seat of my pajamas. She marched down one aisle and up the other, flipping back the covers and wielding licks with her rubber hose. As she approached my bunk, her heavy breathing kept rhythm with her lashing arms. She laid the hose across my rump.

I heard the thump but I laughed at her waste of energy.

On Saturdays, Benny and I often took time out from play to watch the strange cars delivering new classmates. A somber-faced mother, often holding her child's hand, would walk into the main building.

Within a few minutes, the mother would return alone and the car would head down Third Street. With the ever growing number of abandoned children, now past four hundred, we were tossed together like dandelion spores. Many of us slept next to one another with the indifference of strangers.

Mrs. McGoy, who talked of improving our attitude, brought in Lorene Ford, a Sunday school teacher from the First Christian Church. She was a slim, graceful lady with auburn hair and clear brown eyes. She always dressed simply in gray or black. No frills. Mrs. Ford mothered all the children, and we kids loved her.

"I care about you boys. I really do," she said. "I know that you are acting up because of your pain." She talked to us about the goodness of the world and told us about the jobless Okies who ate slumgullion and lived in cardboard shacks along the Cimarron River.

After class, Mrs. Ford handed copies of the Bible to Ned, Benny, and me. "Young men, I want you to read about Moses. He too was an orphan. And I wish to encourage each one of you to memorize the Ten Commandments which he brought down from the mountains."

She believed that the Lord's word would ease our restless minds. On those drizzly nights when the winds rattled our windows, we snuggled under the covers and used flashlights to read our Bibles long past the lights out bell.

I don't know how Benny felt, but I waited a couple of weeks for the high wisdom to make me content. I needed to reach down, pray longer and deeper, read the Scriptures, and quit lifting sweets from Hoyt's Grocery before the angels would bless me with happiness. Every night, I kneeled beside my bed and prayed that the Holmans would come and take me back to Drumright.

Many evenings, we'd lie awake and relive the past. Tonight we talked of our parents. Many of us orphans knew they were out there living another life. Like Benny's mother and father—they had split up and still lived near Tulsa, but they never visited or wrote.

Benny sighed, complaining about his dim flashlight, and brought up the story of Moses and the stone tablets. "Mrs. Ford says he was raised as an orphan, but I bet his folks never pitched him in a hole like this."

Ned smacked his hand on his forehead. "Yeah, why should I honor my parents? My father ran off to Arizona with another woman and my mother dumped me here."

I clutched my Bible and wondered why my mother left me without any warning.

Benny decided we could only find true happiness by revising the Ten Commandments. So he pulled a pencil out of his pocket and canceled the Fifth Commandment from Exodus 20: "Honour thy father and thy mother. . . ." Ned and I did the same.

We now lived by the Orphans' Nine Commandments.

"No one cares if I'm failing in school," Ned said.

School? After the third week of classes, the teacher tossed me out of the fourth grade because I threw spitballs at the girls. During school hours, they locked me in the book room, a high single-windowed closet with shelves of books on one side, a small table, and a metal chair. The smell of oil and sawdust filled the air. Many days I felt comfortable under a veil of loneliness, but on overcast days, I walked the floor and cried until they released me after the evening school bell.

On the better days, I found solace in the tattered textbooks and the encyclopedia that filled one wall. I prized each volume of the *World Book* for the illustrated articles. I read about cowboys, baseball, football, and flew with the Wright brothers at Kitty Hawk. I marched alongside George Washington and watched Jefferson draft the Declaration of Independence. I continued my love affair with books. In my imagination, I escaped the home and ran free. When school began after the holidays, they allowed me back in class but I flunked the fourth grade.

When my eyes tired, the thought of Drumright kept me going. One hundred fifty miles separated me from the Holmans. The idea of returning to Drumright lifted my spirits; and I reached out to the Holmans and to their friendly neighbor, Pearl Blackstock. I wanted them to yearn for me as I yearned for them.

To work this magic, I decided to tweak their interest. Every other week, I lifted two six-pack cartons of Wrigley's Juicy Fruit gum from Hoyt's Grocery store. Back at the home, I visited the kitchen, ripped off pieces of brown butcher paper, wrapped the gum, enclosed a note in each, and mailed them to Drumright. I wrote, "Mother, I try to stay busy, but I'm lonely. Don't let my skates rust." I told Pearl Blackstock, "Tell Benny and Bob to send news about the Cherry Street Gang."

I watched the mail, hoping to receive letters from Drumright. Mother's thank you came, followed by a note from Mrs. Blackstock saying her boys were busy with school. These notes stirred my appetite to receive further news. Other tidbits from Hoyt's Grocery flowed to Pearl Blackstock and the Holmans, and I kept hoping for a reprieve as fall turned to winter.

December arrived with a blinding rainstorm. Wind gusts wailed around the windowpanes and flailed the oaks guarding our door. By mid-month, a shy sun, hidden in sullen clouds, waited to send the smile of Christmas while the building danced with new sounds.

Benny Button borrowed a Victrola and records from Miss Huff's office. With "Jin - gle Bells! Jin - gle Bells! Jin - gle all the way!" floating through the halls, the festive spirit of Santa Claus' reindeer prancing across the snowy fields became real.

We stripped several branches from the campus evergreens. We shaped the greenery into rings of festive arrangements, and tied the wreaths with red bows made from one of Maggie's old dresses.

But even with this feeling for the season—one that no longer found us believing in Santa Claus, but only in the spirit of giving and receiving—we noticed a missing element. I told Benny and Ned, "You guys should have seen the cedar we decorated in the Baptist home."

"Yeah, our dorm deserves a tree." Ned liked the idea.

When we sneaked off on our weekly lifting spree to Hoyt's, I thought we had our answer. There we stumbled into a forest of green stacked near a sign, "Christmas Trees. 50¢ to $3." I mentioned the possibilities to Benny. "Let's borrow one for the dorm."

"The sheriff will toss us in the can." Benny looked down the road.

"Don't worry. His patrol car is never around."

Later in the week, Ned advanced the idea again with Benny. After discussion, we all agreed. Our dorm needed a Christmas tree. We talked over several plans and came up with a doozy.

On Saturday, Ned would enter Hoyt's to shop with five pennies, while Benny and I sorted through the trees. We cautioned Ned to spend only one penny at a time. He should taste a jelly bean, sample an orange slice, then a red licorice twist, being mighty slow in making his decisions to give us time to select the best tree.

"Delay. Delay. That's our game." Benny cheered us on.

The fateful Saturday arrived. A soft snow drifted from out of the night, but by noon an orange sun cleared the streets. As the campus warmed, Benny, Ned, and I whistled our way out the gate and onto Third Street, a dirt road that ran six blocks east up a small rise leading into town. This happy day, coins jingled in our pockets. A dog yapped like a gun. We three friends, wild and out of our skulls, walked down the street weighing the risks of adventure.

"Let's hope Mr. Hoyt doesn't phone Mrs. Huff." Benny feared our superintendent more than he did the sheriff.

"Lord forbid," Ned agreed. "We could get the boot like Maggie's brother got." Ned said Mrs. Huff had shipped Jiggs off to the Pauls Valley Reformatory.

"That's old lady McGoy's doings," Benny said.

Maggie believed that her brother was the sixth kid locked up in the state reformatory without cause. She now wandered around aimlessly, often sitting on the steps gazing into space. Benny added, "Jiggs wasn't a bad kid, just feisty."

We walked on in silence, scuffing our shoes in the loose gravel on our way to Mr. Hoyt's clapboard building on Main Street where Christmas trees filled the porch. We hoped to give one giant fir a loving home.

The store sported a window in the wide entry door. Benny and I stood to one side as Ned peeked through the glass. He turned toward us with a confident grin, then stepped into the store while Benny and I picked through the trees.

"Let's grab one and get the hell outta here," Benny said.

"Keep your shirt on."

Benny yanked one out. "How's this?" Then he answered. "It's a scrub."

He pulled out several more. Still no agreement. Finally, his shaky hands found the perfect tree, a giant ten-footer with limbs tapering to a point. "Here's a beaut! Let's scram."

And scram we did. Benny grabbed the trunk as I locked my arms around the branches. We lugged it off the porch, trotted down Main Street, and turned onto Third Street, heading for home. Possibly the entire village whispered about our escapade behind curtained windows. We had traveled a couple of blocks when I slipped on the gravel and tumbled into the ditch.

Benny lost his grip on the trunk, so the tree landed upright in a large crevice as if it had grown by the side of the road.

Though we stood in view of anyone who might be curious about two boys lugging a tree through the streets, my nervousness spilled out in hilarious laughter. Streaks of dirt dribbled down my sweaty face. Benny picked himself up, grinning as if nothing happened. "Damn it, Roger, get up and quit laughing."

I struggled up and brushed my clothes. Benny glanced around with a happy expression. "Jesus, here comes Ned running wild."

Our pal arrived with news. "I bet Mr. Hoyt saw you guys."

"We're in a hell of a mess," Benny said. Ned pulled out a bag of candy, and we gobbled down a handful of gumdrops. The sugar seemed to ease our anxiety.

"Okay pals, let's go," Ned said. "Roger, you carry the top, we'll saddle the middle on Benny's back, and I'll boost the trunk on my shoulder." We now toted a lighter load as we trooped down the road, but the fear of being caught with a bundle of guilt on our backs made the load all that much heavier. At last we arrived at the dorm and stood the tree in the corner.

Matron McGoy paced back and forth looking over the scene. Finally, she paused and her eyes shifted first to Benny, then to Ned, and finally to me. I shoved my hands into my pockets, trying to think of the best story to tell, my heart thumping like a steam radiator.

"Roger, where'd you steal this tree?" Mrs. McGoy said, wiping a smudge of snuff from the corner of her mouth.

"A gift from an old man," I said.

Benny and Ned nodded in agreement.

"It's a disgrace. You brats are robbing Mr. Hoyt blind."

"No. No. It was a generous gift." The room filled with curious classmates. They giggled and punched each other, guessing as to how we received our noble gift. A couple of boys arranged fluffs of cotton around the tree, and Maggie rushed off to find baubles with which to decorate our prize.

Matron McGoy stomped her foot on the floor. "If you mulish kids don't own up," she pointed to Ned, Benny, and me, "I'm going to cart you off to the reform school in Pauls Valley."

Finally, in exasperation, Mrs. McGoy retreated, banging the door to her room. We smiled at one another.

"Great! We're home free." Benny pulled out his harmonica, sat down on the window sill, and played "Si - lent night, ho - ly night! All is calm, all is bright. . . ." What a beautiful world. Our royal fir attracted sightseers from the girls' dorm, who envied us for having a generous benefactor.

Ned Biddy hung shriveled carrots that looked like orange candles on the branches. Maggie tied on gingerbread cookies and strung dozens of Hershey kisses, honest-to-goodness gifts from Mr. Hoyt. Benny cut a silver star from a Folger's coffee can and fixed it to the top of the tree, where it touched the ceiling.

A colorful collection of gifts rested on the cotton snow. Our tree made the most humble present seem generous. Benny Button received a used, but freshly oiled baseball mitt. Ned bragged about his re-varnished bat, and Maggie pranced around wearing a string of white beads. Mrs. McGoy received a pair of earrings from her husband. She actually smiled and kissed Shaky! We stared in disbelief.

Santa handed me a present: a copy of the *Rover Boys on Treasure Isle*. I appreciated the gift, but I hoped someone would come to visit.

*

Preparing for holidays was fun and exciting but when the festive day arrived, I felt empty. On Christmas day, flaunting the rules, I lay in my bed staring at the ceiling, wishing to hear from or see Mother and Dad Holman. Loneliness gnawed at my soul like hunger.

The parents of several other children visited, but no one came to see me. I did not have a mother or father, a grandmother or grandfather, or an aunt or an uncle, as did several of the other orphans. I couldn't see, touch, or talk to my kin. I never heard from Helen Minter, and I longed for Momma, my earliest love. Surely my own mother thought of me at Christmastime.

I was my own ancestor, next of kin, and progeny. I wondered who would comfort me on this snow-strewn earth. Who could answer the mysterious questions of my birth as I struggled to live within this home of discarded souls?

The holiday break ended. The sky seemed large that Friday night, and a hopeful moon jostled with the evening sun. Quilts of snow covered the prairie, stretched tight like white deerskin on a drum. Finally the sun sank, and I worried that the Holmans weren't moved by the packages of Juicy Fruit gum I had been sending. So I switched to lifting Hershey bars. I boxed three together and mailed them with a note telling the Holmans I longed to see them.

The following week, on a cold evening, the bedtime bell jarred the stillness of the night, and I flipped onto my back. With sleepless eyes, I stared at the moonlight filtering through the frosty windows as forty of my fellow abandonees drifted into the unconsciousness of sleep; their moans and whimpers rippled through the room in a harmony of unease. I listened to their cries for solace. As their dreams deepened, I crawled under the blanket and questioned my journey. This was my third orphanage after my many failed attempts to keep a home.

Mrs. McGoy said I would always be a failure. But regardless of her warning, I took comfort in my prayers for another interview that might lead to a new home. While I lived in the Baptist home, one preacher said the Lord looked after orphans. He was one preacher in whom I felt confident. The One on High would see to it that my aspirations would be realized. Within a month, my dreams for a future revived.

My prayers for help must have been heard. Back in Drumright, Pearl Blackstock had been feeling blue over receiving my reminders from Helena. With her two sons, Ben and Bob, she called on the Holmans. Apparently, Arlie and Emma were also affected by the odd-ball packages and plaintive notes they had received. The Blackstocks sat down with the Holmans to discuss what had gone wrong in my initial trial period. Mr. Holman said I was wild and out of hand. The same description, Mrs. Blackstock insisted, could be applied to any of the boys in the Cherry Street Gang. Ben, Bob, and their mother felt I should be given another chance.

On Friday, January 22, 1937, the orphanage's morning bell rolled us out of bed at 5:30. Frozen earth, unblinking stars, and howling winds plunged temperatures below freezing across the Oklahoma panhandle. Benny Buttons and I pulled on our overalls, spooned down a bowl of Post Toasties, tossed on our Mackintosh coats, and trudged out to the barn as the wind-spun fog swirled around the bare oaks, which stood dark against the snow-covered earth. Nose cold, hands quivering, we fed and hosed fresh water to the chickens.

Warmed a little by the work, we jogged back across the campus to school. All morning, we shivered and doodled airplanes in our notebooks as the classroom felt dank and smelled of wet clothes. The radiators hissed and rattled, but they gave forth little heat as the ancient boiler rumbled and groaned. Finally, with a gurgle and a thump, it shut down. Within an hour, sheets of ice glazed the windows, and our fourth grade teacher dismissed us early.

We jogged back to our dorm where Matron McGoy greeted me with snuff-stained lips. "Roger, the Holman family is returning tomorrow. They wish to interview you again. Get your things together. You might be leaving here."

Her words opened a possibility I thought I'd lost forever.

That night, I hopped into bed hoping Mother and Dad longed for me as much as I longed for them. Would they take me in again? Could they accept my anguished unrest? The next morning, excited and light-headed, I scrubbed my neck and ears. I slipped on a white shirt and a pair of khaki pants, brushed my hair, and clipped on my bow tie. I waited in the reception room, standing at the window where I could catch the first sight of Dad's car when it rolled up the hill. Within a few minutes, I saw a two-eyed shadow crawl out of the morning mist and turn up Murray Street from the south. Then the headlights swept through the window as the Pontiac twisted into the driveway.

I dashed onto the porch, eager with hope. With unsteady feet, Mother stepped out of the car, blotting her cheeks. I don't believe her tears were of the moment, but they were tears for a mistaken time, the months when she didn't wish for us to be apart.

The silence lifted when Dad Holman greeted me with a smile and a firm handshake. "Son, I'm glad to see you're in good health." His smile didn't falter but turned more lively when we walked into the reception room.

I told Mother that I longed to return home. Her arms, which felt so comforting, hugged me close and I felt her tears on my cheek. "Arlie and I missed you." I wiped my face with my sleeve.

"Does this mean you're taking me home?"

"Well, it depends on Mrs. Huff."

It was Saturday, January 23, 1937. Only five months had passed since I had come to Helena, but Mrs. McGoy's unfeeling treatment and the fear that I might never recover the happiness I had found in Drumright weighed on my mind. When you are bound within an institution, time is slow. The past months had seemed like five years.

Within a few minutes, we entered the superintendent's office where we found Mrs. Huff, dressed in a blue suit with a white broach pinned on her ample chest. She was sitting in a leather swivel chair at the head of a long table. She gestured for me to sit next to her. Dad and Mother Holman moved to the other side, talking in low voices.

Mrs. Huff, large in stature and firm in expression, opened the meeting and asked me to stand. "Roger, the Holmans wish to take you again. You must be on your best behavior. Am I making this clear?"

"Yes, ma'am. I understand."

When I sat back down, Mrs. Huff's secretary walked in with a formal paper and handed it to Dad Holman. He leaned back and read the document, pausing for a moment, then another while he rubbed his chin. His facial muscles tightened as he stood up, walked over to the steam-streaked window, and stared out. He lit a Camel, then turned back. I saw an edge of disbelief on his face and a feeling that he wished to be on his way. He looked down on Mrs. Huff, his lips firm as he spoke. "My Lord. An Indenture Contract. The Baptist Orphanage required nothing like this. It's from another time."

A wave of concern consumed me as he walked back and tossed the paper on the table. The air crackled with tension. The morning Santa Fe train wailed in the distance. My stomach tightened, and I grasped the edge of the table, fearful that Dad would leave without me.

Mrs. Huff pushed back her chair and stood up. Her eyes narrowed as she looked at me, then turned to Dad. "Mr. Holman, I can understand your concern, but this contract is in your interest. It doesn't involve William Wheeler, his old guardian, and is less expensive than going to court for a legal adoption."

Mother looked worried. "Oh, Arlie, we shouldn't sign another paper."

"The boy is still unsettled. This agreement will help keep him in line." Mrs. Huff's words of advice faded as her secretary nodded with approval.

At that, Dad's mood seemed to brighten. He picked up the document and took a deep breath as his teeth bit into his lower lip. Then he turned toward Mother. "Now, Emma, perhaps Mrs. Huff is right. The boy can live with us and then be free at eighteen. But if he causes trouble, we can return him with a thirty-day notice."

Mother acquiesced with a mournful sigh. As the three adults signed the formal piece of paper, I felt numb with confusion and wondered how it would be to live under an Indenture Contract.[7]

~14~

We traveled southward in the Pontiac for over two hours. As we approached Tiger Hill, I saw orange-red flares casting dancing shadows across several oil rigs and dozens of silver oil tanks. I loved the bright sights, oily earth scents, and the sounds of the pumping wells. The town of Drumright didn't need a town square, a stately court house, or a civil war cannon. It had character all its own.

At home on Ohio Street, I threw myself across my spacious bed. I felt so fortunate that I could only regard the Holmans' desire to rescue me for the second time as a gift from on high. As I lay there, the familiar aroma from the array of cleaners Mother used to battle dirt rushed into my lungs. The polished hardwood floor revealed the many coats she had applied from her flat tins of Johnson's wax. The spotless windowpanes gleamed from Windex buffings, and the freshly air-dried bedding caressed my skin.

However, the bleak days in Helena had frayed my nervous system, causing me to flunk the fourth grade. Now the Holmans offered me a second chance, and by golly, I would show Mother and Dad a new outlook. I resolved to quit fighting their helping hands like some fluttering, wounded bird and relax. I needed their loving grace.

The Cherry Street gang offered after-school football. But Dad warned me not to display my temper, so I could not let loose with my fists. My restless temperament had already been a trial for him. Now he had a formidable weapon to keep me in line. He said the Indenture Contract had forced a clean-up act on me.

As an outsider who had aroused the ire of several neighbors, could I make new friends and be accepted? Dad gave me a word of good news, though. He said Grandma had returned to Indiana to live with her son. With that comforting thought, I dozed off in the comfort of my own bed.

Within a week of returning from Helena, I enrolled in the second semester of the fourth grade at Edison School. I shared a classroom with my old pal Bob Blackstock, a true friend from the day I met him during his visit to the Baptist Orphanage. Bob said he and Ray Sebring were looking forward to a game of football.

One morning as Bob and I walked to class, he surprised me with a question. "Mom says the Holmans got you under a bill of sale. What's up?"

"Don't spread that tale. The kids will laugh me out of class."

"Okay, okay." Bob rested his hand on my shoulder.

In class, Verma Akin, who prided herself on teaching literature and math, took me in hand. Under her guidance, working with numbers became one of my passions. A column of numbers always totaled to the same figure. This certainty, unlike the uncertain actions of many grown-ups I had known, made good sense to me.

Many bright students and a few toughies attended Edison. A number of kids came to school from the outlying oil leases. Hardworking fathers raised kids whose conduct made for a tough playground. Fistfights with no holds barred often broke out during basketball games.

Near the end of the semester, Nick Barney, a short kid with a burr haircut, bragged his way into our game. He boasted about working

Saturdays in his old man's oil servicing business. Bob said, "He's a tough nut."

One day after class, we were playing a game of basketball when a Negro boy wandered onto the court. He had walked over the Tiger Creek bridge that separated the white and black neighborhoods and asked to join our game. Several boys invited him to play, but after a quiet moment, Nick's upbringing possessed him. "Don't like niggers. Dunbar's across the creek."

I stepped forward, thinking of Uncle Walter. "You're not the boss here."

"Back off, buster," Nick said and shoved me against the base of the basketball goal. With an urge born of fear, I lunged at his chest and coiled my arm around his neck. We crashed to the ground and rolled across the rocky court, busting each other until I felt my eye swelling. Finally, Bob yanked us apart, and Nick straggled off.

That evening at the supper table, Dad asked about my black eye. I told him about my fight with the Barney boy.

"My Lord. You're still wild."

"I stood up for the Negro kid."

"Use your head. You boys could have played over at Bob's house."

"Bob's dad wouldn't let the Negro on his place."

"Anyway, quit fighting. Don't force me to take action again."

I felt a dark force stealing over me—akin to the fear of being set adrift again. I rushed into my room and flopped across the bed. I had assumed that Dad would never threaten to take me back to the Helena orphanage.

For a couple of months, I controlled my temper and avoided any fights. But when the warmth of spring returned, Bob and I skipped class and pedaled out to Tidol Lake. We went skinny-dipping. Late that afternoon, the school principal phoned Mother Holman about my absence.

Before supper, Dad called me into the living room. "Sit down," he pointed to the sofa.

"What for?"

He stood over me, cleared his throat, and folded his arms across his chest. "Why the hell would you and Bob skip class and wander out to the lake?"

"I don't know."

"We need to talk this out." He pulled the Indenture Contract from a folder. He reviewed the provisions, paragraph by paragraph. If I stepped out of line, he could return me to Helena. "Need only a thirty-day notice," he said. "Before you pull some stunt, think about the consequences. You need to develop self-discipline."

"I've had more discipline than I need."

"Don't get smart. It'll keep you outta trouble." In Dad's mind, self-discipline was the answer to my becoming an upright boy.

*

As the months passed, I sought a deeper understanding of Mother and Dad Holman. I started by comparing them to Helen and Will Minter.

Mother Holman and Helen Minter seemed like complete opposites. Unlike Helen Minter, who possessed a fierce spirit which dulled her interest in keeping house, Mother Holman spent her days cooking, wrestling with the sweeper, washing and hanging clothes, and scrubbing the woodwork.

Helen, audacious and wise, remained a commanding figure in my mind. Mother Holman was shy but nurturing in her caring ways. Helen's tall, lean figure looked swell in the latest fashions. Dear Mother, comforting as a powder puff, had a figure no modern fashions could enhance. She looked best in dark, loose-fitting, full-cut dresses. The latest trend of ladies' slacks never hung in her closet.

They both loved me and I loved them, but they showed their affection in contrasting ways. Helen pointed me in the direction she believed would do me the most good: close observation of my fellow

174

man and protecting myself from the crafty schemes of anyone who was out to get me.

Mother, on the other hand, thought good of everyone, fought no evils, never protected herself from those who might wish her harm, and poured her cornucopia of sweetness out for everyone to share. Besides doing housework, she found happiness in helping me realize my boyhood dreams, spending quiet evenings around the radio, and trying to avoid fretting over Dad.

With Grandma no longer shadowing our days, Mother and I developed a more carefree, spirited life. First up, Mother Holman prepared marvelous breakfasts, my favorite meal. She served eggs sunny side up, with a side dish of bacon, sausages, or ham. I savored her homemade biscuits layered with butter and honey. I gained weight and grew stronger.

The month following my return, I suggested to Mother that it would be grand to ride a bike to Edison School like the Blackstock brothers. She agreed to look into the matter if I would do some odd jobs. A couple of days later, she told me to drop by Miller Hardware. "Talk to Jack Schickram; he's one of the partners. Tell him you're shopping for a new bike."

"I've never been in the store."

"Never you mind. Tell him to put it on Dad's bill." I struck off for the town's bountiful hardware store and, like a miracle, I pedaled out the rear delivery ramp on a new Schwinn bike. It was deep red and equipped with a headlight, an electric horn, and a wire basket. The following day, I rode out to the dog pound and chose a brown-and-white street dog. My new pal, Scooter, rode in the basket, and his nose twitched as he sniffed the wind. We flew down Tiger Hill, my shirt flapping. I relished our freedom.

My worldly goods now came through my kitchen conferences with Mother. If I needed a new suit for Sunday school or wanted a baseball glove embossed with Dizzy Dean's signature, a Remington .22 rifle, a model airplane kit with an Ohlsen 30 gas motor, a subscription to *Popular Science*, or anything else, I shared my dreams with Mother, and they often came true.

With Mother's encouragement, and to help cover the costs of my many requests, I scouted the neighborhood for odd jobs. I weeded flower beds, trimmed trees, mowed yards, built and sold whatnot shelves, and delivered the *Tulsa World* newspaper.

*

Dad Holman and Will Minter were alike in their posture, dress, and voices. They both gambled—Will on drilling for oil, and Dad on cards, sports, and roulette. And they loved to tell expansive stories.

Dad Holman looked distinguished in his gray Hickey Freeman suits with matching vest, gleaming white shirts, colorful blue-and-red-striped ties, and stylish Boston felt hats. He performed the banking and furniture shopping and attended my school activities. All of my teachers knew Arlie Holman's phone numbers, both at home and at the refinery.

He lived the life of a well-cared-for bachelor who just happened to have a wife and a son. Yet he wasn't a swaggering figure. He worked long hours as a foreman at the refinery and looked for opportunities to better himself. Other than his habits of gambling and hanging out after work with his friends, he treated Mother with great deference.

However, unlike Will Minter, Dad's social life had a dark side. He loved to gamble and enjoy a shot of Jack Daniels now and then. He gave many evenings over to playing poker, or sitting at a roulette wheel at the Sportsman's Inn, one of several roadhouses on the outskirts of town. His ease with all strata of men was at its peak when he spun one of his tales. The truth didn't matter; it was the telling that held his audience spellbound.

One afternoon he bounced his new Pontiac full throttle into our driveway and waved me over. "Bill, I've had a hell of a scare!"

I leaned inside the car's window. "What's up?"

Record of Will Rogers -

Will Rogers was made a ward of the Oklahoma County court by his
Mother, Mrs. J. H. Becham of El Reno, Oklahoma. Mrs. Becham stated
to the court that Mr. Becham left her before the child was born
and she did not know of his whereabouts.
The Oklahoma County Court turned the custody of the child to Mr.
W. C. Wheeler who operated the Society of the Homeless. He then
placed the child with Mr. and Mrs. W. N. Hardt of Sulphur, Oklahoma.
In January 1935 Mr. and Mrs. Hardt had the child made a ward of
the Murray county court and the court then committed him to the Oklahoma Baptist Orphans', Oklahoma City.
The County court of Oklahoma County shows the childs name as Roger
Becham, but the court of Sulphur in Murray county committed him under
the name of Will Rogers.

> This information given by Miss
> Rice of Judge Blinn's office in
> Oklahoma City, May 4, 1936

Ms. Anna Rice of Judge Blinn's office, Oklahoma County Court,
May 4, 1936, reviews the name of Roger Bechan and Will Rogers.
She reports that Roger Bechan's mother lived in El Reno, Oklahoma.
However, no records have been found to support this observation.
From the files of the Baptist Orphanage, Oklahoma City.

<u>RELEASE</u>

By authority of the Oklahoma County Court, the Baptist Orphans Home of Oklahoma City, releases Will Rogers to W. C. Wheeler, Oklahoma City, Oklahoma, this 15th day of May, 1936.

State of Oklahoma
                    SS
County of Oklahoma

Subscribed and sworn to before me, a Notary Public, this 15th day of May, 1936.

My commission expires March 14, 1940

Baptist Orphans Home releases Will Rogers (Roger Bechan)
to W. C. Wheeler. Oklahoma City. May 15, 1936
(This permitted Mr. Wheeler to collect an adoption fee from Mr.. Holman.)
From the files of the Baptist Orphanage, Oklahoma City.

PETITION

In the matter of___Roger Bechan___

a ___Dependent___ Child} PETITION #4128

In the Name and by the Authority of the State of Oklahoma.

[Date:. September 4, 1936]

Comes now___W. C. Wheeler___ a reputable person and a legal resident of Oklahoma County,

State of Oklahoma, and respectfully represents and states to the court that one___Roger Bechan___

___of Oklahoma County and State of Oklahoma, a child under the

age of sixteen years, is a___Dependent___child in this, to-wit:

That he is of the age of 10 years born on the 7th day of September 1925; that he is dependent for the following reasons that his parents are seperated and divorced; that the mother was given the sole care and custody of the child through a divorce decree granted her upon grounds that the father deserted her before the said child was born. That the father has never seen the child. That the mother Mrs. J. H. Bechan personally appeared in this court and petition and this court to made said child a ward of this court and place him with some person for the purpose of finding a suitable home for adoption. That on the 20th day of May 1932, said Roger Bechan was made a ward of this court and committed into the care and custody of W. C. Wheeler of Oklahoma City, Oklahoma for the purpose of finding a home for adoption.

That W. C. Wheeler hereby petitions this court to have said child committed to the State Orphanage located at Helena Oklahoma for the purpose of finding a home for adoption, for reasons that he has placed said child in a home at Sulphur Oklahoma and they have not completed the adoption, therefore that leaves the boy without a home at this time, and Mr. Wheeler being unable to furnish a home for said child, therefore he would be upon the public for his support, making him homeless at this time, therefore all premises considered he hereby petitions this court to make such order or orders that would deem for the best interest of said child at this time,

Your petitioner prays this court to place him in the West Oklahoma Home for the purpose of finding a home for adoption, and giving them full authority to give the necessary consent when such a home is found.

I, DALE _____
Okla. _____
correct _____
so _____
Juvenile Clerk _____
day of October, 69 _____ 28th

OKLAHOMA COUNTY JUVENILE COURT. Petition No. 4128
William Wheeler writes: "Roger Bechan's parents are divorced
and the father has never seen the child."

WEST OKLAHOMA HOME FOR WHITE CHILDREN

Helena, Oklahoma

Table   II

AVERAGE MONTHLY PER CHILD MAINTENANCE COSTS AT THE WEST OKLAHOMA HOME AT HELENA
1925-1935

Fiscal Year	Food	Cloth-ing	Utili-ties	Sun-dry	Total
All Yrs.	$ 5.19	$2.01	$2.36	$ 6.01	$15.57
1925	11.05	3.92	4.56	11.97	31.50
1926	5.80	2.79	3.05	11.41	23.05
1927	6.50	2.74	2.66	11.84	23.74
1928	5.41	2.00	2.80	7.94	18.15
1929	5.86	2.01	2.00	4.73	14.60
1930	6.19	2.59	2.45	6.12	17.35
1931	6.10	2.31	2.31	5.32	16.04
1932	5.39	2.18	2.23	6.38	16.18
1933	3.65	2.06	2.30	4.97	12.98
1934	3.60	0.81	1.99	3.17	9.57
1935	3.31	1.14	1.93	4.31	10.69

During the past ten years the Helena Orphanage's expenditure on food, for each child, had shrunk by 70%; down from a monthly cost of $11.05 in 1925 to a low of $3.31 in 1935. The state now fed each child on approximately 3 1/2¢ per meal. Oklahoma State Planning Board. *State Homes for Orphans* . . . Chapter III. (Oklahoma City, 1937), p. 50

THE DAILY OKLAHOMAN

November 24, 1937

HOT CRITICISM AIMED AT HEAD OF ORPHANAGE

Mrs. Bassett Returns Mrs. Huff's Fire.

Mrs. Mabel Bassett, state commissioner of charities and corrections, Tuesday fired a blast at Mrs. I. L. Huff, superintendent, for her management of the Western Oklahoma Orphans home at Helena.

Bread Waste Is Claimed

"She broke into print about this," said Mrs. Bassett. "There has been a terrible waste of bread out there. The children have peanut butter and molasses until they are tired. The children would take the wiener out of sandwiches—and throw the bread on the floor.

"There is not a particle of discipline in the dining room. It is like a bedlam. The children have no manners. The children are not to blame. It is the management. I want the children taught manners. They should have good manners.

"I tried to help her work out a system. I spent two days out there and not a thing was carried out. I

Cereal Kept In Storage

"This time when I went out there I found them eating the same bran. "I asked, why not cook cereal? The cook said it was full of weevils. They took out several packages of oats and wheat and cereal and found two packages without weevils. The cook said he thought the cereal had been there all summer. In the storeroom there were about 15 or 16 cases of oatmeal and wheat cereal. It has been there all summer.

"There is no system in the dining room. It is maddening. I believe

(Continued on Page 2. Column 2)

in letting the children talk in low tones."

Mrs. Bassett said it was a joke about Lucy having pies at the institution and she supposed that was what Mrs. Huff referred to about his having delicacies while the children watched.

"He bought three pies, I think, and there was a joke about his making them," she said. "I think he did it because some of the help was of assistance to him.

"I think Lucy went out in the garden and picked a little lettuce and washed it and showed the cook how to cook green tomatoes. There were no rare and luscious delicacies unless the three pies made it"

"Failure to teach children cleanliness and orderliness is not being kind to them," said the commissioner. "When I first went out there I saw many children in school too dirty to be there. I told the teacher they should be sent back to the matron"

Mrs. Bassett said she sent three boys' home last week before school started for the matrons to clean them up, which they did. The children attend school in Helena.

She said Mrs. Huff had

The Helena Orphanage was often headed by political appointees. This accounts for the chaos and intrigue which beset the home.

Indenture Contract

THIS AGREEMENT, made and entered into this **23** day of **January, 1937** _____, 19____, by and between The State of Oklahoma, represented by ~~Mrs. J. L. Huff~~ Superintendent of the West Oklahoma Home, of the first part, and **A. W. Holman** and **Arlie Holman** husband and wife, of _____ **Drumright, creek, County, Oklahoma** _____ County, Oklahoma, of the second part:

WITNESSETH: That whereas, the second parties desire to secure a child from the above named institution and the first party is willing to grant such request:

NOW THEREFORE: The parties of the second part hereby agree to take the child, **Roger Beacham** _____, into their home as a part of their family; to treat such child with kindness and in all respects as if it were their own natural child; to give it proper food, clothing, medical attention, education and moral training until the said child reaches the age of **maturity** years, unless it should die or be married before reaching that age. *30 day notice must be given the institution unless waived by Supt.*

The party of the first part shall have the right at any time to require the return of the child to the above named institution if the best interests of the child should, in the judgment of the above named representatives of the first party, require such return.

The parties of the second part shall have the right at any time to return the said child to said institution at their own expense, provided, however, that if the child be of sufficient age (**18** years) and physical strength to be capable of rendering services of value, then in the event the second parties return the said child they shall pay $ **1.00** per day for each day the child has been in their possession.

Witness the hands of the parties of the second part and the execution hereof on behalf of the party of the first part by the hand of the Superintendent of the West Oklahoma State Home, the day and date last above written.

WEST OKLAHOMA HOME

Mrs J L Huff
Superintendent

Arlie Holman
Mrs Arlie Holman

THE STAR PRINTERY, MUSKOGEE 7938

WEST OKLAHOMA HOME FOR WHITE CHILDREN
releases Roger Beacham, at the age of eleven,
to the Holman family under an Indenture Contract, January 23, 1937

ARLIE & EMMA HOLMAN
Drumright, Oklahoma

"Can you keep a secret?"

"Sure thing."

"Been hunting squirrels near the Cimarron. Damn near lost my life." He lit a Camel with shaky hands. "I bagged a couple and went back to the car to take a nap. Suddenly, three blasts jarred me awake."

"Did they hit you?" I stood in shock as Dad told his tale.

"You'll see." He struggled out of the car and led me around to the rear of the Pontiac. Sure enough, three bullets had pierced the trunk.

"Would any of your gambling buddies shoot you?"

He frowned. "Naw, they wouldn't fire at a fella. Now don't breath a word to Mother."

"All right. All right."

Dad popped the trunk open and pulled out his Winchester pump-action 10-gauge shotgun. It glistened with a blue burnished barrel. He pushed a couple of empty liquor bottles away from the day's kill, and a different scenario flashed before my eyes. I pictured Dad returning to the car, not to take a nap, but to quench his thirst. He must have walked around to the trunk, and when he attempted to eject the shells, his gun accidentally went off. Without a doubt, Dad had riddled his own car!

Our eyes met, and it was as if I saw into his soul. "Dad, supper's getting cold. I'll clean out the trunk."

He trudged through the back door with a sheepish look on his face. That evening he retired early, which gave me a chance to remove the damaging evidence—an empty pint and a fifth of Jack Daniels whisky. I tossed them into the neighbor's trash can where Mother wouldn't see them.

At breakfast, Dad informed Mother, "Emma, the Pontiac needs a tune up."

"Why should a new car be out of sorts?"

"She's got flawed timing, but with GM's guarantee, they'll fix her." Dad and I drove to Jack Hill's body shop.

The following Saturday, we walked down and picked up the car. Driving home with renewed assurance, Dad patted me on the knee. "Son, it's good to share a secret."

However, several months later, Dad told Mother his original version about his hunting experience. She was shocked. Mother told the story of strangers who shot up Arlie's new Pontiac for years afterward, receiving many tut-tuts and pursed lips from her friends.

With each passing year, I began to better understand my place in the family puzzle. The Holmans had never realized the dream of having a child of their own. Dad had resigned himself to it, but Mother had not. She longed for motherhood. Her despair over failing to produce a son for her beloved husband ripped at her heart.

By the time she convinced him of her need to be a mother, she was too old to handle a baby. Lucky for me! I was young enough for the nurturing administered by an obsessive mother, yet old enough not to be a needy baby who would burden a high-strung father like Dad.

Mother's main worry was Dad's friendship with Benny McGrew, a former tool dresser, better known as "Little Red." He hung out at the Sportsman's Bar. Mother pleaded with Dad to stay out of the roadside liquor joints, but her tears only drove him further from home. Her mind was like a disordered pantry cluttered with mason jars containing spoiled peaches and pears. Many an evening I'd find her waiting up for Dad, sitting in the rocker by the front window, lost in a world of worry.

One afternoon when I came in from school, Mother stood in the kitchen preparing supper. The aroma of fried steak, sliced onions, and corn bread filled the air. "Glad you're on time." She wiped her brow with the tip of her apron and slid the skillet of steaks off the burner. "They're done. We'll pour the tea when Arlie comes."

Time passed. The steaks turned cold. "I'm beside myself worrying over Arlie. He already owes Little Red a gambling note."

"Should I go get him?"

She nodded. "But be careful. Arlie has a temper." With Scooter tagging along, I pedaled down the road to the Sportsman's Inn, freshly coated with white paint. I arrived in the parking lot and slid off my bike. Scooter curled around the front wheel.

I opened the door, and curious gazes followed me across the dance hall. The notes of "Keep an Eye on Your Heart," floated from a yellow jukebox. Soft lights gleamed across the mahogany bar, and the stale smell of beer, smoke, and whisky blended together like a pot of sour stew. I walked by several women sitting at a round table. "Just a minute, son." A woman dressed in a short skirt stood in my path. My stomach tightened.

"He's Arlie's boy," a husky male voice called from the end of the bar. He waved me on. I followed a light to the game room. There Wooley Swindle, a hard-living bootlegger and a small-town gambler, offered beer, whisky by the bottle or glass, and a rousing table for high stakes.

I found Dad sitting next to Little Red, a red-haired, heavy-chested man wearing a leather jacket. They sat with a dozen friends, the roulette wheel clicking beside them.

Wooley Swindle, a pink-faced, bald-headed fellow, wore a wrinkled white shirt with the sleeves rolled to his elbows. His smoke-reddened eyes had followed a roulette wheel for too many years. He spun the wheel and clattered out words:

> Come men,
> Have a hunch.
> Bet a bunch.
> Bet to win. Bet to lose.
> Call any number. All kinds of ways.
> Get with it, gentlemen.
> The wheel of fortune is rolling.
> Place your money on the lucky number.
> It's your turn to win.

To the men gathered around the roulette wheel, the spiel was like a beautiful siren beckoning them to a treasure-laden island. As sweat poured down their faces, they spun their wages away, then signed loans with Mr. Swindle or one of their friends. Dad, sitting erect in his gray-vested suit, joined this world of restless men.

Finally, still eyeing the whirling click, click, click of the spinning wheel, Dad leaned over. I pulled his sleeve. This tug brought him back from another loss. He pushed his chips over to Little Red, who stood up and shook my hand. "Arlie, is this your son?"

"Yes, this is Bill." Dad had told me earlier that although his friend had replaced his flathead motor with a V-8 whereby he could run booze, he was an all right guy.

"Young man, did you see my Ford out back? It'll hit a hundred."

Listening to Dad and Little Red talk about customizing cars and running whisky, I realized that the underworld was filled with daring. From Mother's worries over his gambling, I felt the danger, but Dad never accepted the futility of risking his future on chance. "You never know," he would say. "Any day, I may hit a home run."

Dad patted my shoulder. "It's getting late. Better start for home."

That evening after supper, Dad walked into my room. "In Heaven's name. Never embarrass a person in front of his friends. Smarten up. Stay out of bars."

He carried a hammer and the Indenture Contract, which he had stuck in a Woolworth picture frame. He drove a nail into the wall and hung the agreement to the right of my desk, claiming that it would serve as a reminder. "If you don't wise up and develop self-discipline, I'm going to pack you back to Helena."

Dad's threats of dumping me back into the orphanage were more brutal than a licking. He had tossed me aside once, and I had every reason to believe he would drive me back to Helena, hand me a dollar, and abandon me again. In my mind, this mere piece of paper rattled my nerves. Since I had taken notes on several of the provisions, I offered a few pointers to Dad.

"It's not legal. My name is Bechan, not Beacham."

"That's a minor point."

I pointed to the third paragraph. "If I get married, I'm free."

Dad examined the page for a bit. "You're still a teenager. Can't cut it in the world."

In my mind, Dad wasn't one to give advice about self-control since he couldn't avoid hanging out at the roadhouses.

Although I was done with institutional life, my education as an orphan had barely begun. I felt like a hostage, resentful of Dad's warnings, and always dreaming of the day when I would be free from the burden of a contract which I had never signed.

I felt Mother's care and love, but I struggled in my relationship with Dad. Mother encouraged me to attend Sunday school, develop good morals, be honest and trustworthy. And to learn to care for others and be less self-centered.

Dad said that Mother's high-minded ideals were all dependent upon self-discipline.

*

Periodically, without cause or warning, dark clouds held me hostage. I couldn't concentrate. My classwork spiraled downward. Mother arranged an appointment with Dr. Woodson Reynolds, our family physician. "What is causing these episodes?" he asked.

"I don't know. Every month or so, I face the blues."

"These periods of dark thoughts are called melancholy." He prescribed a fowl-smelling tonic and recommended hot baths and more regular hours.

Living within my hurt, I yearned to change. When my mood brightened and in an effort to become more focused, I started a diary in a ringed binder. I inked out a list of the new model airplanes I wished to build, outlined a couple of articles in *Popular Science*, and penciled out the highlights of each week's activities.

In an effort to improve my behavior, I jotted down a list of questions: "How can I control my explosive temper? Why am I so rebellious? How can I learn to follow directions? Why do I keep skipping school? How can I be free of the blues?"

Every week, I went over a list of my failures. I talked to Mother about my problems. "Broaden your interests," she said. "Read one book a week. You will learn how other boys grow into men."

Mother's interest in my reading prompted her to send me to the library. When the Drumright Public Library's door swung open, I paused to admire the arched windows and vaulted ceiling. A heavy silence permeated the place, interrupted by the occasional thump, thump of a rubber stamp. The smell of new books, glue, and volumes covered with cloth bindings filled the air.

There I met Katy Schickram, president of the library board, who was substituting for the librarian. When she gave me my first library card, I felt the deep pride of belonging. Mrs. Schickram asked about my reading interests.

"I liked *The Rover Boys on the Ocean*."

"Must have been a good read," she said. "Now try a true adventure." She took a copy of Richard Henry Dana's *Two Years Before the Mast* from the shelf and thrust it in my outstretched hand.

During the following week, I longed to join the captain and sail aboard the brig *Pilgrim* exploring the coast of California. With the approach of each storm, the crew slipped the boat's anchor and sailed the ship out into the deep Pacific to avoid crashing on the rocky shore. Dana kindled my interest in sailing.

From that day on, I roamed the vaulted home of ideas, explored the stacks, pulled out books, flipped pages, rushing into each story, where I lived apart from my classmates.

I searched for pirate's gold with the Rover Boys; walked with Tom and Huck as they witnessed Injun Joe commit a murder; flew the Atlantic with Lindbergh; helped Smokey the Cow Horse fight off a coyote; lived in a shed with Madam Curie as she extracted radium;

and enjoyed the light of a fireplace with Abe Lincoln. The library became my haven, as it was for many youngsters who sought friends, adventure, and knowledge.

Katy Schickram said, "The public library is one institution which will always fulfill its chartered mission." With an observing mind, she guided me into the life-sustaining world of books.

*

In May of 1940, nearly two and a half years after returning from Helena and with my grades placing me in the top three percent of my class, the Holmans decided to proceed with a formal adoption. Before we made the trip to the county courthouse, I was curious to learn about my early years. One morning, I interrupted Dad's reading of the sports page in the *Tulsa World*. "Did Mr. Wheeler ever mention my father?" He looked askance at me over the top of his glasses. But Mother spoke up.

"Why look back?" Mother looked down and took the final stitch in another doily—one of dozens she had labored over. Then she frowned. "If you open the door to your past, it could be hurtful."

"Didn't Mr. Wheeler give you a file? Mrs. Schickram says that I should have a birth certificate."

"There is no record of your birth. We're not sure about your age," Mother said.

Mother started to explain further, but Dad cut her short and paused for a moment. They looked at each other. Then he broke the silence. "Yes, there's a paper which mentions your parents. It's in our safety deposit box." My heart quickened.

Later that morning we drove downtown and parked in front of the Citizen's Bank. We entered the stately building, and Dad paused at the front desk for a bit to talk with Coin Sellers about Winston Churchill becoming prime minister of England. Then we walked back to the vault, where Dad pulled a polished steel box from the wall and sat down at a table. Papers tumbled out—bank notes, insurance policies, and Mother's family records. Dad rummaged through the items until he found a legal-sized document. "Here it is."

My heart pounded as I read "Petition no. 4128," dated September 4, 1936, addressed to the Juvenile Court, Oklahoma County.[8]

> "The boy [Roger Bechan] is a dependent because his parents had separated and divorced; and that the mother, Mrs. J. H. Bechan, was given custody of the child through a divorce decree granted her upon grounds that the father deserted her before the said child was born. The father has never seen the child."
>
> Signed. W.C. Wheeler
> September 4, 1936

What was this? How could this be? My father had never seen me? All these years I had believed my mother when she said, "I want your father to live with us again." I blew up.

"Dad, my mother lied to me!"

"Perhaps your father's first name is Joseph or John Bechan," Dad said. "One day, Bill, you may solve the mystery."

"Is this an official record?" I fingered the paper and looked at Dad.

"It's a petition to the court, written by your guardian. Since I don't care for the gentleman, I couldn't verify his statement."

"Why's that?"

"Mr. Wheeler, like many court appointees, was supposedly a man of high religious leanings. But he was also a broker."

"And so?"

Dad placed his hand on my shoulder. "When we took you from the Baptist home, Mr. Wheeler required a payment of $700, then levied a fee for three months."

A clear picture emerged. Over the years, my protector had garnered money from several of my adoptive parents.

"Yes, Mr. Wheeler was a man of business," Dad said.

Before I could appear in court, Dad solved the puzzle of my name. Legally, I thought it might be wise to resume my birth name of Roger Bechan.

"No, son. You will need to sign documents with a full first, middle, and a family name. William is more appropriate." So my first name became William after Will Minter; my middle name became Roger; and I received the name of Holman out of respect for Mother and Dad's gift of love.

On May 17, 1940, we journeyed to Sapulpa where we lunched in a swanky dining room. The waitress served red wine, which settled Mother's nerves. Dad looked relaxed. In the afternoon, we appeared before Judge S. M. Cunningham in the Creek County Courthouse. He informed me that he was voiding Mr. Wheeler's guardianship. However, if something should cause the Holmans to give me up again, I was to be returned to the Helena orphanage under the Indenture Contract.

Mother and Dad signed the adoption papers. Mother finally had a son. She cried. Dad shook my hand. At last I had a legal name, William Roger Holman.[9]

~15~

Drumright came alive on Saturday night. Our small family spent those evenings on Broadway Street, and Mother took on a more spirited air when she dressed up for the weekly event. When the sun sank over Tiger Hill and the earth cooled, hundreds of people who lived on the outlying farms and oil leases streamed into town, joining the festivities. The wide sidewalks easily handled the crowd.

"There is no other town like Drumright," Dad said, and he was right. During the early boom, the farmers and native citizens rejected the newcomers, forcing the oil people to cling to one another and creating a fraternity based on need. Now all were united and the heart of Drumright beat with a vibrant spirit. When a well rumbled to life and crude shot into the air, Drumright prospered. The citizens loved the continuing boom, the whirling sounds of the pumping rigs, the smell of light brown crude, and the tales about the local bootleggers and Kansas City Babe, the town's madam.

"Let's park near the Citizen's Bank tonight." Mother loved to view the town's goings-on from the corner of Broadway and Ohio where her friends could find her with ease in Dad's latest Pontiac.

The evening started with the high school's award-winning marching band parading up Broadway. A green and yellow parrot named Jeanette highlighted the band's higher notes with squawks of "Whatcha doin'?" as she strutted back and forth on the City Drug's marquee.

As Jeanette's voice faded, the Salvation Army band, in black uniforms with red trim, played its Saturday night concert on the corner. A big boy on the tuba, a spindly man playing the trombone joined the trumpets and tambourines. Their joyous tunes seemed to project the hope of saving a few sinners from the milling crowd. The major delivered a brief message and led the gathering in singing, "Onward Christian Soldiers." Coins flowed into jingling tambourines as two ladies passed them from one car window to another.

Members of the "Town Council," as Dad called the elderly gentlemen who hung around the Citizen's Bank, rolled Prince Albert cigarettes and chewed Pall Mall tobacco. With their Case pocketknives they whittled figures out of pine as they told tales of the giant gushers of the past.

"When you step around the corner from Ohio Street," Dad said, "you'd better be quick-footed or be prepared to wipe tobacco juice off your shoes."

But nothing dampened the excitement of Saturday night. People gathered to forget the hard times, hear cheerful stories, nod over the latest gossip, or exchange tales of their neediest friends.

Mother liked to remind people of how desperate some couples were. She called them "Two Cup Families." This meant they had to borrow coffee cups from neighbors should they have company.

"Yep, oil people know one day you have chicken and the next you have feathers," Dad said. He felt everyone would be happy if it weren't for the Great Depression, but this dark reality only sent more people out on Saturday evenings.

The street teemed with cars and a few pickups. Mothers, fathers, and children wandered in and out of the shops. People admired the drillers, tool pushers, and roustabouts as exceptional men. They considered wildcatters local heroes. Clusters of sunburnt farmers and oil workers in starched khaki pants and blue denim shirts walked the hilly sidewalks. Professional men, dressed in seersucker suits, mixed with the workers and shared the latest stories that were seldom listed on the police blotter.

Most nights, Bob Blackstock, Ray Sebring, and I sat on the Pontiac's fenders and tossed popcorn at the girls as they strolled up and down the sidewalk in their flowered, billowy dresses. Younger children stood in small groups teasing one another or searching sidewalk crevices for lost coins.

For me, the temptation of hot tamales and chocolate malts was almost as strong as the lure of girls. I felt awkward around them, but when I heard Mr. Nat, a small lean man, cry, "Hot tamales in corn shucks, 25¢ a dozen," I hustled up the hill to his two-wheel cart. My appetite was stronger than my libido, and I was comfortable gorging down the meaty hot tamales.

When possible, I tagged along with Dad when he left the car to shop. He believed in a world economy long before such a term was coined. He had accounts with all the international shops—the Syrian-Lebanese, the English, the Irish, and the Jews. He bought a suit at Kraker Brothers, picked up a scarf for Mother in Deeba's Clothing Store, purchased groceries from Sam Whitlock's grocery, and we later ate at Fred Joseph's Steak House. He took pride in understanding economics. Dad preached about self-discipline but he failed to practice it himself. He liked the largess of buying on credit for to him it was like playing poker. He never seemed to realize any limits.

One evening, we put our packages in the car and walked down the street to talk with the refinery crowd about Hitler's expansion in Europe and the running argument about the Jehovah's Witnesses refusing to serve in the army.

A dour-looking fellow with a matchstick waggling between his lips nodded his head. "A war is on. You can't hide behind religion."

Mother and Dad valued their friendships and loved the Saturday evening social chats which lent color to their lives. Our car was one of the last to leave Broadway after the nine o'clock siren blasted from the fire station to signal "closing time." The merchants, with the exception of the drugstores and the pool hall, pulled down their blinds and switched off their lights. The soft glow of the street lamps punctuated the deepening darkness. With Dad content, Mother appeared relaxed. But the onus of Dad's gambling was about to rattle all of our nerves.

One winter evening in December, eighteen days before Christmas, the last notes from the Salvation Army band had faded into the night as the lights in the drugstores and a few other shops dimmed into a soft glow. Dad walked down Broadway to Ben Russell's Billiard Hall as I dozed in the backseat, exhausted from parading the sidewalks.

BANG! BANG! Two rapid shots rang out, followed by a third, shattering the evening calm.

"Gunshots!" Mother cried.

"Yeah. Three of them!" I crawled out of the car and looked down the hill. A woman standing in front of the Marquette Pharmacy let out a piercing scream.

"My Lord, could it be Arlie? Bill, see what's going on." Mother's hand fluttered near her face as if she were fighting for air.

Just then, Dad came running up the hill. "My God, Little Red's dead." Dad looked spooked.

Mother, speechless with relief, sank down in her seat.

Dad said he was standing outside the billiard hall talking to Ben Russell when Wooley Swindle came to the door. "Say, Ben, is Little Red in your place?"

Ben gestured toward the back room. "He's playing dominoes."

"That rascal," Wooley grumbled. "Been stealing liquor out of my warehouse."

"Jesus," Ben grabbed him by the arm. "Don't tear up my place.

189

Wait here. I'll get him." So Ben brought Little Red out.

"I watched the two walk across the street," Dad said. "When they started to get in the car, Wooley pulled a gun and blasted Red. He lived for a bit. His eyes were open. Then, without a word, he turned his head to one side and died." Tears streaked down Dad's face. "Yeah. Old Wooley shot him in cold blood."

We listened to the wail of an ambulance. Mother wondered aloud on this unfortunate event. "With Little Red's death," Mother said, "Dad's gambling debts will probably be cancelled."

Dad turned to Mother. "Red sold his IOUs to Wooley last week."

"I hope your Mr. Swindle doesn't cause us any trouble." Mother wiped her eyes.

"Let's forget tonight." Dad spoke in a whisper. The milling crowd thinned as we drove down Broadway and headed for home.

Months later, Wooley Swindle settled Dad's note for less than a quarter of its worth because he needed cash for his defense. Mr. Swindle came to trial in Superior Court. He retained Lawrence Jones, a noted criminal attorney from Bristow. Although everyone knew Little Red never carried a weapon, Lawyer Jones convinced the jury that his client had fired in self-defense. Several prominent business-men testified that Mr. Swindle was an upstanding citizen. "Why," they said, "he has always voted and paid his taxes on time." The jury came in with an acquittal. Wooley Swindle walked free.[10]

There was something about living in Drumright that fascinated Dad. Perhaps the nature of day-to-day life wove a spell around those who lived with uncertainty of the future. In the early days, after the criminals gunned down two police chiefs, the citizens elected "Fighting Jack Ary" to establish law and order. This drove many of the robbers, gamblers, and bootleggers out of town. But within a few months, several straggled back. Some found prosperity through the Prohibition years from 1920 to 1933. Selling bootleg liquor and killing off rival intruders, these lawbreakers gave Drumright the reputation as a tough town.

With the end of the nation's prohibition, the local church fathers in alliance with the American Temperance League organized to protect the righteous. They restated the premise: "Hard liquor is the curse upon the innocent." The majority of the citizens attended church and led upstanding lives. They continued to vote to keep Creek County "dry"—another way of saying "you can't sell liquor here." Thus, they provided fertile ground for the bootleggers and gamblers.

Dad understood both camps—churchgoers and roughnecks. He knew men. Many workers, after a hard day's labor, enjoyed the camaraderie of playing cards and sharing a drink. The old adage around the oil fields was, "Don't trust a man who doesn't drink."

This was my small world: a family that was reshaping me; a village ripe with adventure and vice; and a school determined to ready me for what the world might hand out.

*

In 1941, as we in Drumright lived in a haven apart from man's madness, the war in Europe and Asia raged with millions of casualties. We read daily reports about Japan's invasion of China and listened to Edward R. Murrow's broadcasts as Hitler's forces invaded France and stormed into Russia.

That September, I started the ninth grade in Drumright High. We freshmen, distanced from the older classes by our greenness, felt apprehensive about meeting our new teachers who challenged our naivete. One teacher in particular, Lou Ann Pinkston, seemed bent on waking us from our primal sleep, wiping the mother's milk from our cheeks and dusting us with wake-up powder.

Her pioneer face, sculpted cheekbones and wind-burnt complexion, looked as though she worked in the Oklahoma wheat fields. But this face belied a remarkable mind. Mrs. Pinkston used civics and history to erase our previous parroting of family politics and pushed us to visualize the history of our time, our place in it, and how best to cope with all of its realities. To this end, I wrote a term paper about Wendell Wilkie and his support of President Roosevelt's proposal to establish the United Nations. Mrs. Pinkston beamed her approval, giving me an "A."

"Bill," she said, "you must go to college. With your strong will, your love of history, and your gift with words you could become a leading lawyer."

Mrs. Pinkston gave me a new goal. I'd attend the University of Oklahoma and become an attorney.

But, meanwhile, I did what all the teenagers did on slow Sunday afternoons. I went to the movies.

My pals and I frequented the Tower Theatre, which was filled with smells of buttered popcorn. A dusty ribbon of light hovered over our heads as the screen filled with John Wayne's manly walk and various big-busted actresses revealing their cleavage. When the lights popped on, we stepped up the aisle and stumbled outside into the glaring sunlight.

One Sunday when we emerged from our dark cocoon, crowds of people were milling up and down Broadway.

It was December 7, 1941.

"My Lord, the Japs have bombed Pearl Harbor," one man shouted. At this a woman screamed, "Oh no! My son is stationed right there!"

We boys reacted by boasting of the military might of the United States and Bob swore, "Hell, we'll whip those Japs in a month."

But as older friends rushed off to the services and word was received of several of their deaths, war became real to all of us. Bob changed his tune, saying if the war lasted long enough, he would join the air force.

Our war efforts centered around rationing of foods and fuel.

Sugar, butter, and meat were in short supply as was gasoline for cars. But these were minor inconveniences. All in all, we lived in a protected enclave from the brutal realities being faced by people in England, Europe, and the Pacific islands.

During my sophomore and junior years, my interest in running around with my friends grew stronger. Bob Blackstock, Ray Sebring, and I made a noisy threesome as we headed up Pennsylvania after playing football with the Cherry Street Gang. We shoved each other in playful jousts as we reviewed the afternoon game with Bob teasing Ray about dropping one of Jack Sellers' key passes.

Bob was tall, broad-shouldered, and walked with a rolling stride like an old friend rushing to meet you. With a mature face, framed with coal-black hair, he was remarkably handsome. He drew people to him because they wanted to share his enthusiasm. My pal, from the beginning, made the world seem like a brighter place.

Ray, a husky youngster, was the strongest weight lifter in high school. Shifting from one foot to the other in a lumbering motion, Ray bragged about earning four letters in football.

We finally made it into Norwood's Confectionary Store where we listened to a hit parade tune, Harry James' "You Made Me Love You," blaring on the radio. We continued horsing around and teasing each other to draw attention to ourselves from the pretty coeds sitting at the round wire-legged tables. I envied Bob and Ray's easy way with the girls. Socially, I was ill at ease. Tall and lanky, I couldn't play high school football. Big-footed, I couldn't dance. Instead, I invested my time in classwork, delivering newspapers, and running around with my pals.

Once we ordered our Cokes, we laid off the teasing, put politics aside, and got down to the usual subject: Kansas City Babe, the town's notorious madam. She ran girls out of her Sinclair Rooms, and she whetted our curiosity about all things feminine. Bob claimed the Babe was a legend in the oil field, like Calamity Jane was to the

West. She loved to shoot dice and belt down a shot of booze.[11]

I told my friends that when I delivered papers to the Sinclair Rooms in the early morning hours, I was tempted to wander down the narrow-planked hallway—lighted by a dim red bulb—to catch a glimpse of ivory-skinned Firehouse Anne, one of Babe's sexy girls. The guys down at the newspaper's delivery office said she had bouncy boobs and long, shapely legs. They claimed she had a number of boyfriends when Bob Wills and his Texas Playboys performed at the American Legionnaires Hut. Babe's rooming house stood next door.

On those Friday evenings when western swing music filled the hut, Bob Wills sang out, "Take it away Leon, AH-haaa." Then the guitar melody of "Dance all night, dance a little longer . . ." drifted down Broadway. Hundreds of folks danced, and several men stayed a little longer to visit Kansas City Babe and her girls.

One day when Ray skipped the fun at Norwood's, Bob and I dropped by his dad's tire shop. We found Ray changing a bicycle tire.

"Hey, old fossil," teased Bob, "when you going to give your old man an honest day's work?"

Ray, with sweat staining his cotton shirt, took a break. "I fancy you guys have been in Norwood's croaking stories over a Coke."

Bob patted him on the back. "The word's out that the Babe has stashed cartons of Jack Daniels among the hollyhocks in her backyard." Bob asked Ray if that was legal.

Ray shrugged his shoulders. "You guys don't know the Babe. You don't even know her name, do you? I do, and its Hazel Hoskins."

"So, what's up, old philosopher?" Bob asked.

"She dropped her car off yesterday. And, boys, she's not anything like y'all imagine."

"Have you been in the Sinclair Rooms?" Bob said, gasping.

"Not like that. Right now she's mighty sad."

"Why so?" Bob looked puzzled.

"She wants me to bury Fluff, her toy poodle. It died in the night."

"Can we help?" Bob asked. "We'd like to meet Hazel Hoskins, as you call her. What do you say?"

"I could use some muscle. But don't get buggy-eyed when the Babe comes out. This is a serious time for her."

Bob and I looked at each other and smiled. Would we see a painted dance hall floozy? Would she have rouged cheeks and big boobs bouncing under a red satin dress? For the first time, we had a chance to see a real, honest-to-goodness, call-house madam.

Down the alley we three grave diggers trudged. Ray lugged a pick, Bob toted a shovel, and I carried a cardboard box. We entered the back gate to find that the Babe had cut back a row of hollyhocks and outlined a burial plot.

"Okay, guys, turn to," Ray ordered. "Bill, take the pick and open the hole." I wielded the pickax until I paused for a break.

Before I could regain my breath, Bob jumped in with a shovel and tossed up a mound of dirt.

Suddenly the screen door squeaked open. I turned to see a woman I thought was the maid carrying a small dog lying on top of a pink pillow. She looked like a plump housewife, plain-faced with no make-up. A blue-and-orange-print house dress reached down to touch her brown oxfords. A black bracelet clung to one of her wrinkled arms.

"We're ready, Mrs. Hoskins," Ray said. "We've brought a box for Fluff." With these words, Bob and I met the notorious Kansas City Babe. The light went out in our movie script dream. No painted lady, no enticing breasts; she looked like any other woman crying over the loss of a pet.

The burial proceeded as I placed Fluff in her casket. Then Bob lowered the toy poodle into the ground with her head to the west. The Babe sprinkled a handful of dirt on top and mumbled words about dust to dust. Ray covered the grave. The Babe tearfully handed Bob a wooden cross decorated with Fluff's leather collar and a pink ribbon. "Place her marker where it will withstand the wind."

With the flat of the shovel, Bob tapped it deep near the edge of the grave. Babe bowed her head and said farewell to her beloved companion. Her simple words of love brought tears to our eyes.

Babe warmly embraced us and slipped a silver dollar into each of our grubby hands before turning to reenter her rooming house. We moped back to Ray's place and went our separate ways.

I learned about the real world that day.

*

Dad accepted a more responsible position at the refinery, giving him less time to frequent the roadside taverns. I admired his work ethics. He often said, "Hard labor shapes a boy into a man." This credo became mine. Bob Blackstock and I continued to peddle papers for the *Tulsa World*. But I searched for another job, hoping to earn a weekly check.

On the south corner of Broadway, where Pennsylvania divided the town, there stood a red-brick building housing the weekly *Drumright Journal*. One afternoon after school as I passed the corner, I heard the clank and whirr of machinery pounding up from the basement. I walked downstairs, and while admiring the print shop, up walked Gordon Rocket, the owner. I introduced myself.

"Say, Bill, how would you like to become a printer's devil?" I jumped at the chance to work after school. Throughout the week, I tossed used Linotype slugs into a gas-fired iron kettle and melted them down, creating fresh "pigs" of lead. I helped set type for the headlines and locked the lines up with zinc engravings for forthcoming issues. Then I sorted the type back into the cases. Our only foundry face was Century Old Style, which was easy to read. I now came home each evening smelling of carbon-black printer's ink, hot molten lead, binder's glue, and newly milled paper. To me it was intoxicating.

After I apprenticed for a year, Mr. Rocket asked if I would like to run the printing press. I jumped at the chance, but he said I must first work as the fly-boy, helping to run the monstrous three-ton Babcock newspaper press as it spun, thundered, and clanked out the weekly news. Within a month, I could run the brain-boggling machine by myself.

I took on the challenge of work with the same wild spirit I had on the playground. Work became play. I made a game of listening to the Linotype's tinkling brass mats set slugs of type into a story. I enjoyed the clanking sound of the printing press as it impressed inked type onto paper. Thus began my interest in printing and typography.

With my first check, I dropped by the Citizen's Bank and opened a savings account which Dad matched dollar for dollar. This began my ever growing nest egg for college. And I paid Coin Sellers a sum of $50 for the injuries I had inflicted on his mare and filly in the summer of 1936. Dad said he was mighty proud that I had settled an old debt.

As I paused to ruminate on the positive influence which Mother and Dad had played in my life, I came to value the Bible's Fifth Commandment: "Honour thy father and thy mother: that thy days may be long upon the land. . . ." In spite of what I considered Dad's earlier and unjust use of the contract, I honored my loving mother and concerned father who welcomed a traumatized boy into their lives.

This small town of Drumright, perched on three hills, covered by prairie grasses and scrub oaks struggling out of arid crevices in rocky soil, with chugging oil wells echoing through the valleys, evolved into the core of an eternal universe, where events unfolded with new meaning and my life became more secure.

I had found my small place in a large world.

Part Four

Searching for One's Beginnings

❧

There must be a mind
within our minds which cannot rest
until it has worked out,
even against our conscious will,
the unresolved questions of our past.

EDWIN MUIR
An Autobiography

~16~

But true to the essence of my peripatetic life, changes came to my small world. In early January 1944, Dad, having sworn off gambling, decided to accept a challenge. The B.F. Goodrich Company offered him a responsible position to supervise the construction of a new plant in Miami, Oklahoma.

This meant moving away from Drumright. Mother and I were reluctant but curious. Could we adjust? I would have the most difficult hurdle—a larger school, strangers for classmates, and missing my work at the newspaper. Mother would have all her familiar accouterments—husband, son, and home.

Dad gave us no choice. "It's a done deal."

We moved 150 miles northeast on Highway 66 to Miami in the corner of Oklahoma touched by Kansas and Missouri. Dad said this city of 10,000 people prospered from cattle and lead mining. For a town of its size, it had more millionaires than any other in the state. We saw that reflected in its busy Main Street shops, a city airport, bus line, the number of chauffeur-driven cars, and the multitude of estates with their parklike lawns.

In Miami, Mother loved her spacious, two-story brick home. She settled in by finding the best grocer for deliveries, a stylish hair salon, the friendliest neighbors, and a young housemaid. Mother said, "Life is better here."

I was happy for Mother but distressed over the disruption in my daily life. I enrolled in Miami High School, but I missed my friends, my school, and my town. I wanted to go back and walk up Tiger Hill and smell the aroma of oil drifting in the air. My separation from the familiar stirred up my restlessness.

Dad called a family conference. He and Mother agreed that I could return to Drumright and graduate if I completed my junior year in Miami and worked on construction at the B.F. Goodrich plant during the summer.

Springtime arrived early in Oklahoma that year, the winds softened and the white buds on the wild plum trees appeared like confetti tossed in the air. One Saturday in April, I walked into Wiley's Pharmacy, and at the soda counter I met a young lady like no other. Barbara Louise Switzer—sky-blue eyes, black hair, pink cheeks, she was a tall, willowy girl brimming with delight and mischief. She wore a blue-and-purple summer dress with white lace at the sleeves.

Barbara was a force one couldn't ignore at Miami High School. In the following days I noticed her emceeing assemblies in the auditorium, playing a cello in the school orchestra, acting in student plays, and winning first place in the class tennis tournament. She often created banners to announce student meetings or sports events. Most attractive to me, I never saw her without a friendly smile.

The following Saturday, I asked for a date and within a few weeks we became a couple. We walked close to each other, her hand fell naturally into mine, and I sensed a mutual bond. We dated through the spring and summer, and her sunny temperament bedazzled me. My heart beat with a rush I had never felt before! I remember chattering with happiness, thinking an angel had brought us together.

But my inquiring mind asked, "Wait a moment. Meet her parents. Gain some insight into the family." I visited her home where I found her vital German father working in the garden and her auburn-haired mother busy keeping Barbara's younger sister and brother corralled. The Switzer family was open and relaxed with me.

During the hot summer months I worked on construction at the B.F. Goodrich plant placing all my earnings in my college savings account. During this period of burdensome labor, disturbing thoughts floated up from my past. Though I wished to forget, the memory of my birth mother's love still lingered in my mind, but her leaving without an explanation had left a raw wound.

I was torn by conflicting emotions: I loved Barbara with a boundless passion and craved her warmth but felt wary of commitment. Would my unsettled nature disillusion her? Would she reject me as my mother had done? My orphan years had left me with inexpressible fears.

Barbara learned that I was adopted, but she was not dismayed. She said when she saw me and Dad together, she knew he was my father. "You two walk alike, look alike, dress alike, and smile the same. Are you sure Mr. Holman is not your real father?"

"Yes, I'm certain. But let's not talk about my unlucky years."

"Bill," she assured me, "your bad luck is all used up. You're going to have a wondrous future."

I loved her optimistic spirit. But my fears and conflicting feelings held sway.

*

In the fall of 1944, I rode the Greyhound bus back to Drumright. As I approached the outskirts of town, I heard the thumping pump rigs and saw hundreds of white houses scattered across the rolling hills, making this village of friendly people a place of wonder and excitement. I lived in an apartment on Tiger Hill and earned my board and room by driving an ambulance, often delivering patients to and from hospitals in Oklahoma City and Tulsa. I was pleased to be back in Drumright, but I still experienced episodes of depression.

After a few weeks of classes and arduous nights of driving, my thoughts turned back to Barbara Switzer. Fresh waves of excitement flowed with affection, tenderness, even bewilderment at times. We renewed our courtship with touching letters and weekend visits.

When I graduated from Drumright High School, I returned to Miami and asked Barbara Louise Switzer to share life's adventures with me. My cheerful optimist said yes. On September 1, 1945, we were married in a single-ring ceremony before a Baptist minister. Although the war had ended, I spent several months in the U.S. Navy V6 reserves earning two years of college under the G.I. Bill.

My dream of attending a major university came true when I enrolled at The University of Oklahoma. The campus, with its red-brick gothic structures surrounded by formal gardens and sweeping lawns, presented daily rewards. I pursued law briefly. But I left the field to my fellow classmate, Bob Blackstock, when I went to work as a student assistant in the Bizzell Library. The library held a number of rare collections. I became interested in the art of fine bookmaking when I viewed an exhibit of medieval manuscripts and books illustrated with gold initial letters and decorative borders.

By 1949, Barbara and I had two sons only a year apart. David and Roger brought home to me the preciousness of family life. I questioned how my father could have abandoned my mother. And why did my mother, blessed with the miraculous bond of motherhood, abandon her six-year-old child? I saw myself as a protective father. I looked forward to holding a responsible position and providing my children with a secure and loving home.

One spring evening as I walked out of the library feeling optimistic about graduating in June, a bolt of melancholy sprang out of the sky and clubbed me with despair. This was the first episode of depression to strike in over six months. Wretched memories of my orphan years unfolded. I couldn't concentrate. I refused to eat. Books no longer grabbed my attention, and I couldn't work. I skipped classes and lay on the sofa. Determined not to let these somber clouds overwhelm me, Barbara made an appointment with the student counseling center. Dr. Albert Jensen, a psychologist, helped me to tap into the debris of each abandonment, each rejection and failure.

The doctor encouraged me to search into my beginnings and possibly find the source of my despair. "Many orphans are born out of melancholy genes," he said, handing me an article on depression.

"You mean, it's an inherited trait?"

"Yes, in many cases." he said. "Where did your birth mother go? Perhaps she and your father are living today." He advised me to seek information through the courts, the orphanages, and the various adoptive homes. "Contact Helen Minter. She is the most likely person to know about your parents."

Barbara phoned Helen for an appointment. The Minters lived only thirty miles away in Oklahoma city. We had kept our lines of communication open through letters. We drove to the city in our old but sporty 1932 Model A Ford. The emotion that swept through me as I stepped onto Helen's front porch with Barbara and my two sons made me weak in the knees.

Will Minter was calm as Helen glowed with parental happiness over our visit. "Barbara, Bill possessed a wild, spontaneous love of life," Helen said. "He had fire in his blood and challenged any grown-up who tried to lord it over him." But she never mentioned my parents.

Barbara finally came out with the weighty questions. "Can you tell us where Bill's mother went? And who was his father?"

Helen's smile vanished, and she grew pensive. "I can't talk about any of that. I can't."

I pushed ahead of Barbara and faced Helen. "Surely you can reveal my father's name."

"I'm sorry, but I can't go there." Helen turned aside. Will Minter remained silent.

"It wouldn't cause any harm." I struggled with how I could make her talk.

Barbara laid her hand on my arm, and I felt a sense of caution. Having experienced Helen's iron will as a youngster, I stepped back. I didn't wish to rupture my relations with the Minters.

Through the years that followed, we visited the Minters a number of times, always hoping to learn of my parents. But they took the secrets to their grave.

From out of this disappointment, I made a vow: I'd never pause until I found my beginnings. I wouldn't give up until I had the true history of Roger Bechan.

In 1952, after receiving an undergraduate degree from the University of Oklahoma and my masters degree in Library Science from the University of Illinois, I accepted the position of Head Librarian of a small college in Edinburg, Texas. I spent four years helping to build the book collection for the college to be accredited into the Pan American University. The library also served as the city's public library. Thus, I gained a view of a library from two perspectives. I decided that my interests in public libraries was strongest.

In 1955, I applied for the position as Head Librarian of the Rosenberg Library in Galveston. With funding provided through a bequest from Henry Rosenberg, this was the oldest public library in continuous operation in Texas. The institution was now receiving public funds, but it was still governed by an independent board of directors. William Morgan, the president, emphasized that I would be accountable only to them.

I asked Mr. Morgan, "To whom does the library's board report?"

"Only to God," he said.

The Rosenberg Library was one of the finest of its size in the country. In addition to its general collections, the institution held a rare collection of incunabula, first editions, and examples of fine printing. And there were outstanding collections in Texas history including manuscripts, maps, artifacts, and early historian imprints.

Despite my fascination with the venerable Rosenberg Library, the lack of affordable housing began to discourage us from living on Galveston Island.

When I was approached by the San Antonio Library board, Barbara and I first visited the city to see what housing that city presented. Barbara was pleased to see that the size and prices fit our budget. In 1957 I accepted the position of Director of the San Antonio Public Library. I reported to an advisory library board and a city manager, a radical change from the independence of Galveston.

But I was inspired by the Spanish elegance of the city and the fine nobility of the public library. For three years, I was content with my work and my home. During the last year of my tenure the San Antonio Library received the American Library Association's John Cotton Dana Award for interpreting its services to the community.

Then one Sunday afternoon as I worked alone in the library preparing a new budget, the tedious figures plus the overcast day brought on an unease. I wanted to escape. Remembering the new book exhibit the staff had installed the day before, I wandered downstairs to inspect the collection.

As I entered the exhibit room, I was transported from the mundane world of budgets to one of beauty and art. Here on display was an array of fine books from the library of Robert Tobin—a veritable bookman's feast. Mr. Tobin's collection of fine printing included such creative books as Doves, Kelmscott, Ashenden, and Updike. I wandered from case to case seeing names I knew: Grabhorns, Cranach Press, and Bruce Rogers. Suddenly, the title page for Adrian Wilson's *Printing for Theater* leaped "onstage" and touched me. I had to read the book.

I found the keys and opened the case. Gone was any thought of work as I retreated, with book in hand, to my office where I had the comfort of an armchair. Who was Adrian Wilson? Who was Joyce Lancaster, the actress-wife whose roles were listed in the dedication?

The afternoon sped by while I caught up on their careers in theater and bookmaking in San Francisco. This richly illustrated book was a perfect form for this diary of their lives: colorful, sensual, dramatic, forthright, and natural. No fusty leather binding would do; it was bound in natural linen over boards.

Tobin's book exhibit revived my interest in typography and printing, and made me realize that San Francisco was the center of fine bookmaking in the United States. Within a week, I purchased a Chandler and Price printing press and several fonts of Bruce Rogers' Centaur type. I gave up golf and printing became my avocation. I took my son David, then twelve, into our print shop and taught him to hand set type and run the press. We issued several pieces of ephemera and looked forward to other projects.

About this time, members of the Library Commission of San Francisco beckoned. I hesitated at first to move my family, but when San Francisco mayor George Christopher called and offered me the position as director of their library, I said yes to living in that beautiful city with its incomparable vistas of the Pacific and the historical ambience going back to the 1600s.

In October of 1960, I was appointed City Librarian of the San Francisco Public Library, a main library and twenty-seven-branch library system that had been under public criticism as inefficient and antiquated. At thirty-five, I became the youngest head of one of the largest public libraries in the nation. My arrival began with a rush of newspaper publicity and great expectations. I relished the challenge and felt confident that I could transform this much-maligned system into an institution of which the citizens would be proud.

We learned how to use the streetcars, ferries, and buses that facilitated travel in and around the city. And later, we purchased a small sloop so we could explore the magnificent bay, learning to navigate in treacherous fog and finding calm overnight anchorages in the lee of Angel Island.

But our most rewarding discovery was the camaraderie we found with the various printers that I had admired from afar in San Antonio. We were welcomed into Ed, Jane, and Bob Grabhorn's print shop on Sutter Street. We visited the private presses of Lew Allen, Mallete Dean, and Andrew Hoyem, and other bay area printers. Adrian Wilson, who lived at No. 1 Tuscany Alley, became our best friend after Barbara and I enrolled in his course on typography and book design.

We were emboldened by Adrian's encouragement and purchased a Colt's Armory printing press. We launched our own imprint—Roger Beacham, Publisher—using the name under which I was released by the state of Oklahoma.

Barbara designed and I printed on weekends, letting my avocation become more and more a part of both of our lives. We printed our first book in 1963.

Mayor Christopher, influenced by the library commission and the Friends of the San Francisco Public Library, increased the library's budget, and the staff modernized the cataloging system. Then we removed thousands of books from the closed stacks and created subject departments. The spirit of rejuvenation continued as the Friends of the San Francisco Public Library attracted writers such as Aldous Huxley, Eric Hoffer, Christopher Isherwood, Mary McCarthy, and Arthur Hoppe to speak at their meetings.

This renaissance of the library took six years of intense devotion. Then my interests in fine printing and twentieth-century literature led me away from public library life.

I had been in contact with Dr. Harry Ransom, president of the University of Texas at Austin, who asked if I'd come aboard his team to help in their quest to build one of the world's finest literary collections. In 1967 he offered me a professional appointment in the Humanities Research Center. I accepted only after I negotiated a nine-month contract. I wanted my summer months free to pursue my interest in book design and printing.

Dr. Ransom's charisma and persuasive personality raised private and public funds in the millions with which the university acquired over thirty million literary manuscripts, one million rare books, five million photographs and one hundred thousand works of art. Highlights include the Gutenberg Bible (c. 1450), the world's first photograph by Niepsce (c. 1826), manuscript collections of George Bernard Shaw, Ernest Hemingway, T.S. Eliot, and D.H. Lawrence, to name a few.

I look back now and see my early interest in Little Blue Books as my incunabula that launched me into a career centered around authors and manuscripts. My world had come full circle.

One of the collections that Dr. Ransom wanted me to examine was in England. Now I needed a passport. Not having a birth certificate sent me to the Oklahoma Society for the Friendless in Oklahoma City with hopes of finding my early records. Unfortunately, the building had been torn down, and Mr. William Wheeler had passed away. In time, after submitting a copy of my adoption record, the U.S. State Department issued my passport.

A few months after returning home from Europe, we reviewed Mr. W.C. Wheeler's 1936 petition to the Oklahoma County Juvenile Court and were intrigued by his statement that my mother, Mrs. J. H. Bechan, was given custody of me through a divorce decree. Believing that my father's name would appear in these records we drove up to the Oklahoma County Courthouse. But after an extensive two-day search, we never discovered any records under the name of Bechan. Was Mr. Wheeler's story of my mother's marriage and divorce a fabrication?

Several years later, in February 1979, I received a letter from Harold Miller, a book collector and fellow orphan in El Paso. He enclosed a news article from the *El Paso Times* for January 23, 1979, telling how, after a fifty-eight-year search, he had found his birth mother. Mr. Miller, now wanting to assist other orphans, reported that Judge Charles Halley of the Oklahoma County Juvenile Court was, at his discretion, releasing court documents to a few applicants.[12]

So Barbara and I flew up to Oklahoma City and appeared before the judge. We requested that my records be opened. "Possibly my birth certificate will be in the files. Also, I wish to know about my birth family," I pleaded.

The judge said he didn't believe that certain abandoned children should probe into their past. "The beginning, for many orphans, is not a happy one."

I informed Judge Halley that I not only needed a birth certificate but I had a hunger to see, to touch, to understand my own blood family. Only they could reveal answers about my genetic being, my medical and psychological makeup. He arbitrarily denied my request.

A few years later, after a new judge had taken office, I renewed my search. I appeared before Judge Nan J. Patton in Oklahoma County Juvenile Court and asked permission to examine the court's files. She reported that, for lack of storage facilities, many of the files for the 1930s had been discarded. But she approved my request to examine the court's ledger.

Under the watchful eye of a court clerk, I thumbed through the red Morocco-bound ledger to the entry made on May 20, 1932 (Oklahoma County Court. Juvenile Docket No. 8, Entry 4128). "Roger Bechan / Dependent . . . wherein the said Roger Bechan was declared to be a dependent child and made a ward of the Court and committed into the care and custody of W.C. Wheeler living in Oklahoma City . . . for the purpose of finding a suitable home into which home said child might be adopted." There was no date of birth, no home address, and neither of my parents' names was listed. My beginnings remained a mystery.

We moved on to the Oklahoma Historical Society Library, where we searched for the name of Bechan in newspaper clipping files, phone books, city directories, and cemetery records for Oklahoma County. Finally we read through the 1920 Census, and much later the 1930 census for both Oklahoma and Canadian County. But we never turned up my mother's name. We became discouraged with our quest in Oklahoma.

Barbara and I turned in another direction. What about the Hardt family in Sulphur? Could they provide any information? A computer search turned up James and his brother Edward Hardt, now living in Sacramento, California. Barbara and I drove out and interviewed them.

Edward, still the quiet, shy person, welcomed our visit. "We shared great times together," Edward said. He talked about the Saturday he came home from visiting his cousins. "Dad had traded his Plymouth in on a Chevrolet. My parents never mentioned your name again."

James Hardt, blustery and mulish as ever, knew pieces of the puzzle. His folks disliked Mr. Wheeler because he demanded monthly payments for my trial adoption. "So my parents went to court and hid you in the Baptist home under the name of Will Rogers."

Barbara and I were shocked to learn why the Hardt family changed my name to Will Rogers and abandoned me in the Baptist Orphanage. But the Hardt brothers didn't possess any information about my birth mother or father.

In the late seventies we visited the Baptist Orphanage in Oklahoma City. After we parked on the oval driveway and looked out, I saw that the Old North Building had been razed and replaced by a number of cottages. My thoughts turned to Bessie Riney, my beloved matron, and I wondered where she might be. And did the elderly Negro still serve possum and sweet potato stew to the boys down by the lake?

I stepped out of the car and entered the orphanage's new office and visited with the supervisor. She reviewed the institution's change from the dormitory system with one matron attempting to care for fifty children to the more nurturing cottage plan where eight children lived with a foster mother and father.

I picked up a directory of former classmates and requested a search for my papers under the name of Roger Bechan. But the files failed to deliver any information

"Look under Will Rogers," Barbara suggested.

There they found a folder with papers relating to the Hardt family, Mr. Wheeler's 1935 legal maneuvers to regain custody from the Baptist Orphanage, and the Holman family's taking me into their home. This proved to be a rich find.

But again we failed to discover any information about my birth parents.

A year later, thinking that we might uncover further information, we drove up to Helena, Oklahoma. Perhaps the West Oklahoma Home for White Children held additional files. We arrived in the small village and headed out to the orphanage. To my dismay, the old main building had been razed and coils of razor-blade wire covered the fences. Several battle-jacketed guards, wearing bulletproof vests, patrolled the grounds with automatic rifles. The state had converted the orphanage into a state prison.

The years slid by, and my wife and I continued to search court documents, census files, marriage and death records for Mrs. J.H. Bechan. We had yet to find her forename. There are fewer than thirty-five Bechans in the national phone directory. It is likely that her family is Czech because a good number of central Oklahoma communities like Prague, Mishak, Yukon, and Hatshorn were settled by Bohemians at the turn of the century. We read the ship manifests from the ports of Galveston, New Orleans, and New York for the Bec'ans (many anglicized their names to Bechan when they settled in America). We found an extended family of Bechans in Massachusetts.

But we never found a Bechan family with a relative who either moved into or out of Oklahoma.

My frustration over my failures grew stronger with the passing years, as did my episodes of euphoria followed by depression. I had gone through several years of psychotherapy with Dr. Tracy R. Gordy. He said that a good number of abandoned children remain prisoners of their past, suffering various depths of melancholy. He guided me through experimental treatments with Lithium, Nardil, Xanax, and, later, antidepressants such as Lexapro. These seldom had the desired effect. I continued to soar to lofty highs, working sometimes around the clock.

As long as I lived on one of those enchanted peaks, I was happy. But when depression hit—often without cause or warning—I fell into a state of gloom. I saw life as a coin flipped high in the bright sunlight: it sparkled with promise as it soared ever and ever upward, but was tragically bereft of hope once it hit the ground.

*

In late May 1993, a few years after retiring from the University of Texas, and having spent over forty years in an unsuccessful search for my birth parents, I felt thwarted by officials and their hidden records. As a youngster, when my mind grew anxious, I had run to Bell Isle Lake, and my longing to be on the water had never left me.

With my wife by my side, I escaped to the sea. We sold our home and our small sailboat to put us at the helm of a thirty-six-foot Morgan-designed "West Indies" sloop. We named her *Teddy* after Erling Tambs' and his wife's remarkable voyage as narrated in his book, *The Cruise of the Teddy*.

One afternoon, we hauled anchor in Miami's Biscayne Bay and threaded our way out through the seaward buoys. With only a compass and the stars to steer by, we set an easterly course for the Abacos, a bright cluster of islands in the northeastern Bahamas. With a towering fifty-four-foot mast setting a mainsail and a billowing white genoa, *Teddy* cut through the seas with a remarkable turn of speed. Within an hour, the sky turned gray and a northwesterly picked up. As the winds tossed pearls of water across my shoulders, I felt the mystery of mankind and how brief a time we have to fulfill our dreams. *Teddy* rose on the crest of each wave and settled back into a trough of foaming water, "and the great shroud of the sea rolled on," as Melville wrote, "as it rolled five thousand years ago."

Was my search for my mother and father to be as disastrous as Ahab's quest for the white whale? Would I pass into that great darkness without learning about my beginnings? Why did Mother walk out of my life that sunny day in May? What personality traits did I inherit from her?

What about my father? Did he like to hunt, to fish, and to sail? What was my nationality: was I English, German, or with my fair complexion, could I be Swedish? And did I have a brother or sister? And why, after a search of over forty years, hadn't I been able to find my most secretive father, the most hidden of all men?

The following day, we rounded Indian Cay Light and headed east toward Great Sail Cay where we anchored for the night. The following morning, we continued to navigate across the treacherous shoal waters. We both stood at the helm as we talked and studied the watery world around us.

Barbara said, "You're one of the luckiest of men. You used up all your bad luck as a youngster. Since shedding the Indenture Contract, you have lived a charmed life."

Since graduating from college, I had been rewarded with a professional career, new suits that replaced the orphan's hand-me-downs, a tall-masted sailboat and offshore adventures, and a hilltop residence overlooking the San Francisco Bay. Good fortune had gifted me with a cell of purposeful living in the midst of a tumultuous world.

But no experience has been more rewarding than our remarkable marriage. My wife and I have shared interests not only in our chil-

215

dren, but in literature, art, book design, printing, traveling, and sailing. I am one of the fortunate men, and no doubt there are many, who has enjoyed the full measure of his wife's love, as well as her gift of intelligence and talent.

In the gray hours of the fourth day, after passing Green Turtle Cay, I scanned the eastern horizon and there, like an old friend's smile, the Man-O-War Cay light rose out of the sea, blinking a warm welcome. Without a Loran position instrument, we had steered a compass course to a quiet haven on the chart. Were we just two fortunate landlubbers or were we, after forty years and five sailboats, seasoned sailors? We like to think the latter.

Teddy rushed around the headland, and I eased the mainsail as we sailed through the channel into the lee of the harbor. When the chain clattered out of the forepeak and the anchor dug into the sandy bottom, it came to me. I needed to be as diligent in my genealogical quest as I had been in learning to navigate the treacherous Bahamian waters. No mother or father departs this earth without leaving some trace behind. I needed to find their mark on the chart of life with less emotion and a truer compass. Somewhere, another beacon would guide me to a safe harbor and away from an anchorless past.

～17～

When we returned home, I abandoned the judges and the courts and instead searched for Paul Minter, my so-called Uncle Paul, who had befriended me as a child. Could he shed light on the mystery of Joseph Bechan, my father? Or was Uncle Paul or Will Minter my father? But their home phone numbers were no longer listed.

I finally found Paul Minter's former secretary. She thought Dr. Walter Dardis' son might know how to locate the Minter family. Through a computer search, I found Dr. Walter Dardis Jr. in Pueblo, Colorado. I phoned him and asked if he knew the whereabouts of the Minters. He said that he hadn't kept up with the family. "Call my sister in Oklahoma City. Her name is Romilda Heyser."

I phoned her. She also remembered the Minter family, but hadn't followed them for years. "Talk to Lucy O'Toole. She was Father's nurse when he had his office in the Petroleum Building. She knew the Minters."

I called Mrs. O'Toole. It was June 16, 1993, and she was at home in Oklahoma City.

"Hello. This is William Holman in Austin, Texas. Is this Lucy O'Toole?"

"Yes, it is."

"Were you once a nurse for Dr. Walter T. Dardis?"

"Back in the thirties. Who did you say you are?"

"Mrs. O'Toole, you probably don't remember me, but when I was a small boy, my mother regularly brought me to Dr. Dardis for check-ups. Later, I lived with Helen Minter."

"The Minters have passed away."

"I understand."

"And as I recall, your name was Roger."

"Yes, Roger Bechan."

"Did you know that your mother and Dr. Dardis were close friends?"

"I loved to visit his office. He often handed me treats."

She hesitated for a moment. Then she spoke in a firm voice. "I'm at that age where I needn't keep secrets anymore." A long pause hung in the air. "Dr. Dardis was your father."

With my heart thumping, my mind floating in a fog of confusion, I slumped in my chair. Dr. Dardis was the last name I had expected to hear. Finally I stammered, "Mrs. O'Toole, I must talk with you further. May I fly up and see you tomorrow?"

"That'll be fine. This may have been painful for you to hear, but I feel it needed to be told."

Lucy's revelations lifted the curtain of intrigue hanging over my life, but I remained bewildered, even while jubilant. Questions flooded my mind. Would she know when and how Dr. Dardis and my mother met? Why didn't my father rescue me from the Society for the Friendless? Were Helen and Will Minter related to my father? I couldn't wait to fit the pieces of my life's puzzle into place.

The following morning, after a hastily arranged flight, my wife and I arrived on Lucy's doorstep in Oklahoma City. Mrs. O'Toole, a lady with brilliant red hair and white porcelain skin, took us into the past with her tales. My "teller of truths" talked about my mother, my father, and me. She brought all three of us together so naturally that it seemed a Broadway play was being performed before our eyes.

She said it was time I knew about my father. "You look like him. You have his lanky frame, large facile hands, and unusual ears. And look at those blue eyes. They look like your father's. Yes, you are the doctor's son. But I'm hesitant to share these memories with the Dardis children. They would be so shocked and I swore to keep his secret just as the Minters did."

"But what about my mother?"

"I only knew your mother as one of the doctor's patients. Mrs. Bechan was not a young woman, but tall with fine features and wavy hair turning gray. She appeared to be in her mid-thirties, possibly forty." She said that Mother would enter the reception room, greet her briefly, then walk back to the doctor's office. Some days she came alone and other days I tagged along. "On one occasion, when your mother and the doctor were having problems, she walked out of the office and left you with a box containing your clothes."

"A cardboard box?"

"Why yes, a small box. The doctor asked me to take you home for the weekend. My sister helped to care for you."

"Your mother was waiting in the office when I took you back on Monday." This was lost to my memory, but it came alive with Lucy's telling.

Lucy said that when my father learned that my mother had abandoned me in Mr. Wheeler's home, he was devastated. "So through his friend Will Minter, who had an office in the Petroleum Building, he asked Helen Minter to rescue you from the home."

I was shocked to learn that Helen Minter's care was enlisted by my father. Lucy said that hard times, together with his wrong choices in life, broke my father's health. In March 1942, Dr. Walter Dardis Sr.

was brought low by a lingering illness that took him too soon. He died at sixty-two.

Then I thought about my mother. In the thirties and forties, an unmarried mother faced ostracism and shame. To some it was the most burdensome sorrow apart from death. Death is final and the deepest of griefs. But society's scorn for a fallen woman lives on. Gossip no doubt plagued her. But why, knowingly and willingly, could she have abandoned me? Momma and I could have survived together, as I survived alone.

Why did my mother keep me from learning that Dr. Dardis was my father? I couldn't understand the world into which I was born, a perplexing milieu of deceptions and lies.

Joseph Bechan proved to be a myth. As T.S. Eliot said, "It is the human will to see things as they are not." The true story of Dr. Walter Dardis Sr. proved more incredible than the lie.

After all the years of not knowing who I was, who my parents were, or where I stood in the world, I was now a man with a birth father. And surprise! Surprise! I had a half brother and half sister. Having blood relatives and blood ancestry, life held a whole new vocabulary that I was anxious to learn.

I felt humbled by the weight of Lucy's courage but was uneasy with her desire not to share her memories with the Dardis children. I found it hard to keep such a secret. My wife and I couldn't see how new lies could fix old lies. I decided to explore my new roots as a friend rather than a family member and see how it went.

My half sister, Romilda Dardis Heyser, lived in Oklahoma City. I called to let her know that her father had been my family doctor and I would like to know more about him. She invited us to come by her home.

With warm memories she spoke of her father's impact on his patients' lives and how they held him in esteem. My wife and I felt the shock of revelation might cause undue stress. We let our visit be as a friend of the family.

A month passed from the day I talked with Lucy O'Toole until I visited my half brother, a physician in Pueblo, Colorado. I called Dr. Walter Dardis Jr. and told him the same story about being a patient of his father when I was a small boy.

"On your next trip north, drop by," he said. "I'll be pleased to meet you."

The morning of our arrival in Pueblo, Walter was standing by his driveway. An active skier and outdoorsman, he looked vigorous and healthy. He invited us into his home with its low architectural lines and its neat lawn and gardens. "Tell me what this visit is all about."

My brother's demeanor—healthy enthusiasm, smiles, and heightened curiosity—finally brought these words from my wife. "Dr. Dardis, I see you studying Bill's face and lanky frame. I think you see someone familiar. I'm going to tell you something which you may not know. Bill is your half brother." A long silence hung in the air.

He turned to me with his eyes wide with bewilderment. After he recovered, he asked, "Are you certain?"

"We have talked to Lucy O'Toole," Barbara said. "She knows the story."

It was as if his family's past collapsed around him. My wife told me later that she regretted saying it the way she did, but it was too late.

After a pause, Dr. Dardis said, "Bill, I know one thing. You look more like my father than I do." This was the confirmation I had hoped for.

We took a lunch break. Then my newly found brother opened his wall safe. With pride he displayed his father's gold stickpin, the roaring lion with two rubies for its eyes and a diamond in its mouth, the object of my fondest memories as a young boy. Later he made copies of Dardis' genealogical charts and pictures for my files.

He said that his father was born in 1880 and raised in Winchester, Tennessee. He earned a degree in pharmacy from the University of the South in 1903. A prominent Episcopalian school, the university was referred to by many as the Harvard of the South. In his graduation photograph, he is wearing an academic award medal.

He moved to Oklahoma in 1905, where he worked as a pharmacist and earned his degree in medicine from the University of Oklahoma in 1911.

Before we parted, he told me that he would phone his sister. "Romilda will talk to Lucy, and if she verifies the story, I'll believe it."

Barbara wondered how Romilda Heyser might cope with the news.

But Walter said, "She needs to know."

We left the telling to Walter and headed west.

Naturally, within the Dardis family this revelation stirred discussion, and with a few members, a lengthy debate. I told my wife, "This will shock Romilda."

"She'll come around," Barbara said.

A few weeks later, we drove up to Oklahoma City. Romilda treated us to a steak dinner. She couldn't believe that her father had a child outside his marriage. "What makes you think we are related?"

"Lucy says Dr. Dardis was my father."

"She doesn't know that for a fact. And you don't look like my father."

"If you compare our photographs . . . we look like twins."

"Could you be Will Minter's son?"

"Mr. Minter was childless. That is why he adopted Jay Cole."

Romilda wished to create a story of her own, shaped with questions and doubt.

"Bill, you have unrealistic expectations," Barbara later said. "Just because you are Dr. Dardis' son doesn't mean you will be accepted by these people to whom you are a stranger. It is going to take time. Lots of time."

Finally, after over a year of denial, Romilda suggested a DNA test. My brother and I shared the expense, and all three of us gave blood samples.

On April 26, 1995, the Diagnostic Network of America issued a formal report. In summary, they reported that the chances of the three of us being half siblings was a positive 99.90 percent. I felt enriched, after these many years, to learn I had gained a father, a half-brother and a half sister.[13]

Over a period of sixty years, I had never known a relative. Were my restless nature, fiery temper, and determined will largely shaped by the trauma of the numerous homes or were family genes a determining factor?

My quest was aided by my brother's desire to spend two weeks together. His plan involved escaping from civilization by provisioning his four-wheel-drive vehicle for sleeping and eating. We struggled over abandoned mining roads around Copper Mountain, crossed the Continental Divide, and camped in the mesa country once peopled by the Pueblo cliff dwellers. Then we drove west over boulder-strewn trails into Moab and spent a week exploring the red canyon lands of Utah.

This exploration of soul and geographies proved edifying, because we discovered we shared many traits. We both are restless adventurers, approach and solve problems similarly, meet people easily, and examine life with a common perspective. We are both skeptical of sham and pretense.

Walter and I felt compatible and at ease. I admired my brother's sterling character and insight into the human condition. Our journey of discovery proved a success.

*

It is difficult for an abandoned child to understand himself. He has been caught up in a struggle to survive in which insight plays a minor role. It was only when I found my father that I could walk back in time.

Curiosity about the history of the Dardis family led me to the Tennessee State Library, where the family came to life. An article in the *Franklin County Historical Review* reported that my great-great-grandfather, James Dardis Sr., and his brother, Thomas, had immigrated from the County of Westmeath, Ireland, to the United States in 1795.[14] In Franklin County, Tennessee, the Dardis family were prominent leaders in the community and owned land and a prosperous mercantile business.

Barbara and I drove to Tennessee to meet with Charles Woodruff, who had compiled a genealogy of the Dardises. He said that the family, down through the years, was known for its industry: they were active, possessed a fierce independence, pursued professional goals, and earned a reputation for their determined wills and turbulent Irish tempers.

Mr. Woodruff wrote an account of my great-great-uncle, Thomas Dardis, a redheaded Irishman.[15] With a keen wit and sharp humor, he had the confidence of a young attorney who had been elected to the Tennessee State Legislature. In 1808, he became embroiled in a heated debate with General John Cocke, and they took up arms. Thomas Dardis was killed in the duel. Years later, Sam Houston gave Andrew Jackson details about the Cocke-Dardis affair. Jackson was astonished to learn the Cocke had fashioned a body-fitting iron shield to wear underneath his clothes during the duel.

We now sought information on the Dardis family in Ireland. From the library in the County of Westmeath we received a publication which traced the family's surname back to the thirteenth century, and listed several of their land holdings. The importance of the family's role in Irish history is evinced by seven Dardistowns to which they had given their name.[16]

*

Despite the Holmans' love and my gaining of self-esteem, during the

9039. DECREE OF ADOPTION.

STATE OF OKLAHOMA, CREEK COUNTY.   IN COUNTY COURT.

In the Matter of the Adoption of_____Roger Beacham_____

BE IT REMEMBERED, That on this____17th day of_____May 1940_____A. D., 193____,

_____there coming on for hearing the petition of_____

antx Mr and Mrs A.W.Holman_____

_____ to adopt

_____Roger Beacham_____, and there being present in__

Court the said petitioner s___ and the said child, whose adoption said petitioner____ pray, and_____

_____ and_____

_____, the_____of said child,

and the Court having examined the said petitioner s___ and the said__Ray, G, Burns_of said

child, each separately; and the saRay G.Burns having in open Court executed and filed herein ____

written consent to such adoption,____the said Ray G. Burns being the Superinten-

dent of "West Hoklhoma Home", and said Roger Beacham having heretofore

been made a ward of the Court of Oklahoma County, Oklahoma, and by said

Court placed with the West Oklahoma Home.

_____

_____

_____

I LEE SNIDER, Court Clerk for Creek County, Oklahoma hereby certify that the foregoing
is a true, correct and full copy of the instrument hereinafter set out as appears on file in
Court of Creek County, Oklahoma, dated at Sapulpa, Okla. th__1 7_____ ___unty

                              LEE SNIDER, Court Clerk

                        By_____Deputy

_____

_____

_____

DECREE OF ADOPTION, May 17, 1940 CREEK COUNTY COURT, OKLAHOMA
Roger Beachan (Roger Bechan) is adopted by Mr. and Mrs. Arlie Holman.

Drumright Public Library. Dedicated in 1936.
Severely damaged by tornado in 1956.
Photo courtesy of Eileene Russell Coffield

William Holman visits his mentor
Mrs. Katharine Faust Schickram who was one
of the founders of the Drumright Public Library.

BARBARA SWITZER HOLMAN
October 1945

BARBARA HOLMAN
at the helm of the sloop *Teddy* heading for the Bahamas

WILLIAM HOLMAN
sailing Teddy in the Bermuda Triangle.

D N A

DIAGNOSTIC
NETWORK OF
AMERICA

26 Apr 95

		Lab No.	Race	Blood Drawn
Sibling 1	Romilda Heyser	364	W	7 Apr 95
Sibling 2	Walter Dardis, MD	365	W	4 Apr 95
Alleged Half-Sibling	William Holman	357	W	12 Apr 95
Case Number 130				

System	Sibling 1	Sibling 2	Alleged Half-Sibling	Half-Sib Index
D12S11	12.29	12.29	12.29	3.16
	13.22	13.22	10.64	
D17S79	3.37	3.37	3.78	60.87
		2.58	2.58	
D6S132	3.46	3.46	3.46	2.36
			3.98	
D7S467	5.96	5.96	5.96	2.10
	7.00	7.00	9.03	

WILLIAM HOLMAN can not be excluded as the half-sibling of ROMILDA HEYSER and
WALTER DARDIS, MD. The combined half-sib index (the odds in favor of half-sibship) is 953.
The relative chance of half-sibship, assuming a 50% prior chance, is 99.90%

I hereby certify that the above testing was conducted according to currently accepted medical
standards, and that the results and conclusions, including the probability of half-sibship were
verified by me and are correct as reported.

Douglas R. Oliveri, Ph.D.
Laboratory Director

Sworn to and subscribed before me this 26th day of _April_, 19 _95_, at Austin, TX.

Notary Public-Texas

My commission expires _3-14-98_

MOLLY LONG FARREL
Notary Public, State of Texas
My Comm. Expires 3-14-98

1005 WEST 41ST STREET • SUITE 200 • AUSTIN, TEXAS 78756 • (512) 451-1083 • FAX (512) 451-1084

Positive DNA Test (April 26, 1995) by Diagnostic Network of
America proved that Walter Traynor Dardis, Jr.,
Mrs. Romilda Dardis Heyser, and William Holman were half siblings.

Walter Traynor Dardis, Jr. and William Holman
Pueblo Colorado, 1996

DR. WALTER TRAYNOR DARDIS, SR.
Graduation photograph, University of the South, Sewanee, Tenn. 1903
(Roger Bechan's birth father)

WILLIAM HOLMAN, DIRECTOR
San Francisco Public Library

bleakest days, I kept Momma alive in my dreams. Through these many years, I have often wondered if she cried for me as I have cried for her. No doubt, after she abandoned me, she couldn't help but be burdened with a mournful heart. Yeats said, "The world's more full of weeping than you can understand."

I have never been able to comprehend how a man and a woman can come together, bear children, then abandon them knowingly and willingly without a justifiable cause. They discard their own kind, and when you toss your own child away you are bereft of a miraculous gift.

Momma has never been silent over these many years, for my memories of our early days are filled with familial feeling. Living at home in Bethany and riding the trolley remains more real to me than events that happened yesterday. It is difficult to understand how a mother who left decades ago can remain so close, yet so unknown and out of reach. Samuel Johnson said, "Curiosity is the thirst of the soul." Is she resting in a stoneless grave without a spreading elm to shade her? Does anyone pay her visits? I long to know her past. What was her family's history? Did she love literature and writing? Did she appreciate art and design?

*

I look back with the advantage of maturity and am awed by the journey of the youngster who inherited the burden of his biological parents' wrong turns. He lost his mother, his father, his home, his name, and his innocence. During his unsettled teens, the state forced him to live under an ignominious Indenture Contract. And for six decades, he lost the insight into his genetic past—the vital key that sheds light on one's personality and physiological being.

I had several identities tacked onto me as I was shunted among orphanages and adoptive homes. Most people take their names for granted because they have worn them since birth, but as Roger

Bechan I became Bill Minter, Billy Hardt, Will Rogers, Roger Beacham, and finally William Holman. I found it difficult to shed one label before someone stamped me with another. In the Baptist Orphanage, I never felt comfortable with the name of Will Rogers. This was the name of a famous man, who was known throughout the world. It wasn't me.

Freud said that the mind has a mind of its own, and sometimes I feel like I have lived one life within another. Roger Bechan, the name given to me by my mother, had been etched into my soul as a youngster. There are nights when my passions and dreams are still centered there. Occasionally, when I am attending a social affair and someone introduces me to another party, I pause. Should I tell them in the silent corner of my mind I think of myself as Roger Bechan although everyone calls me William Holman.

Two and a half years after being released from the Helena orphanage, the name changes ended when Arlie and Emma Holman proceeded with a legal adoption, giving me a permanent signature: William Roger Holman.

Like the Baptist Orphanage's trampled grass which turned green and flourished in the spring, with few exceptions, the children who grew up there matured and pursued successful careers. An orphan learns early on that he is responsible for what happens in the future no matter what has occurred in the past. He is endowed by a sense of his own self.

I became City Librarian of San Francisco's Public Library system; J.C. Watson, my runaway buddy, held a responsible position with Phillips Petroleum; John Henshall served as an educational counselor for a Texas college; and Leroy Harris became a talented craftsman. And we all led purposeful lives by nourishing our own children into maturity.

These accomplishments reflect the hidden strengths many orphans and foster children use to build a bright future. With sensitive antennas honed to a perceptive understanding of our fellow man, many youngsters were forced to function in the midst of anarchy. Few orphans experienced the sheltered world provided by the average family. Adversity somehow created a fierce desire for success. We faced hardships early and prevailed, gaining a resiliency which fostered an inner confidence that armed us for life.

After I graduated from college, I took the Indenture Contract to an art supply shop where they matted and placed it into a gilded frame. I have kept it hanging above my desk for these many years as a reminder of life's many vicissitudes, and how the human journey, regardless of one's childhood trauma, is at once a gift, and always a challenge.

End Notes

1. State of Oklahoma. Oklahoma County Juvenile Court. Juvenile Docket. No. 8, Entry: 4128. May 20, 1932.

2. "Will's Namesake, An Orphan, Sad Before Portrait," *The Daily Oklahoman*, August 18, 1935, p. 14.

3. Truman H. Maxey. "Heartache to Happiness: The Story of Oklahoma Baptists' Child Care Ministry, 1934-70." *Oklahoma Baptist Chronicle*. Vol. XVIII, Spring 1974, pp. 6-29.

4. State of Oklahoma. Oklahoma County Court. Baptist Orphans Home releases Will Rogers to W.C. Wheeler. May 15, 1936.

5. "Hot Criticism Aimed at Head of Orphanage," *The Daily Oklahoman*, vol. 46, no. 320, Wednesday, November 24, 1937, page 1-2.

6. Oklahoma State Planning Board. *State Homes For Orphans and Veterans in Oklahoma. A Preliminary Study of Present Facilities*

and Conditions. Oklahoma City, 1937, Chapter Three, Table II, p.50.

7. State of Oklahoma. Indenture Contract. January 23, 1937.
8. W.C. Wheeler, "Petition in the matter of Roger Bechan, Dependent Child," *Petition in the Juvenile Court within and for Oklahoma County, State of Oklahoma*, September 4, 1936.

9. State of Oklahoma, Creek County Court. 9039. Decree of Adoption. In the Matter of the Adoption of Roger Beacham. May 17, 1940.

10. "Acquitted on Murder Count," *Drumright Weekly Derrick*, Friday, March 20, 1942, p. 1.

11. D. Carl Newsom. *Drumright! The Glory Days of a Boom Town*. Evans Publications, 1985. pp. 191-194.

12. Edna Gunderson, "Adoptee Finds 'Mom' 58 Years Later," *El Paso Times*, January 23, 1979, p.1-D.

13. Diagnostic Network of America. DNA. "Sibling 1: Romilda Heyser, Sibling 2: Walter Dardis, MD, Alleged Half-Sibling: William Holman. Relative chance of half-sibship . . . is 99.90%." Austin, Texas. April 26, 1995.

14. "Dardises of Franklin County," *Franklin County Historical Review*, Volume XX, Number 1, 1989, pp. 38-40.

15. Charles M. Woodruff, "The Duel Between Thomas Dardis and John Cocke," *Franklin County Historical Review*, Volume XX, Number 1, 1989, pp. 41-47.

16. Hubert Gallwey, "The Family of Dardis," *Riocht na Midhe, the Journal of the Meath Archaeological and Historical Society*, 1976. pp. 56-77.

Epilogue

William Roger Holman has received recognition in two parallel careers: first as an innovative director of metropolitan library systems, and second as an award-winning book designer and fine printer.

After a successful tenure at one of the loveliest public libraries in the nation—the Rosenberg Library in Galveston—Holman introduced modern library practices to the San Antonio Public Library. Building on that success, he was asked to bring the same kind of order to the San Francisco Public Library. A recognized renaissance in services and collections of that institution followed, with enough notice that Chancellor Harry Ransom of the University of Texas asked Holman to join him through the budding years of the Humanities Research Center.

Over the years, he has designed and published books such as: *Jasper Hill's Letters of a Young Miner*, 1964; David Kheridan's *Bibliography of William Saroyan*, 1965; Edward Dahlberg's *The Leafless American*, 1967; Neal Austin's *A Biography of Thomas Wolfe*, 1968; Hazael Beckett's *Growing Up in Dallas*, 1986; Harold

Billings' *Texas Beast Fables,* 2006, and designed or printed over a dozen other titles.

In 1972, he issued a colorful folio volume entitled, *This Bitterly Beautiful Land: A Texas Commonplace Book,* which many consider the most beautiful book ever published in Texas. It was printed on handmade paper and consists of quotations about Texas selected by Al Lowman and woodcuts by Barbara Whitehead.

On the national scene, Holman's work in bookmaking was recognized for his Platt & Slater's *Travelers' Guide to California . . . .,* 1963, and Harold Billings' *Edward Dahlberg, American Ishmael of Letters,* 1968. Both were included in the American Institute of Graphic Arts 50 Books of the Year Awards.

Holman received a bachelor's degree from the University of Oklahoma and a masters degree in Library Science from the University of Illinois. He is a lifetime member of the American Library Association, and was elected chairman of the ALA Friends of the Library Committee. He served on the Board of Directors of The Book Club of California, 1961-1967. He has served as a mentor for the Orphan Foundation of America and represented the group on national television (CNN. "On The Road," Dec. 27, 2001).

William Holman's professional career is recognized in two books: Peter Booth Wiley, *A Free Library in This City* (San Francisco: Weldon Owen, 1996), and Nicholas A. Basbanes, *Patience & Fortitude; A Roving Chronicle of Book People, Book Places, and Book Culture* (New York: HarperCollins, 2001).

He is married and has two sons. His avocations are book collecting and sailing.

A Note on the Type

The text of this book was set in Sabon,
a typeface of rare beauty and great clarity.
It was designed by the distinguished
German typographer Jan Tschichold.
(1902-1974)
Introduced in 1966, it is based
on the 16th-century letter forms of
the French typecuttter, Claude Garamond.

Book Designed by
WRH